The Third World in the Global 1960s

Protest, Culture and Society

General editors:

Kathrin Fahlenbrach, Institute for Media and Communication, University of Hamburg.

Martin Klimke, German Historical Institute, Washington, DC / Heidelberg Center for American Studies (HCA), University of Heidelberg, Germany.

Joachim Scharloth, Department of German, Dokkyo University, Tokyo, Japan.

Protest movements have been recognized as significant contributors to processes of political participation and transformations of culture and value systems, as well as to the development of both a national and transnational civil society.

This series brings together the various innovative approaches to phenomena of social change, protest and dissent which have emerged in recent years, from an interdisciplinary perspective. It contextualizes social protest and cultures of dissent in larger political processes and socio-cultural transformations by examining the influence of historical trajectories and the response of various segments of society, political and legal institutions on a national and international level. In doing so, the series offers a more comprehensive and multi-dimensional view of historical and cultural change in the twentieth and twenty-first century.

The Third World in the Global 1960s

Edited by

Samantha Christiansen and Zachary A. Scarlett

Berghahn Books
New York • Oxford

First published in 2013 by
Berghahn Books
www.berghahnbooks.com

Library of Congress Cataloging-in-Publication Data

The Third World in the global 1960s / edited by Samantha Christiansen,
Zachary A. Scarlett.
    p. cm. — (Protest, culture and society ; v. 8)
    Includes bibliographical references and index.
    ISBN 978-0-85745-573-4 (hardback : alk. paper)
  1. Youth protest movements—Developing countries—History—20th
century. 2. Youth—Political activity—Developing countries—History—20th
century. 3. Student movements—Developing countries—History—20th
century. 4. Students—Political activity—Developing countries—History—
20th century. 5. Developing countries—Social conditions—History—20th
century. I. Christiansen, Samantha. II. Scarlett, Zachary A.
    HN19.T43 2012
    305.23509172'4—dc23

                                                            2012012569

British Library Cataloguing in Publication Data

A catalogue record for this book is available from the British Library

Printed in the United States on acid-free paper

ISBN 978-0-85745-573-4 hardback
ISBN 978-0-85745-574-1 ebook

Contents

Illustrations follow page 85.

Foreword
The Third World in 1968

Arif Dirlik

About 10 years ago, I received an invitation to contribute an essay to a volume
on 1968. In the course of a conference on which the volume was based, the
editors had realized that nothing on the Third World had been included, which
seemed like a serious absence. My essay was intended make up for this absence.

When I sent in my essay, it was with the title above, "The Third World in
1968." Somewhere during the editorial process, someone in his/her wisdom, assuming, I suppose, that the "in 1968" part was redundant in a volume entitled
1968, took that part out of the title, leaving just "The Third World," which more
or less made a mockery of the introductory paragraph where I had written:

> The ambiguity built into the title of this chapter is intentional. A Third
> World perspective on 1968 requires a double vision. First, it demands
> recognition that as idea and reality the Third World was conspicuously
> present in the events of 1968, not only in the many different areas en-
> compassed by the term "Third World" but also and more importantly
> in the First (and Second) Worlds; it is reasonable to suggest that the
> emergence of the Third World as a challenge to the First but also as a
> substitute for the Second World of Soviet and Eastern European Com-
> munism was a crucial aspect of 1968. Second, it enjoins us to recognize
> the many contexts that shaped the participation of people in the Third
> World in the events of 1968. This raises the question of whether or not
> 1968 can serve as a marker in Third World histories in the same sense
> that it has come to mark a watershed in First and Second World histo-
> ries and, for that very reason, of the dialectic between the general and
> the particular in the construction of 1968 as a historical marker.[1]

I cite this paragraph not to get back at the editors of that volume for the
discrepancy their editorial work created between the title and the substance of
my essay, but because the issues raised in that paragraph serve as an appropriate
introduction to the present volume.

My essay in the earlier volume was the sole representative of the Third
World, and made an effort to cover a number of countries (The People's Republic of China, India, Turkey, Egypt, Ethiopia, and Mexico) to illustrate the

tri-continental spatial scope of 1968, on the one hand, and the diversity of the movements spawned in the globalization of the protest activity of that year. The present volume undertakes a similar task, but at a much larger scale, in greater detail for a wider number of societies, and richer and more varied subject matter. It is a welcome addition to the scant literature on an important subject: the contradictions in Third World societies that 1968 brought to the surface, and the longer-term consequences for radical politics of the particular course the events of 1968 took in different societies, that also varied in duration and temporality in different contexts. The volume is of obvious historical significance, which is not unrelated to its political significance as a reminder of the importance of both 1968 and the "Third World," which appear in a negative light these days not just for their detractors but even those who were participants in the events of the time. The depoliticized post-revolutionary post-colonialism that has acquired popularity with the retreat and corruption of Third World radical politics has repudiated not just the commonalities but also the solidarities of earlier Third World movements, in the process calling into question the very idea of the Third World. The events of which the year 1968 became the temporal symbol have been discredited, partly because of their own degeneration into a mindless radicalism in the face of political repression that allowed few alternatives, and partly because the victory of global capitalism has successfully recast in a negative light the efforts of an earlier age to hold it in check.

The events of 1968 worldwide were directly inspired by the crisis of colonialism, and the implications for capitalism of de-colonization, but also by the seeming crisis of "actually existing socialism," until then the only challenger to capitalism. The crisis gave renewed hope to Third World struggles for liberation, autonomy, and new modes of development that would avoid the pitfalls of capitalism as well as of Stalinist Communism. It is probably futile, and unnecessary politically, to ask whether it was the urban revolt in the First World that inspired the Third, or the anti-colonial struggles of the Third that inspired the First, as a ready, and empirically verifiable, dialectical interplay of the various movements is quite apparent throughout the 1960s (if not earlier) and into the early 1970s. But there is probably good reason to describe 1968 as "the year of the Third World," not because the Third World was responsible for the events of that year but because the Third World was everywhere in the consciousness of political activists. It was a mobilizing idea for those involved in the struggles against colonialism and newcolonialism. Among First World radicals and progressives, solidarity with the Third World represented a new measure of political radicalism. 1968 may well be described as the political coming of age of the Third World that had assumed visibility with the Bandung Conference of 1955, but now became a focal point of radical activity globally.

Both 1968 and the Third World have disappeared into the past. But that does not mean that they have not left important legacies that are still invoked against the continuing injustices of the capitalist system, and colonial legacies that refuse to go away despite all the brave talk about post-coloniality. The more constructive legacies of 1968 are still visible in the flourishing placed-based politics of the Global North, which have regained strength in response to the globalization of capital and the crisis of the environment. In the Third World, and globally, the solidarities of an earlier day are still invoked in the construction of social movements that have taken over from political parties the task of protecting livelihood and freedom against an increasingly oppressive regime of capital.

The context of contemporary struggles is different from that of an earlier day, with its clearly delineated divisions between the East and the West, colonialism and anti-colonialism, or the First, Second, and Third Worlds. Neo-liberal policies since the 1980s have succeeded in consolidating the global power of a ruling class that has assumed a transnational visage through the recruitment into its ranks of newcomers from the former Second and Third Worlds. Earlier divisions have been scrambled by changes in the global political economy. The past is not sufficient to guide or explain the present, and it may be necessary on occasion to forget the past in order to recognize what is different about the world. But forgetting may also serve as a blinder on reality. For some, memories of 1968 are uncomfortable reminders of a bygone past, but despite all the effort to "forget" them, they refuse to go away because of the persistence of the contradictions that are the legacies of the past to the present. On the other hand, those memories are still of some inspiration to those engaged in oppositional movements—now, more than ever, movements for survival—that themselves need to go global if they are to have any hope of effectiveness, not to speak of success. Studies such as those in this volume, to the extent that they contribute to the preservation of those memories, are not of merely of academic historical but also of contemporary political significance.

Notes

1. Arif Dirlik, "The Third World," in Carole Fink, Philipp Gassert, and Detlef Junker (eds.), *1968: The World Transformed* (Cambridge: Cambridge University Press, 1998), 295–317.

Introduction

Samantha Christiansen and Zachary A. Scarlett

The shadow of the Third World hangs over the study of the radical protest movements of the 1960s in Europe and the United States. When thinking about this decade, Third World actors such as Ché Guevára, Frantz Fanon, Amilcar Cabral, and Ho Chi Minh often spring to mind alongside the likes of Rudi Dutschke, Daniel Cohn-Bendit, Stokely Carmichael, and Tom Hayden. Scholars have long acknowledged that individuals, groups, language, ideology, tactics, and, indeed, the very idea of a Third World liberation movement inspired student groups and activists in Europe and the United States. These scholars have referred to the Third World as providing a "mandate for revolution"[1] and of "receiving unprecedented attention"[2] from activists in the West.[3] Many radicals hoped that a new "Third World International" could be formed out of the solidarity between Western and non-Western students.[4] As Max Elbaum notes, in the 1960s, "Third World Liberation Marxism-Leninism" came to replace Soviet Marxism, effectively differentiating one generation of leftist dissent—what became known as the New Left—from an older generation.[5] The editors of *1968: The World Transformed* note that "with the fading of the Marxist and Soviet models, the heroic factory worker and peasant had been replaced by the heroic Third World freedom fighter."[6] Scholars have also examined the effect of the Third World on specific student movements. Timothy Brown and Quinn Slobodian both point out that the state visits of Tshombe and the Shah of Iran galvanized West German students, leading to the massive outpouring of dissent in 1967 and 1968.[7] Meanwhile, Kristen Ross's study of May '68 traces the origins of the French student movement to the Algerian Civil War.[8] As each of these authors demonstrates, the Third World became the vehicle for the social, cultural, and political transformation in the West.

The Third World not only inspired many students to take to the street in the 1960s, it also provided a model for the radicalism of the decade. Many activists in the Civil Rights Movement, for example, saw the Third World as a natural ally.[9] The Third World and the Black Power movement became so intertwined in the 1960s that many in the United States no longer differentiated between the two causes. Decolonizing the Third World meant freedom at home for African-Americans, and vice versa.[10] The Third World also impacted many white students. As Todd Gitlin notes, the antiwar movement's inability to end the Vietnam War also caused many white middle class youth to turn to the revolutionary tactics of the Third World.[11] This frustration also tore apart the Students for a Democracy Society (SDS), one of the foundational organizations of the 1960s.

What emerged out of this factionalism was the Weather Underground, a group that, as Jeremy Varon notes, believed that only the Third World revolutionary, and not the white middle class in the United States, could actually stop the monolithic force of American imperialism. The Weathermen saw themselves as a compliment to the Third World revolution, struggling against imperialism inside the centers of power.[12] The Red Army Faction in Germany, meanwhile, asserted that anyone who identified themselves with Third World revolutionaries—and not the proletariat—were themselves part of the new revolutionary vanguard.[13]

And yet, despite its importance to activists and revolutionaries in the West, the Third World remains *terra incognita* in the scholarship on the 1960s. To be sure, there are a number of excellent studies on individual countries in the Third World,[14] as well as numerous discussions of Third World countries that appear in global examinations of the 1960s.[15] Still, the Third World as a body politic has yet to be considered. And if we are to produce a truly global understanding of the 1960s, we must, as Martin Klimke suggests, take up the case of the Third World, not as it was in the minds of Western students, but as it exists in history and on the ground.[16] It is here in which we will encounter both familiar and novel aspects of the struggles of the 1960s, and confirm as well as challenge previous categories and notions about this decade.

The present study in no way represents a complete survey of the 1960s in the Third World; indeed, such a task would exceed the length of this book. While we are pleased to include case studies that spread across Africa, Asia, and Latin America, we recognize that for every new contribution to the field offered by this volume, there are just as many silences. The reader will no doubt wonder why Pakistan and Bangladesh, Turkey, Ethiopia, Peru, Egypt, and a host of other countries are not included. To be frank, it is not because they are not important or do not fit into the Third World matrix, but simply because we could not cover every aspect of this rich and nuanced decade. We therefore consider this book to be the opening, rather than the decisive, remarks on the Third World in the 1960s.

The case studies that follow offer a diverse sample of the Third World experience in the 1960s. They illuminate new features and novel paradigms of the 1960s that are not discussed in most studies of Western student movements. In such a reexamination there are some questions that arise at the outset. What is the Third World and how can we analyze the Third World as a part of 1960s radicalism? Does the periodization of the 1960s even fit with the Third World? If not, how should one think about "the 1960s" as a historical period in the Third World? Finally, for the sake of global context, what are the similarities and differences between the activism of the Third World and the movements of Europe and the United States, and how can exploring them increase the understanding of each arena? Instead of rehashing themes with which many readers will be familiar, this introduction focuses much more on the differences between Western and Third World movements in an attempt to break down old paradigms and discuss new categories.

Time and Place: Why the Third World? Why the 1960s?

We have purposefully chosen to include the term Third World in the title of this volume. We do so knowing the controversy surrounding its usage, as well as its implied global hierarchy based on a modernization paradigm.[17] We also understand that the term has become outmoded since the end of the Cold War.[18] Although we reject its pejorative connotation, we use the term in this volume to elucidate its meaning in a specific historical epoch.[19] For one, it allows for the distinct grouping of different countries with the shared historical experience of colonialism, which shaped some of the protest movements of the 1960s. Second, the term helps distinguish a group of countries that hoped to avoid Soviet and American influence during the Cold War, with varying degrees of success.

Despite its Western origins—the term comes from a French sociologist[20]—the idea of the Third World was realized in political practice with the formation of loosely based political, cultural, and social groupings articulated at the 1955 Bandung Conference.[21] It was at Bandung that leaders from countries throughout the Third World recognized the importance of non-alignment and pledged to remain neutral in the Cold War. We may therefore conclude that the countries in this volume share a similar, although certainly not homogenous historical experience during the Cold War. This "flexible network" of loosely bound states operated via "degrees of affinity" rather than a "hard sense of uniqueness."[22] Although the term Third World may be outmoded today—replaced by the vague (and equally questionable) Global South—we stand by its value as a historical idea of vital importance during the Cold War. Discarding the term would be to erase a historical situation that did indeed play a central role in the global protest movement of the 1960s. From this perspective, applying the modern concept of a Global South to the 1960s is anachronistic and temporally disjointed. Because of its importance, the idea of the Third World, as well as a lengthy examination of the term's origins and variations, occupies the first section of this volume.

If Third World is indeed a useful term, then how does it fit into the idea of the 1960s? Was the 1960s even a decade of any great significance to the Third World, which experienced almost non-stop social and political agitation since the end of World War II? This question of periodization is perhaps one of the most difficult to answer because the borders of "the 1960s" are so complex and hazy. Indeed, the 1960s had multiple trajectories, and it therefore seems logical to contend that it has multiple periodizations. In the West, one may begin an analysis of the 1960s, or at least the Civil Rights Movement, with the Montgomery Bus Boycott of 1955.[23] It was in Montgomery that Dr. Martin Luther King, Jr., first rose to national prominence. Perhaps the spirit or the ethos of the 1960s in the Third World emerged in 1947 with the independence of the Indian subcontinent, where a great tide of anti-colonialism signaled the final destruction of the French and British empires. Or, as Frederic Jameson contends, perhaps the 1960s began somewhere in the late 1950s, in the streets of Algiers, or in the

Ghanaian capital of Accra, or outside of the gates of Dienbienphu or maybe even in Havana, which validated the *foco* theory that provided a theoretical basis for Western youth and global revolutionaries.[24] Indeed, the impact of Ghana's independence in 1957 could serve as an excellent starting point—not only did Ghanaian independence stir the entire continent of Africa, but it also made an important impact across the Atlantic. Dr. King's visit to Ghana in the year of its independence inspired the young members of the Civil Rights Movement to look toward Africa in their struggle for equality and justice.[25] The point is that we need to allow ourselves flexibility in our understanding of time. The 1960s is a general timeframe, not a hardened structure into which we can place the vast movements and ideas examined in this volume.

And yet the protest movements explored in this volume were distinct from the anti-colonial struggle in Ghana or Algeria discussed above. If the 1960s were born in struggle against colonialism, then they matured in a very different milieu. With that in mind, the Third World in the 1960s may be conceived of in two overlapping waves. The first wave, which ended in the mid 1960s, consisted of movements that focused on the anti-colonial struggle for national independence. Indeed, between 1945 and 1965, more than 50 independent states emerged, most of them in the Third World.[26] Activists in the second wave, however, fought against neo-colonialism and the project of the nation-state, which tended to subvert progressive activism in favor of stability.[27] Indeed, many of the charismatic and progressive nationalist leaders of the anti-colonial movement had lost power by the early and mid 1960s, and were replaced by leaders who were more authoritarian and less tolerant of dissent.[28] What replaced the radical anti-colonialism of the earlier part of the decade was therefore a frustration with the inefficiency and injustice of postcolonial society, the lingering presence of colonial institutions, mentalities, and influences, and the subordination of the socialist agenda to that of the nation.[29] The new elites of the Third World realized that the radicalism and progressivism of the anti-colonial agenda was difficult to merge with the new project of nation building. As Frederic Cooper notes regarding the process of decolonization in Africa, "Politicians built a powerful challenge to colonial regimes. But once in power, such leaders understood all too well how dangerous such claims were."[30] The nation-state, as it turned out, was simply unable to create an equal and just society, and instead began to repress any challenge to its power. It was this political, social, and cultural environment that sparked the protests of the second wave of the 1960s.

By focusing on the this second wave in the Third World, this volume presents case studies that have by and large not been considered in analyses of the decade. However, the "two waves" of the 1960s is a soft rather than hard point of demarcation. The themes that comprised the anti-colonial nationalism of the earlier part of the decade often echoed in the social movements discussed in this volume. As Prasenjit Duara notes, the movement against colonialism was not simply fought for the transference of power, but was also "a movement for moral justice and political solidarity against imperialism."[31] The second wave of the 1960s in the Third World was in many ways the same fight, although the disputants had changed. Even in the Americas, where many nations had experienced independence well before much of Africa and Asia, the ideological battle against imperialism, neo-colonialism, and the abuses of the nation-state also fueled countless protests in the 1960s.

In addition, it's important to recognize that colonial rule was still present in some parts of the Third World during the 1960s, even if the white elite considered their country to be independent. Indeed, this volume contains accounts of anti-colonial struggles against minority white rule in Rhodesia and South Africa. Even those states that had gained formal independence still had to contend with the continued influence of the Western powers.[32] This presented a difficult dilemma for many activists in the Third World. On the one hand, strengthening the nation-state was the surest antidote to neo-colonialism. On the other hand, a strong state often came at the expense of individual rights and political dissent. Many activists thus had to walk a very fine line between the nation-state and neo-colonialism.[33] The second wave of the 1960s therefore became a movement against the former colonial powers who sought to manipulate the Third World, as well an attempt to gain access to new institutions and rights, which were often suppressed in favor of projects of nation-building and modernization.

The beginning of the decade may have hazy boundaries, but it clearly marked a "moment of transition" in the Third World, just as it did in Europe and the United States.[34] But what of an end to the decade? Many participants and scholars have recognized that the energy of the 1960s in the West was transferred to other important movements, such as the women's rights and nuclear non-proliferation movements, the fight for gay rights, and numerous environmental causes, among others. The 1960s in America and Europe did not end, it simply diffused; the same can be said for the Third World. Marking an end to the 1960s in the Third World is to suggest that either the activists were victorious in their respective struggles, or that they were silenced by their opponents. The events of 1960s should be understood as situated within struggles against oppression that continued in subsequent decades—the most notable being against South African apartheid. As in the West, the 1960s continues to shape social movements and collective action throughout Asia, Africa, and Latin America, suggesting that the ideas of this decade had no clearly definable ending.[35]

Common Ground and New Territory

There are certain hurdles one must surmount in order to create a global framework that properly captures the social movements of the 1960s. Scholars must primarily define certain similarities and differences that existed between the West and the Third World. Pointing out these differences will help identify new paradigms and patterns that will help scholars draw a more global portrait of the 1960s. Of course, differences and similarities between different countries and continents abound. Instead of becoming bogged down in an infinite comparative analysis, this study takes a more thematic approach to the Third World.

One important catalyst that sparked social movements in Europe and the United States, as well as in the Third World, was an active concern over education and education reform. In fact, education reform provides an excellent example of the intersections between First, Second, and Third World movements. The importance of education reform has been well documented in the scholarship on Western student movements in the 1960s.[36] The Western education system was outmoded and ill-prepared for the massive influx of new students after World War II. As several studies in this volume point out, this was also the case in the Third World. Education reform was an impetus for broader social movements, first encouraging mobilization and then fostering a rebellious milieu that quickly expanded beyond college and secondary school campuses. Many students began to see the university as a microcosm for society's ills. For example, Congolese students' complaints about the continued Dutch influence at Lovanium, the county's most prestigious university, eventually came to represent President Mobutu's refusal to Africanize Congolese society. Seminary students in Rhodesia felt the same way; the racist policies of the Church denied the students their African heritage at their school, just as did white rule in Rhodesia. In Brazil, students entered into an intense and prolonged dialogue about the meaning of education and its role in Brazilian society. They also protested against the collaboration between Brazil's Ministry of Education and the United States government, and the imperialistic relationship between these two countries. Similarly, students in the Philippines coalesced around the Movement for the Advancement of Nationalism, and demanded less US influence and more Filipino say in the education system. As these cases demonstrate, protests that began at universities often became emblematic of deep-seeded problems in these individual societies.

Despite this and other similarities, there are countless historical developments unique to the Third World experience in the 1960s. Highlighting the differences between the West and the Third World, which occupies the majority of this section, is not meant to obviate a broader global perspective, but rather to suggest new categories of analysis and new ways of understanding the radicalism of the 1960s. This is particularly illuminating when considering the source and simultaneity of the Third World 1960s. Scholars of the 1960s have long attempted to locate a common impulse that drove students and activists into the streets in the West. These scholars have reached varying conclusions; some claim that the influence of the mass media galvanized Western students.[37] Others claim that a certain *zeitgeist*—what George Katsiaficas refers to as the *eros* effect[38]—swept over the generation. Still others have identified the political and cultural climate of the Cold War as a main reason for the many social movements in the 1960s.[39] While these models may fit Western cases, it is difficult to apply some of these explanations to the Third World. For example, television did not enjoy the same widespread dissemination and impact in the Third World as it did in Europe and the United States, where viewers tuned into the nightly news and found on their screens the horrors of the Vietnam War. Furthermore, information in many parts of the Third World was censored on a more pervasive level; radio and print media were heavily regulated, and in many cases, operated by the state. The mass media thus proves inadequate as a general explanation for the scope of these movements in the Third World.

Furthermore, the Cold War resonated very differently in the Third World than it did in the First and Second. For one, the Cold War was far more than a "cold" battle of ideologies in the Third World. Proxy wars orchestrated on behalf of the superpowers were part of the day-to-day experience of many young Third World nations (and nationalists) in the 1960s, and the reality of assassination, political imprisonment, and outright massacre amounted to much more than an ideological debate. And yet, there was also a certain distance to the Cold War. In the Third World there was an open engagement with and blending of various ideologies that seem diametrically opposed to the blustering political battles of the First and Second Worlds. Leftists in much of the Third World embraced an ideology that blurred the Sino-Soviet split, and aid-dependent governments often walked a thin line between economic systems in order to maintain relations with both sides of the Cold War.[40] Such perfidious behavior was not accepted in the First or Second Worlds. Third World leaders also used the Cold War to advance their own politics. The Cold War presented many governments with an easy excuse to deal harshly with internal dissent. The trade and arms deals made in the name of ideological alignment (or non-alignment) were more physically present as an aspect of the Cold War for Third World dissidents opposing a military *junta* than for activists facing a comparatively less armed police force in the West.[41]

The diversity of participants and activists in the Third World 1960s also indicates that many of the categories and classifications used to understand the Western 1960s are untenable in the context of the Third World. For example, although heavily disputed, the 1960s in the West is often categorized as a "youth revolt."[42] Scholars have asserted that the fusion of "youth" with consumer societies acted as catalysts for the unrest of the 1960s in the United States and Europe.[43] Applying this term to the Third World, however, holds little value, despite the important role that students played in the anti-authoritarian revolts of the decade. Instead of classifying the 1960s in the Third World as a youth revolt, this volume illustrates that a host of institutions participated in the myriad social movements discussed herein. Churches and religious institutions, NGOs, radical nationalist movements, various left and right wing organizations, and (in the case of Indonesia) the army all played an important role in the Third World 1960s. While the movements in 1960s in the Third World were driven by younger people, "youth" as a category, with its own language, style, habit, or mentality, was not an essential part of many of these protest movements. Ideology, resources, familial and societal links, and a host of other factors took precedence over youth as a distinctive social category.[44]

Not only does this volume present new actors and institutions that were important to the Third World in the 1960s, it also challenges the mythology that came to embody the Third World in the West. Todd Gitlin notes that the radicals of the 1960s in the United States "increasingly found exemplars and heroes in Cuba, in China, in the Third World guerrilla movement, in Mao and Frantz Fanon and Ché and Debray."[45] And yet, one will notice that these "heroes" of the Third World are not central figures in this volume. That is not to deny the profound impact that these people had on the world in the 1960s. This volume, however, has consciously decided to focus on the characters, actors, and dissidents that are not often present in the Western discussion of the Third World. It is therefore not a study of the "heroic Third World guerrilla," but instead a look at those who were on the ground, who were in the arenas, who were waging their respective fights, and who sometimes came and went too quickly to make a global impact. We should therefore think of the Third World in the 1960s with a more complete list of characters: Ché Guevára and the Jamaican dancehall crowds, Frantz Fanon and the Indian journalist, the Cuban guerrillas and the Rhodesian seminary student. The goal is to compare and contrast the Western *imagination* of the Third World and the Third World as it existed on the ground in the 1960s, populated by those who are often invisible in popular memories of the decade. The merger of these two realities can provide a more complete, and indeed more global and dynamic, landscape of the 1960s.

Despite this expanded list of the activists who affected their respective societies in the 1960s, the Third World lacked any significant or united countercultural movement. The counterculture was an important if not central characteristic of the Western student movement.[46] Groups like the hippies, the Situationists, or *Kommune I* saw cultural freedom as the key to political liberation and infused cultural space with political meaning. The Provos in the Netherlands, for example, staged large public provocations such as a free bicycle program in order to draw attention to the negative impact that the automobile had on society. Others, like the Situationists and the members of *Kommune I* placed great currency in the impact of the spectacle, and attempted to shock a complacent society out of its lethargy by exposing the pernicious effect of bourgeois culture.[47] For many of the countercultural groups, challenging cultural norms was a means to also confront social and economic inequities. The Situationists, for example, believed that art "needed to find its role in the transformation of everyday life" and that artists were to "agitate and polemicize against the sterility of and oppression of the ... ruling economic and political system."[48] The counterculture in general became an international phenomenon, and also acted as a key means of organizing youth in Europe and the United States.[49] It was, in the end, one of the cornerstones of the 1960s in the West.[50]

This volume is noticeably devoid of any equivalent countercultural movement that resembles the Western experience. That is not to say that culture as a point of contention or as a political by-product was absent from the Third World experience during the 1960s. Indeed, as James Bradford's chapter demonstrates, reggae and the culture surrounding this musical genre played a major role in the Jamaican protest movement of the 1960s. And of course active countercultures emerged in places like Brazil and Mexico,[51] and formed around new modes of expression throughout the Third World. Culture was central to the 1960s in the Third World; activists infused their political demands with culture symbols and constructed meanings. But the ethos of the Western countercultural movements—a desire to completely remove oneself from society—is less in the forefront in the Third World. The idea of "turning on, tuning in, and dropping out," as US countercultural icon Timothy Leary prescribed, is not present in many of the case studies of this volume. One of the reasons for this is that the actors and dissidents in this volume had nothing to drop out from. Many felt that they did not have a place in society, whether because of racism, authoritarianism, or the lingering effects of colonialism. These activists believed that dropping out of a society in which they had no rights was useless. Many others were still actively engaged in the crafting of new nations. The 1960s in much of the Third World was therefore a movement to drop *in* to society, a battle for inclusion and for representation.

There is also a notable difference in the pitch and level of violence in the Third World as compared to the Western experience. Of course, Europe and the United States were not without their incidents of violence during the 1960s; Italy experienced a prolonged period of intense violence, while certain organizations in West Germany and the United States turned toward terrorism after realizing the ineffectiveness of nonviolent tactics. And yet, as Arthur Marwick observes, the 1960s was characterized by a "measured judgment" from the authorities.[52] According to Marwick, the freedom of the student movement, and particularly the counterculture, to act without massive interference was due to the "existence in positions of authority of men and women ... who responded flexibly and tolerantly to their [sic] demands."[53] Such tolerance and flexibility did not generally exist in the Third World. Almost every case study presented in this volume—from Brazil and Mexico, to the Congo and South Africa, to the Philippines and Indonesia—contains instances of extreme violence, most often originating from the state or other institutions of authority. This made some of the protest movements of the Third World in the 1960s rather short lived. Activists were readily harassed, arrested, imprisoned, physically abused, and sometimes executed. Violence therefore became a tool of the Third World authorities, an antidote to dissent that leaders in the West were unwilling or unable to use.

This does not, however, exonerate the West from any sort of violent reaction to dissent. By and large, the Western states used violence against their own people less than the authorities in the Third World, although the nature of

Western capitalism relied on the deprivation and continued political injustice of the Third World. While the authorities proved flexible and tolerant of dissent in their own country, their entire system in part relied on the continuation of violence in the Third World. The United States, for example, may have moderately tolerated the Yippies or the New Left, but they would not tolerate the Vietcong, or anyone accused of being a part of that revolutionary group in Southeast Asia. The same can be said of France; measured judgment was observed in the streets of Paris in May 1968, but not in the streets of Algiers several years before that. Cases of this nature abound. The victims of this violence in the Third World were not the political elites, but instead were often the very actors and characters included in this volume. The students, farmers, activists, and dissidents bore the brunt of violence not only from their own leaders, but from many Western countries alike.

No Roadmaps for New Directions

In light of these differences, is it still possible to claim that a global protest movement did indeed exist in the 1960s that encompassed Europe, the United States, and the Third World? Yes—the 1960s was the weaving together of individual (national) strands of history. These strands can stand alone, but the tapestry that they produced represented a semi-cohesive whole. One can therefore choose to study these national strands, or step back and examine the entirety of their individual efforts; this volume does both. Each chapter focuses on individual Third World social movements of the 1960s; the reader, upon finishing this book, however, will have gained a wider understanding of the decade. This in-depth and prolonged discussion of the Third World, when considered alongside the myriad studies of the 1960s in Europe and the United States, will produce a truly global topography of the decade. Studying the Third World, and the case studies presented in this volume, however, requires what Arif Dirlik has called a "double vision"—the reader must hold in his or her mind both the individuality of each case study, as well as the recognition that the examples presented herein represent one part of a larger narrative that took on a global shape in the 1960s.[54]

To make this task more manageable, the present volume is arranged along thematic rather than geographical lines. Grouping together case studies with similar stories, narratives, actors, and examples better illuminates some of the major themes of the 1960s in the Third World that stretched across both temporal and geographical boundaries. We recognize the power that such groupings hold, however, and emphasize that the purpose of this volume is not to build borders, but to cross them. Thus, the reader will find that many of the chapters might also fit well in another section, or come together in a completely new pattern if viewed side by side. These new connections are precisely what we hope to accomplish, and see this structure as an introductory schematic—open to change, interpretation, and new directions.

The first section, "Crossing Borders: The Idea of the Third World and the Global 1960s," offers four chapters that examine the historical development of the term *Third World*, as well as the ways in which the idea of the Third World gained currency during the 1960s. These chapters together illustrate that just as the Third World itself was a dynamic arena with a multiplicity of (sometimes competing) voices, so too were the imaginary and discursive spaces of the "Third World." Together, these chapters point to wide-ranging, and at times even fluid, notions of the Third World that moved across borders in all directions. In addition, as this section endeavors to highlight, the "Third World" has always existed in a conceptual dialectic. In all of the definitions of Third World, we see ideas of First and Second World defined and negotiated as well.

As a point of departure, Christoph Kalter explores the initial usage of the term *tiers monde* and its journey through time and space to the usage employed by the French radical Left of the global 1960s. The essays that follow, in this section and throughout the volume, represent different trajectories of this idea, sometimes overlapping, sometimes wildly divergent from previous usages. Within these variations, one particularly salient feature of the term is the fundamental inspiration of Third World as a potentially revolutionary force (like the Third Estate during the French Revolution). This prediction of revolutionary prospective remained common throughout many of the different ideological manifestations. Indeed, as Kalter illustrates, Frantz Fanon saw the discursive power of the term *Third World* alongside its literal power and used it as a unifying identity (in the form of Third Worldism) for a potentially global collective of formerly colonized Third World revolutionaries. The Third World then could rally around a shared experience of oppression and abuse (as did the Third Estate) on one hand, but also a shared identity based on a collective power that, if united, could undoubtedly overwhelm the global power dynamic. The term *Third World*, for Fanon and those that agreed with him, was certainly not a pejorative term—it was the reclamation of an idea and a militant position.

Similar notions of empowerment are seen in the periodicals examined by Avishek Ganguly. In India, we can observe a flipping of the lens—rather than a worldview—in which when we look into the Third World Other, we see an articulation of the First World Other. The view of the 1960s from the Naxalite perspective, and their supporters', was decidedly more guided by the revolutionary forces in the Third World, and the actions taking place in Europe and the US were more echoes of the battles at home. Certainly there are expressions of solidarity, and even a shared identity on a basic level, but the Third World worked from a self-defined position of influential dominance, and in doing so, on at least a discursive level, placed the First World into a more Third World–centered world order.

That is not to say that the term was applied in the same way across different countries. Zachary Scarlett illustrates how this recognition of the revolutionary potential of the Third World was present in Chinese students' imaginations and put to very China-centric usages. By positioning Mao Zedong as a glorious leader of global anti-imperialism (vis-à-vis Third World Revolution), the symbol did more to define Chinese students' sense of their own revolutionary identity during the Cultural Revolution than to collectively empower the Third World. In fact, as both Scarlett and Ganguly's work demonstrates, the Maoism of different Third World interpretations took a decidedly non-China-centric trajectory, and responded to locally relevant issues. Thus, while Chinese students imagined that they were inspiring the poor masses of the world, many of their would-be followers had adopted only certain facets of Maoism and moved on.

Of course this is not to cynically imply that the expressions of solidarity were not genuine—or that students (in China or elsewhere outside the Third World) were unable to see beyond their own myopic experience. Indeed, as can be seen in Konrad Kuhn's chapter, the idea of the Third World had a massive mobilizing appeal in Europe, and solidarity with Third World struggles presented a new, and highly effective, framing opportunity for humanitarian aid organizations. Famine and disaster imagery may have been fundamentally othering in their representations, but they also provided a starting point, or a foothold, for First World actors to engage with the negative consequences of imperialism and neo-colonial exploitation. Furthermore, the issue of solidarity with the Third World victims built bridges between organizations with different goals, and to some extent, a new, more informed, politicization of aid and compassion work. These bridges extended across borders and linked not only First World activists with Third World activists, but opened new channels of movement resources to which the Third World gained access. Indeed, in the issue of solidarity and aid we see a widening of the cast of players engaging in the global 1960s on both sides of protests.

All of the chapters in the volume demonstrate that the idea of the Third World was mobile, highly malleable, and far from monolithic. In the second section, "Fresh Battles in Old Struggles: New Voices and Modes of Expression," we explore four case studies that deal with protest movements that began long before, and in many cases extended long after, the 1960s. This section demonstrates that the 1960s did not exist in a temporal vacuum and that these movements are part of a long history preceding, and following, the sensational moments of the late 1960s. Within these protracted struggles, however, the presence the global milieu of the 1960s is visible, as are new modes of expression and negotiation that emerged during the decade. Thus, this section illuminates the effect of the 1960s on longer campaigns of resistance as well as placing aspects of the 1960s into a clearer historical context.

As Colin Snider's chapter demonstrates, university reform in Brazil is rooted in a larger dialogue between the state and population over the direction and development of the nation, the role of education, and eventually, the role of democracy. As Brazilian students negotiated with the state, the 1968 *Reforma Universitária* represented a significant success in and of itself, but in the larger struggles for democratization, the decade was less clearly victorious. The students' ability to form new alliances and the adaptability of the students' campaign to the introduction of military rule marks only one aspect of the longer process of negotiation and contests for power.

While Brazil's students were contending with a new regime of power in the form of military rule, other cases in the section present cases of old power facing new consciousness. White dominance and racist oppression was certainly not new in the 1960s, nor was resistance to these institutions. However, the 1960s did mark a point in which "blackness" as a mobilizing identity crested. The influence of both the US Civil Rights Movement and the Black Power movement in South Africa and Jamaica, as presented in this section in the chapters by Chris Saunders and James Bradford, are two of countless examples illustrating black empowerment as one the most mobile and lasting ideas circulated in the 1960s. The racist roots of colonial domination were clearly present in the policies of apartheid under which South African blacks lived every day, and the presence of oppression was irrefutable and certainly deeply entrenched in local societal structure. Yet, as Saunders' chapter demonstrates, in the 1960s a globally informed black consciousness drew inspiration from writings by authors with origins outside of South Africa; Frantz Fanon, Dr. Martin Luther King, Jr., and Malcolm X expressed a black solidarity and identity that echoed and embodied the idea of a Third World revolutionary potential. This empowerment would take many more years to manifest into actual freedom for blacks in South Africa, but the struggle against apartheid became ideologically and physically more global in the 1960s.

Similarly, as James Bradford demonstrates, the influence of Black Power in Jamaica's poor quarters led to expressions of both outrage and hope. The Rodney riots represented black frustration with continued oppression, and the politicization of music, in the form of reggae, embodied another mode of black consciousness. Both the riots and the reggae drew on international notions of black consciousness and Third World empowerment, but also placed the identity in a very personal and local mode of expression. Nicholas Creary's chapter also presents a case in which black seminary students contended with a newfound sense of empowerment. In this study, however, the focus of white domination is the church. Creary brings a new dynamic into the discussion of race and the 1960s. Analysis of race in the 1960s often centers on governmental policies, but there were certainly institutions of power outside of the government exercising racist oppression as well. As Creary's contribution deftly reminds us, the 1960s unsettled that power in various corridors.

In addition to the tension between white domination and black oppression, this section also illustrates important moments of cooperation on issues of race.

Saunders and Creary both provide examples in which white and black students were able to see a common identity beyond (or at least beside) race and oppose the injustice together. These alliances offered shining examples in the 1960s that a movement built of new, globally informed ideas of justice was possible.

The struggle against racism was not new, nor was it won, in the 1960s. Neither was the struggle for university reform or democratization in Brazil. Indeed, very few of the issues of the 1960s were actually new at all. The 1960s, in these chapters, represented a new engagement with old issues. This new engagement also took novel forms and allowed for fresh voices to come forward. These studies demonstrate that while much of the action of the 1960s took place in the street and on college campuses, it also occurred in quiet seminary halls, cricket fields, the offices of military dictators, and dancehalls.

In the final section, "Unfinished Business: Challenging the State's Revolution," we present four case studies in which students in Mexico, the Philippines, Indonesia, and the Congo challenged the state's claim to represent a revolutionary or postcolonial government. In each of these cases, students ask a fundamental question: "What do we do now that the revolution has supposedly already taken place?" This question was particularly important for the Third World. The French and American Revolutions aside, students in Western Europe and the United States all looked at social and cultural transformation as something that was to come in the future, and did not have to contend with governments that claimed that revolutionary politics was a thing of the past. Of course, as these four studies point out, despite the state's claim to represent a revolutionary or post-colonial government, they were anything but. Indeed, what prompted students in Mexico, the Philippines, Indonesia, and the Congo to take to the streets was the fact that these supposed "revolutionary" governments had become, over varying amounts of time, defenders of the status quo. They may have claimed the revolutionary or postcolonial mantle, but in reality they displayed the same entrenched, conservative, and unyielding qualities of many Western governments. What the students in each of these countries came to realize in the 1960s was that postcolonialism in the Congo, guided democracy in Indonesia, institutionalized revolution in Mexico, and nationalism in the Philippines were constructed notions used to maintain order and to propagate the power of individual leaders or mass political parties. The goal of the students during the 1960s was to tear down this façade.

Challenging the state's revolutionary monopoly meant making nationalist claims, a theme that each author highlights in their respective studies. These four chapters therefore work to unsettle common approaches to the 1960s, which often do not focus on nationalism. The reader will notice that these nationalist claims manifested themselves very differently. In the Philippines, for example, the Movement for the Advancement of Nationalism (MAN) heavily criticized the Philippines' industrial and economic policies, Marcos's close relationship with the United States, and the continued influence of foreigners in the Philippines' national affairs. In Indonesia, however, students made the opposite claims, demanding *more* American influence in the Indonesian university. Nevertheless, both sets of students relied on nationalist repertoires in an attempt to change policies in their respective countries. So, too, did students in the Congo, who criticized the government for its reliance on colonial tactics (especially when it came to disciplining dissent), and demanded that Mobutu Africanize the Congolese university. Even in Mexico, a state that gained independence well before the Congo, Indonesia, or the Philippines, students still relied on what Julia Sloan calls a "history of revolutionary nationalism to justify their position."

The students' nationalism upsets the binary between activists and the state that is present in many instances of unrest in the 1960s. As each of the authors in this section demonstrates, the students' demands, as well as their rhetoric, often overlapped with that of the state. At times this blurred the line between state and student, and occasionally allowed for the state to absorb the student movement more easily. Pedro Monaville, for example, demonstrates that Congolese students and President Mobutu both claimed to represent the interests of a postcolonial society. Meanwhile, in Indonesia, there was little distinction between the army and the main student group, the Indonesian Student Action Front, as Stephanie Sapiee's chapter points out. Despite fierce disagreements in the Philippines between Marcos and the main student movement, Erwin Fernandez's study shows that in the end "its [the student groups'] objectives fit well with Marcos's nationalism." Even in Mexico, where the students and the state fought a fierce battle that ended in horrible violence, students protested more against the current iteration of the Institutional Revolutionary Party (PRI) and its ossification, than against its revolutionary heritage. As Julia Sloan's chapter points out, the PRI was able to placate dissent when it rediscovered its populist past and incorporated many activists from the 1968 student movement into the bureaucracy.

Each of these case studies, despite their differences, brings forth a unique strand of the 1960s experience: that of challenging a ruling elite that is not necessarily anti-revolution, but relegates revolutionary politics and culture to history. And this, in essence, became the central conflict for the student groups discussed in this section. Where each government claimed to be the official caretaker of a revolutionary society, the students saw elites, hierarchy, contradiction, and the status quo. The 1960s was an exercise in reclaiming the revolutionary mantle from an older stultified generation of leaders. In the end, however, the ruling parties and elites could not abide such a challenge to their power or a disruption to the status quo, and so dissent was often met with bloodshed and violence, both from the government and (in the case of Indonesia) from the students and the army.

While the sections discussed above represent a unique theme or narrative that can be found in each of the chapters, we hope that the reader will continue to approach the Third World as a loosely bound collective body. Getting bogged down in the particularities of each case study is to lose the scope and dimension of the broader Third World experience. The opposite is also true; approaching this collection of essays from a purely global perspective is to obviate the nuance of each individual case. What is required of the reader is a very delicate balance that allows for the global, national, and local to coalesce into a single history. The chapters in this volume do not claim to define the Third World experience of the 1960s. They serve to open the field and to begin a new conversation. If this volume unsettles or upsets notions of what the 1960s means, what the Third World means, or how they might come together in a scholarly conversation, then our aim has been achieved. This is an exciting step in what promises to be a rich and highly nuanced discussion that will include voices from and about the 1960s. In the end, what this volume hopes to demonstrate is that a truly global analysis of this decade is impossible without an in-depth and prolonged conversation about the Third World.

Notes

Samantha and Zachary would like to thank Timothy S. Brown, Martin Klimke, and the three anonymous readers for their very helpful comments regarding this introduction and collection.

1. Jeremy Varon, *Bringing the War Home: The Weather Underground. The Red Army Faction, and Revolutionary Violence in the Sixties and Seventies* (Berkeley: University of California Press, 2004), 7.
2. Arthur Marwick, *The Sixties: Cultural Revolution in Britain, France, Italy, and the United States* (Oxford: Oxford University Press, 1998), 16.
3. David Barber, however, disagrees with the New Left's commitment to the Third World. He contends that the failure of the New Left was partially due to their inability to understand their whiteness and privilege and to truly embrace both the Black Power movement and liberation struggles in the Third World. See David Barber, *A Hard Rain Fell: SDS and Why it Failed* (Jackson: University of Mississippi Press, 2008), 8–9.
4. Max Elbaum, *Revolution in the Air: Sixties Radicals Turn to Lenin, Mao and Che* (New York: Verso, 2002), 53.
5. Ibid., 48.
6. Carole Fink, Philipp Gassert, and Detlef Junker (eds.), *1968: The World Transformed* (Cambridge: Cambridge University Press, 1998), 25.
7. Timothy Brown, *1968: West Germany in the World* (Cambridge: Cambridge University Press, forthcoming); Quinn Slobodian, "Corpse Polemics: The Third World and the Politics of Gore in 1960s West Germany," in Timothy Brown and Lorena Anton, eds., *Between the Avant Garde and the Everyday: Subversive Politics in Europe, 1958–2008* (New York: Berghahn Books, forthcoming); Niels Seibert, *Vergessene Proteste: Internationalismus und Antirassismus 1964–1983* (Münster: Unrast Verlag, 2008).
8. Kristin Ross, *May '68 and its Afterlives* (Chicago: Chicago University Press, 2002).
9. Maurice Isserman and Michael Kazin, *America Divided: The Civil War of the 1960s* (Oxford: Oxford University Press, 2000), 277.

10. Cynthia A. Young, *Soul Power: Culture, Radicalism, and the Making of a U.S. Third World Left* (Durham, NC: Duke University Press, 2006), 3.

11. Todd Gitlin, *The Sixties: Years of Hope, Days of Rage* (New York: Bantam Books, 1993), 262.

12. Varon (2004), 53.

13. Ibid, 70.

14. Keith Brewster, *Reflections on Mexico '68* (Malden, MA: Wiley-Blackwell, 2010); Eduardo Valle, *El ano de la Rebelion por la Democracia* (Mexico City: Oceiano, 2008); Elaine Carey, *Plaza of Sacrifices: Gender, Power, and Terror in 1968 Mexico* (Albuquerque: University of New Mexico Press, 2005); Enrique Dussel, *Beyond Philosophy: Ethics, History, Marxism and Liberation Philosophy* (Lanham, MD: Rowman & Littlefield Publishers, 2003); "Solidarity Under Siege: The Latin American Left, 1968," *American Historical Review* Vol. 114, No. 2 (April, 2009): 348–375; Quito Swan, *Black Power in Bermuda: The Struggle for Decolonization* (New York: Palgrave Macmillan, 2009); Christopher Dunn, *Brutality Garden: Tropicalia and the Emergence of a Brazilian Counterculture* (Chapel Hill: University of North Carolina Press, 2001); Andrew Ivaska, "Of Students, 'Nizers,' and a Struggle over Youth: Tanzania's 1966 National Service Crisis," *Africa Today* Vol. 51, No. 3 (Spring 2005): 83–107.

15. Mark Kurlansky, *1968: The Year that Rocked the World* (New York: Ballantine, 2004); Jeremi Suri, *Power and Protest, 1968: Memories and Legacies of a Global Revolt* (Cambridge, MA: Harvard University Press, 2003); Philipp Gassert and Martin Klimke, *1968: Memories and Legacies of a Global Revolt*, Bulletin of the German Historical Institute, No. 6 (2009).

16. Martin Klimke, *The Other Alliance: Student Protest in West Germany & the United States in the Global Sixties* (Princeton, NJ: Princeton University Press, 2010).

17. John Isbister, *Promises Not Kept: Poverty and the Betrayal of Third World Development* (Bloomfield, CT: Kumarian Press, 2003), 32–41.

18. For a discussion of the term *Third World* and its meaning, particularly after the end of the Cold War, see Mark T. Berger, "The End of the 'Third World?'" *Third World Quarterly* Vol. 15, No. 2 (June, 1994): 257–275.

19. For an in-depth discussion of the historical origins of the term *Third World*, see Christoph Kalter's chapter in this volume. As the subject is addressed at such length in the first chapter, we won't duplicate the discussion of the historical development of the term in this introduction.

20. Alfred Sauvy, "Trois Mondes, Une Planete," *L'Observateur*, 14 August 1952: 14.

21. For a discussion of the Bandung Conference and its impact on the Third World, see Vijay Prashad, *The Darker Nations: A People's History of the Third World* (New York: W.W. Norton, 2007).

22. Frederick Cooper, *Colonialism in Question: Theory, Knowledge, History* (Berkeley: University of California Press, 2005), 9.

23. See Marwick (1998) and Gerd-Rainer Horn, *The Spirit of '68: Rebellion in Western Europe and North America, 1956–1976* (Oxford: Oxford University Press, 2007) for a prolonged discussion of the "long 1960s." Both scholars begin their analysis of the 1960s with a discussion of the various political and cultural movements that emerged in the 1950s in Europe and the United States.

24. Sohnya Sayres (ed.), *The 60s, Without Apology* (Minneapolis: University of Minnesota Press, 1984).

25. Thomas Borstelmann, *The Cold War and the Color Line* (Cambridge, MA: Harvard University Press, 2003), 205.

26. Clifford Geertz, "What was the Third World Revolution?" *Dissent* Vol. 52, No. 1 (Winter, 2005): 35–45.

27. Although Latin America and the Caribbean did not follow the same trajectory as Africa and most of Asia, these countries still had to deal with a distinctive form of colonialism. The Monroe Doctrine and the United States' continued forays into the Caribbean and South America meant that these countries were nominally independent, but not free of outside interference.

28. Geertz (2005), 35.

29. Prasenjit Duara (ed.), "Introduction: The Decolonization of Asia and Africa in the Twentieth Century," in *Decolonization: Perspectives from Now and Then* (New York: Routledge, 2004), 10.

30. Cooper (2005), 18.

31. Duara (2004), 2.

32. The Congo is perhaps the clearest example of Western influence in a nominally independent power. The United States first supported the assassination of Patrice Lumumba, and then saw that Mobutu Sese Seko was able to come to power. In 1968, President Mobutu ordered the slaughter of students protesting against Western influence in Congolese society. For a discussion of the Congo in 1968, see Pedro Monaville's chapter in this volume. For a general analysis of the United States' manipulation of the Congo, see David N. Gibbs, *The Political Economy of Third World Intervention: Mines, Money and U.S. Policy in the Congo Crisis* (Chicago: The University of Chicago Press, 1991).

33. Partha Chatterjee discusses the development of the nation-state in the Third World, tracing its normalization as a means of political and social organization to the Bandung Conference. He also discusses the ideal of a strong state in the face of colonial oppression. See Partha Chatterjee, "Empire and Nation Revisited: 50 Years After Bandung," *Inter-Asia Cultural Studies* Vol. 6, No. 4 (2005): 477–496.

34. Horn (2007), 229

35. In addition, the social movements of the 1960s have, in some ways, set the tone for subsequent dissent. Directly confronting the nation-state, as protesters did in the 1960s, has become *the* cornerstone of political protest in many Third World societies, especially because other outlets to engage with the state—democratic institutions, open forums, political rights—are unavailable to many citizens. See, Lisa Thompson and Chris Tapscott (eds.), *Citizenship and Social Movements: Perspectives from the Third World* (New York: Palgrave MacMillan, 2010), 26.

36. See Marwick (1998), 281–287; for a discussion of education and university reform in West Germany, see Nick Thomas, *Protest Movements in West Germany: A Social History of Dissent and Democracy* (New York: Berg, 2003), 127–145; for a discussion of the Fouchet reforms, see Andrew Feenberg and Jim Freedman (eds.), *When Poetry Ruled the Streets: The French May Events of 1968* (Albany: State University of New York Press, 2001), 5; for a discussion of the evolution of radicalism at the University of California, see Isserman and Kazin (2000), 167–168.

37. Robert Daniels, *Year of the Heroic Guerrilla: World Revolution and Counterrevolution in 1968* (New York: Basic Books, 1989); Klimke (2010) also discusses the importance of mass media in forging a deep connection between West Germany and the United States, 3.

38. George Katsiaficas, *The Imagination of the New Left: A Global Analysis of 1968* (Boston, MA: South End Press, 1987).

39. See, for example, Suri (2003) and Klimke (2010), 206. For a perspective of the Cold War and the Civil Rights Movement, see Thomas Borstelmann, *The Cold War and the Color Line: American Race Relations in the Global Arena* (Cambridge, MA: University of Harvard Press, 2001).

40. Egypt is a particularly strong example, in which both Gamal Abdel Nasser and Anwar Sadat attempted to balance their policies between nationalism, leftism, capitalism, and radical Islam, as well as pressure from the Soviet Union and the United States. The pressures of the Cold War shaped the reigns of each of these men. See John Waterbury, *The Egypt of Nasser and Sadat: The Political Economy of Two Regimes* (Princeton, NJ: Princeton University Press, 1983).

41. For a discussion of the Cold War and its impact on the Third World, see Odd Arne Westad, *The Global Cold War: Third World Interventions and the Making of our Times* (Cambridge: Cambridge University Press, 2005).

42. Scholars such as Detleft Siegfried have challenged the utility of this concept of "youth revolt." See Siegfried, "Understanding 1968: Youth Rebellion, Generational Change and Postindustrial Society," in Alex Schildt and Detlef Siegfried (eds.), *Between Marx and Coca-Cola: Youth Cultures in Changing European Societies, 1960–1980* (New York: Berghahn Books), 71.

43. Martin Klimke and Joachim Scharloth, "1968 in Europe: An Introduction," in Klimke and Scharloth (eds.), *1968 in Europe* (New York: Palgrave, 2008), 2.

44. Of course, the idea of youth revolt does lend itself particularly well to the case of Mexico, particularly in the counterculture of Mexico City, as discussed in Eric Zolov, *Refried Elvis: The Rise of the Mexican Counterculture* (Berkley: University of California Press, 1999).

45. Gitlin (1993), 263.

46. Peter Braunstein and Michael William (eds.), *Imagine Nation: The American Counterculture in the 1960s and '70s* (New York: Routledge, 2002); Julie Stephens, *Anti-Disciplinary Protest: Sixties Radicalism and Post-Modernism* (Cambridge: University of Cambridge Press, 1998); Marwick (1998).

47. For a discussion of the Situationists, see Rene Vienet, *Enrages and Situationists in the Occupation Movement in Paris, 1968* (Brooklyn, NY: Automedia, 1992). For a more extensive discussion of *Kommune I*, see Brown (forthcoming).

48. Thomas Hecken and Agata Grzenia, "Situationism," in Martin Klimke and Joachim Scharloth (eds.), *1968 in Europe* (New York: Palgrave, 2008), 24.

49. Klimke and Scharloth (2008), 6

50. For a general overview of the counterculture in Western Europe and the United States, see Jeremi Suri, "The Rise and Fall of an International Counterculture, 1960–1975," *American Historical Review* Vol. 114, No. 1 (February, 2009): 61–68.

51. Dunn (2001); Zolov (1999).

52. Marwick (1998), 13–14, 19.

53. Ibid, 13.

54. Arif Dirlik, "1968 in the Third World," in Carole Fink, Philipp Gassert, and Detlef Junker (eds.), *1968: The World Transformed* (Cambridge: Cambridge University Press, 1998).

Part 1

Crossing Borders:
The Idea of the Third World
and the Global 1960s

Chapter 1

A Shared Space of Imagination, Communication, and Action

Perspectives on the History of the "Third World"

Christoph Kalter

Does the Third World still exist? Stating the growing empirical diversity of the societies grouped together under this overall label, economists and political scientists have repeatedly proclaimed the "end of the Third World" since the 1970s.[1] In the 1980s, the Third World concept came under attack from a theoretical perspective: Post-structuralist critics condemned it as an essentialist and, indeed, Eurocentric approach, confronting it with what they described as a multiplicity of margins outside the realm of Western modernity.[2] In 1989–1991, the end of the Cold War and the collapse of the socialist Second World seemed to finalize the doubts that social scientists had been raising for years as to the empirical and theoretical validity of a world view dividing the globe into three parts for analytical—but also for economic, political, military, and ideological—purposes. Since the 1990s, new dynamics of global interconnectedness and the triumph of the new paradigm "globalization" have furthered the decline of the three-worlds concept. The term *Third World* itself may even disappear from usage altogether. Thus, a better way to put the question, and, indeed, the central enquiry of this chapter is: What *was* the Third World?[3]

Given the paramount importance of the cosmology of the three worlds for the second part of the twentieth century, comparatively little historical research has been done on the genealogy of the concept and its myriad effects on political, social, and cultural representations and actions.[4] This is particularly true in regard to the history of "1968" and the counter-hegemonic movements of the "long" 1960s[5] all over the world.[6] The connection between "1968" and the Third World is still frequently reduced to the impact of the Vietnam War for Western protest movements in the 1960s. Although extensive and important work has been done on this aspect, I would like to emphasize several aspects that have sometimes been neglected. First, this war was perceived by contemporary 68ers as being part of a larger Third World problematic shaped by the confrontation of "imperialism" and "anti-imperialism." Second, representations as well as techniques of protest used by the Western opposition to the Vietnam War were only partly new, while on the other hand dating back to the Algerian war, the Cuban revolution, and other founding experiences of Third Worldism in the 1960s. Third, the Vietnam War set aside, "1968" was also taking place *in* various Third World countries ranging from Senegal to Mexico, China, India, Turkey, and many others, thus turning 1968 in a global phenomenon.

For many of the protesters of the 1960s—as will be argued in this chapter—the Third World was essential: the concept allowed for a radical critique of existing systems of power and representations while permitting them at the same time to elaborate equally radical alternatives. The Third World stimulated the transnational mobilization of protest movements. It had profound effects on worldviews and self-images of intellectuals and activists. To begin with, this chapter provides an overview of the making of the "Third World" in the social sciences and political discourse of the long 1960s. More specifically, it will address the situation in France, where the concept was invented in 1952, established as a scientific paradigm in 1956, and, around 1960, turned into a highly politicized symbol in the context of post-war consumer capitalism, the Cold War, and the process of decolonization, especially the Algerian war. It will be argued that this symbol spread globally and created a space of imagination, communication, and action shared by, but at the same time specifically divided between, the First and the Third Worlds, thus producing its fundamental ambivalence.

The Making of the Third World: Consumer Capitalism, Cold War, and Decolonization

Given the centrality of notions like "development" or "progress" for the idea of the Third World, the concept's history in a broader sense must be traced back at least as far as the eighteenth century. While Christian notions of a teleological history of salvation lingered on, they merged with a developmentalist paradigm emerging in scientific discourses and new time concepts emanating from the socioeconomic and cultural upheavals caused by the Industrial Revolution. To- gether, these strands shaped the idea of constant material und immaterial "prog- ress" in natural and human history.[7] As for the latter, progress and "civilization" were thought to be originating in the rationality of "the West"[8] and its specifically "modern"[9] societies, but at the same time were ascribed universal validity. Hence, the duty of Western civilization seemed to be spreading its particular mode of societal organization to the rest of the world. In the course of the nineteenth century, this "White Man's Burden" or "civilizing mission" was foundational for the legitimatory discourse of European colonialism in Asia and Africa.[10] After the First World War, Europeans warranted their ongoing colonial rule in these territories (as well as the mandate system of the League of Nations) under the heading of their *mise en valeur,* or development.[11] While Europeans, as a result, had firmly established the belief in development by the mid twentieth century, the related concept of "underdevelopment" brought forth in the aftermath of the inaugural address of US President Harry S. Truman in January 1949 was a terminological innovation. This powerful innovation induced a set of semantic shifts as well as new institutions and practices that shaped the transition from European colonial rule to the US-dominated, post-colonial "development age" of the subsequent decades.[12]

The new signal term *underdevelopment* was also the starting point in the invention of the Third World. When, in 1952, economist and demographer Alfred Sauvy (1898–1990)[13] created the term *tiers monde* in an article entitled "Trois mondes, une planète" in the French magazine *L'Observateur*,[14] he referred to the underdeveloped countries outside either of the camps of the Cold War. In defining the Third World for the first time in history, Sauvy thus combined the recently established notion of underdevelopment as socioeconomic backwardness plus demographic pressure with a geopolitical argument: The competition between the developed societies in the capitalist First and the socialist Second World, Sauvy thought, was centered on, shaped by, and even originated in the existence of a Third World.[15] Although it was underdeveloped, and although it was ignored, exploited, and disdained like the Third Estate had been on the eve of the French Revolution, the Third World held a central place in contemporary world politics. Like the Third Estate some 160 years earlier, the Third World was striving for recognition and power. It constituted—and that was Sauvy's equally central and predictive claim—a potentially revolutionary force.[16] By relating the upcoming non- or even anti-European revolutions of the Third World to the French and Western histories of enlightenment and progress, Sauvy, a liberal Republican himself, endowed the project of Third World emancipation and development—which he thought were inseparable—with a historical legitimacy that stemmed from a European, indeed Eurocentric, worldview. The resulting ambivalence was to mark durably the concept of the Third World.

Sauvy, the head of the French Institut National d'Études Démographiques (INED) between 1945 and 1962, had invented a new geopolitical space, a new world; his close collaborator at the Institute, anthropologist, sociologist, and Africanist Georges Balandier (born in 1920) was to transform Sauvy's journalistic catchphrase into a paradigm of the emerging "modern" social sciences. In 1956, Balandier edited the first book ever to have the Third World on its cover: the contributions in *Le "tiers monde": Sous-développement et développement* displayed a multidisciplinary approach.[17] Economists, political scientists, sociologists, ethnologists, geographers, demographers, and historians were explaining the past, present, and future of what they understood to be the underdeveloped world. Adding a third criterion to the economic and geopolitical features identified by Sauvy (insufficient development and a neither-nor position in the Cold War), they stressed a historical commonality of underdeveloped societies. All of them, so went the argument, were still or had been until recently colonized by European powers. None of the contributors, actually, used the term *tiers monde,* but since Balandier published their articles under this overall heading, they neverthe-less effectively contributed to the discursive institutionalization of the concept. One step further in setting up this new discourse was the launching of the review *Tiers Monde* by the French Institut d'Étude du Développement Économique et Social (IEDES) in 1960.[18] While books bearing *tiers monde* in their title became more and more frequent in France since 1961,[19] from 1963 onward, the French term was translated first into English, German, or Swedish,[20] then into possibly every other language of the contemporary world. Quickly, the rather off-the-cuff invention of a French professor had become a global success story.

But what made the idea of the Third World so attractive? In the eyes of con-temporaries, the concept had great plausibility, since it allowed conceptualizing three parallel, but also partly interdependent economic, geopolitical, and histori-cal reconfigurations of the post-war world. The first of these changes was the emergence of a US-dominated economic world system whose center of gravity was the "Atlantic integration" of Western nations.[21] Their economies benefited above all others from the rapidly growing quantity of international trade. Until the oil crisis of 1973–1974, the West experienced a "golden age," characterized by three decades of unprecedented growth creating enormously prosperous so-cieties of mass consumerism.[22] This overabundance contrasted all the more dra-matically with what simultaneously came to be perceived as the dreadful misery of two thirds of the global population; by contrast to the happy few in the First and the competing Second World, material conditions, societal organization, and the people of the Third World were now looked upon as being essentially poor and underdeveloped.[23] Thus constructing their need for development—a perception soon to be shared by many Africans, Asians, and Latin Americans themselves—the Third World became an object and actor of Cold War rivalries. While trying to export theories and practices of "modernization"[24] and devel-opment, the First and Second Worlds strived to prove the superiority of their respective societies and, by doing so, create allegiances in the new Third World and its "young nations."

In addition to the developed/underdeveloped divide, the Cold War, then, became the second important frame in defining global politics and Third World characteristics. Despite what many people had been hoping for, the forceful anti-Hitler coalition, resting for a large part on the economic strength of the US and the human potential of the USSR, was definitely over by 1947. The old al-lies had become superpowers fighting each other by every means possible—every means except open warfare in direct confrontation, which was, with regard to the destructive potential of nuclear weapons on both sides of the iron curtain, no longer an option. Washington, DC, and Moscow became the defining centers of their respective political, economic, and military "camps" in a bipolar world. But bipolarity was not total, and many territories did not want to conform to the East-West dichotomy and its Cold War. Rather, they constituted a third space of global politics, a Third World acting on the two superpowers as well as experiencing enticements and pressures from them—often resulting in dreadfully hot proxy wars.[25]

The third reconfiguration of the global post-war era reflected in the concept of the Third World was decolonization. The Second World War had accelerated the end of Empire, leading to the formation of new nation-states in the former colonies. The decolonization of Asia—with the exception of Indochina—had been completed by 1950. In the following decade, national liberation movements appeared in Africa, claiming and obtaining the end of colonial rule. In 1960, the peak year of African decolonization, 17 new nation-states were founded, and after 1962–1963, only Portugal and a few settler colonies in Southern Africa still resisted the general trend toward transfer of power on the continent. In the light of this process of paramount importance for twentieth-century history,[26] the colonial past or present as well as the existence of anti-colonial parties, movements, or governments became an important element of contemporary definitions of the Third World.

As we have seen earlier, the Third World concept was established in the context of European social sciences as a means of talking about non-European societies, thus constructing them as the Other of Europe. This one-sided discourse, though, was not to last very long. Following the landmark Afro-Asian Bandung conference in 1955,[27] the term *tiers monde*—which had *not* been used by the participants of the conference—came to be employed more frequently by French, but also North African journalists and intellectuals in Paris.[28] The real breakthrough, though, was the final stage of the Algerian war. One of the most violent conflicts in the history of decolonization, the confrontation between the French army and the Algerian national liberation movement Front de Libération Nationale (FLN) started in 1954.[29] By the end of the decade, it had turned into a massive military and political conflict, thrusting the interconnected Algerian and French societies into a state of civil war unparalleled by any other colonial war before. This dramatic process brought about a strong politicization of the term *Third World*, expanding its use outside the accustomed realm of scientific and journalistic discourse. But there was even more to it: through the Algerian war, the Third World became a de-Europeanized concept, a nodal point for political identities inside, but most of all *outside* the West.

From Third World to Global Third Worldism: Fanon and the Impact of the Algerian War

When a radical, leftist publishing house in Paris edited *Les damnés de la terre* (The Wretched of the Earth) in 1961, the book encountered an immediate and long-lasting success and was soon to be translated into no less than 17 languages.[30] Its author, Frantz Fanon (1925–1961), born and raised on the French island Martinique in the Caribbean, had studied medicine in France where he published his first book in 1952. *Peau noire, masques blancs* (Black Skin, White Masks) reflected the author's personal experience and intellectual force as well as his familiarity with French philosophy. Postcolonial studies still emphasize its lasting importance for a theoretically and politically relevant critique of racism. One year later, in 1953, Fanon became the head of the psychiatric hospital Blida-Joinville in Algeria. In 1956, he left his post and joined the FLN, since then working for its newspaper *El Moudjahid* (The Freedom Fighter),[31] and traveling around Africa as a theorist and ambassador of the Algerian liberation movement, attending conferences and meetings with governments and national liberation movements in Ghana, Mali, Cameroon, and Angola.[32]

In his 1961 anti-colonial manifesto, *Les damnés de la terre,* Fanon depicts the impending end of Empire not as a withdrawal generously consented to by the ancient colonizers, but as a "colonial revolution" forced upon them by the—explicitly violent—agency of the colonized. In Fanon's view, decolonization was a multi-faceted process of political, social, economic, but also cultural emancipation collectively undertaken by the colonized subjects. In the process, so Fanon argued, the colonized deconstructed the universalist pretences of the "civilizing mission" as an ethnocentric superiority complex and a discourse designed to legitimate the racialized control Europeans had been exerting over them. According to Fanon, colonial revolution—that is, decolonization—was a national(ist) project, responding to the specific situation of each colonized collective, but also a transnational reality, a movement of solidarity transcending the boundaries of Algeria or Africa and stretching out into the entirety of what Fanon referred to as the Third World.

Fanon's book, thus, marks a turning point in the history of the Third World concept. For the first time, a black anti-colonial activist publicly used a phrase originally coined by white French social scientists in an affirmative manner, designating not only the author-self, but a potentially global collective of colonized revolutionaries. The "Wretched of the Earth" to which Fanon referred were no longer found exclusively (or even primarily) in the factories of the industrialized First World,[33] but rather among the revolutionary peasant "masses" of the agrarian Third World. In the mind of Fanon, colonial revolution would not only free the colonized, but in fact was a starting point—and a precondition—of nothing less than the liberation of all humanity from capitalist exploitation, racism, and violence. Fanon, arguing that the Third World people were the "new men," constructed them as the counter-model of a decadent Europe and its painfully patent incapacity to live up to its own, outdated claims of being the center of humanity, history, and progress.

Following Fanon, it became possible for Third World people to speak *for* themselves in a terminology that initially had been created to talk *about* them. This recontextualization of the Third World concept transformed it into a marker of anti- and postcolonial identities and practices, into a means of empowerment of the South that combined with a programmatic decentering of the West.[34] Nearly a decade after its invention, the Third World thus took on an ambivalence that remained fundamental in the years to come. From now on, it was a concept constantly oscillating between the depiction of a "Third World Other" on the one hand, and the assertion of a "Third World self" on the other. For the political and intellectual leaders and, probably to a far lesser degree, for the people in Asia, Africa, and Latin America, the Third World became a powerful resource of political organization and legitimacy. Those in charge of national liberation movements or post-colonial nation-states used it as a "mobilization myth"[35] in their struggle for national independence, social revolution, "autochthonous" modernization, or, unfortunately, in the setting up of autocratic regimes and in securing their personal power. On an international level, Third World solidarity was called for—indeed, strived for—and at least partially institutionalized as an alternative to the Cold War binarity and as a weapon against "neo-colonialism" and "dependency."[36] For several decades, the Third World structured the collective articulation of interests shared by heterogeneous actors in the "Non-Aligned Movement," the "Tricontinental," or in the "Group 77."

Starting with the Bandung and Belgrade conferences of 1955 and 1961, the Non-Aligned Movement was constructed by advocates of "peaceful coexistence" and strict neutrality on the one hand, and militant anti-imperialists on the other; accordingly, it vacillated between a doctrine of disengagement and a doctrine of combat.[37] In contrast to this hesitancy, the confrontational "anti-imperialist" stance of the Cuba-led Tricontinental movement was very straightforward: In spring 1967, in a famous letter addressed to the OSPAAAL[38] formed at the first Tricontinental Conference in January 1966,[39] Ernesto "Che" Guevara called for the creation of "two, three, many Vietnams" as a means to encircle "the repressive forces of Yankee imperialism."[40] As for the Group 77, it was less belligerent, but at least equally visible: Founded in 1964 during the first United Nations Conference on Trade and Development (UNCTAD), it assembled a loose coalition of Third World countries articulating shared demands in the United Nations. The Group 77 targeted primarily the deterioration of the terms of trade and the structural disadvantages for Third World countries in the world market. In 1974, this battle culminated in a UN resolution demanding the construction of a "New International Economic Order" (NIEO).[41]

This kind of collective politics and politicized self-images made available by the groundbreaking work of Fanon and centered on the notion of a (post-) colonial but potentially revolutionary, underdeveloped but morally superior Third World is being referred to as "Third Worldism" in the Anglophone scholarly literature. This ex post facto term accounts for the ideas and practices of national liberation movements, of transnational Third World coalitions, of the "first-generation Bandung regimes" up to the early 1960s and the more explicitly Marxist-Leninist "second-generation Bandung regimes" of the late 1960s and 1970s in the Third World.[42] But there is more to it: "Third Worldism," and especially its French equivalent "*tiers-mondisme*,"[43] are also meant to include the attraction experienced by First World activists to the politicized concept of the Third World. Just as Fanon and others were appropriating this concept and giving it a wider and different meaning, the Third World traveled back to the First, where its semantics also expanded further. As a means of designating the Third World Other, the concept continued to be used in Western social sciences, its media, and mainstream political discourse. But in the context of the Algerian war and the Cuban revolution of 1959 it also became highly relevant for left wing radicalism in France and elsewhere in "the West."

Alliance, Projection, or Mutual Constitution? The Third World and the New Radical Left

What we refer to as the "new radical left" came into being in France, West Germany, Italy, the US, and other Western societies since around 1956, the year Balandier edited *Le tiers monde* and Fanon joined the FLN. It was a heterogeneous, transnationally related set of political actors, comprising the Nouvelle Gauche, the New Left and Neue Linke, as well as "old" dissident left currents like Trotskyism or Anarchism. Later on, Maoism was equally part of the radical left. Its components thus were not only distinct, but sometimes rivals or even sworn enemies in the field of the political left. Together, they were at the core of—though not identical with—the counter-hegemonic movements of the long 1960s in the West. What justifies, despite important differences, their common labeling as the "new radical left," are their even more important commonalities: first, the radical left stood for Marxist-inspired politics aimed at socialist revolution, but nevertheless clearly dissociated itself from the traditional left incarnated by the old socialist and orthodox communist parties alike. The radical left accused reformist socialists and social democrats of giving away the idea of revolution. As for the communists, the emerging radical left interpreted the 1956 revelations of Stalinist crimes and the bloody suppression of the Hungarian uprising of the same year as painful proof of the corrupt nature of the Soviet Union, which had completely given up the promise for a better world it had originally stood for. Apart from being a dissident, but powerfully voiced new left minority, the second and equally decisive commonality of the radical left was that it conceived of itself as being radically anti-colonial or anti-imperialist and had a strong interest in and commitment to what came to be known as the Third World. It unconditionally backed the process of decolonization, thus dissociating itself from the missing or only incomplete and hesitant support socialist and communist parties were willing to give to the "colonial revolution" of Third World actors.

Thus, the radical left and the Third World not only emerged roughly at the same time—the threshold from the 1950s to the 1960s—but they were to a great extent mutually constitutive. The new radical left in France and elsewhere largely contributed to the propagation and the politicization of Third World-representations. Together with actors of the Third World it institutionalized a set of discourses that motivated political action in the (ancient) colonies *and* in Western societies. Conversely, those Third World representations, as well as the concrete interactions with its representatives, made it possible for the radical left to create a distance from the "old" left, to develop new perspectives on worldwide revolutionary politics, to recruit new activists—in short: to exist as an independent political force. As can be shown through the widespread reception of the preface that Jean-Paul Sartre, Europe's most famous public intellectual,[44] wrote for Fanon's *Les damnés de la terre* in 1961, the idea of a Third World functioned as a mobilization myth in the Western societies as well: Conflicts of leftist minorities with left mainstream parties could be articulated through the concept of the Third World; a new radical left could be institutionalized; the sparkling enthusiasm for Third World revolutions motivated activities—for example, supporting the FLN by means of propaganda or illegal actions—that had long-lasting effects on worldviews, self-images, and practices of the radical left and Third Worldist protest movements in the West.

Many of the French protesters of 1968, for instance, had not organized their first demonstrations in May or June of that same year, but already during the Algerian war. In the Parisian spring of 1968, they could rely on a network of political friendships built up some years earlier in the student union UNEF,[45] the dissident circles of the communist UEC,[46] in the "anti-fascist" FUA,[47] or in the radical left party PSU,[48] all of them highly engaged in the opposition against the Algerian war. As for the American war in Vietnam, French activists conceived of it as being part of the global colonial revolution theorized by Frantz Fanon, Kwame Nkrumah, and Che Guevara, but also by Jean-Paul Sartre, Régis Debray, or the authors of the French periodical *Partisans*.[49] In their view, the violent repression with which police forces met Parisian street riots in 1968 not only resembled the brutality the same police had deployed against Algerian migrants and French protesters in 1961–1962,[50] but also was paralleled with the "war crimes" US troops were thought to be committing systematically in the jungle of Vietnam. While the Vietcong was suffering from toxic gases deployed by American soldiers, Parisian students, it was claimed, were suffering from the very same gases deployed by French police forces.[51]

As this example indicates, for the Western radical left, the Third World not only allowed for making sense of the changes brought about by the end of Empire while relating them to other defining configurations—namely, the Cold War and the perceived simultaneity of plenty in the North and scarcity in the South. Moreover, the Third World could be used politically: the "colonial revolution" was interpreted as a revolutionary space interconnected with First World struggles, giving them new, decisive impulses. "Anti-colonial" revolutions in the Third World would help "anti-capitalist" revolutions in the West. The stamina of the Third World, successfully fighting asymmetrical wars against seemingly superior Western enemies, made the small minority of Western left radicals feel they had a powerful ally in a common cause being fought for by the "oppressed masses" all over the world. Paris, Berlin, Prague, Berkeley, Tokyo, Algiers, Dakar, Havana, Mexico, or Hanoi: In the eyes of the radical left, it was all the part of the "same combat," whose actors were partaking in nothing less than a joint "world revolution." Western minorities being marginalized in their own societies felt they were finally joining what they saw as the victorious majority of the world's population. If revolution was possible in the Third World, it had to be possible at home, too.

The new radical left's ability "to imagine and claim common cause with a radical Third World subject involved multiple translations and substitutions; it required the production of an imagined terrain able to close the multiple gaps between First and Third World subjects."[52] These transpositions, which were needed to construct a common cause, were more or less convincingly grounded in theoretical and empirical arguments about the necessity and reality of joint "anti-imperialist" action. But at the same time they were not exempt from stereotyped idealizations of the Third World that combined with the collapsing of strong disparities existing between the First and the Third World, or within the Third World itself. In this perspective, decolonization was not only a Third World reality, but also a screen on which the First World radical left was projecting its concrete political objectives—as well as its rather vague desires for making history and experiencing adventure, for attaining change, purity, heroism, and grandeur that were supposedly incarnated by the Third World. Stereotyped perceptions of difference as well as romantic or political projections of a Self on its Other, of course, were potentially and sometimes effectively mutual: Third World actors as well held stereotyped ideas about Third and First World realities, and they too could "use" First World activists to further their own political goals or suppress their political opponents by means of propaganda or material support.

Describing these projections, distortions, or "instrumental" approaches should not, though, prevent us from acknowledging the remarkable destructive *and* constructive potential of the Third World concept for the new radical left and the counter-hegemonic movements in the West as well as for Third World actors themselves. All over the world, the Third World allowed for a radical critique of existing systems of power and representations that were considered to be effective globally ("imperialism"), but at the same time to be rooted locally—i.e., to take on a specific form in any given society (e.g., "colonialism" in Portuguese Angola, corruption of "neo-colonialist" elites in Senegal, "exploitation" of migrant workers in France, "racism" in the US, "apartheid" in South Africa, "authoritarian" or "fascist" structures of society in Western Germany, etc.). Mediated through the Third World were not only critiques of these and many more existing structures and semantics, but also the continuation and modification of others. This applies, for example, to the Marxist tradition, which in the process of constructing the Third World, came to be revitalised and enriched by approaches originating in Algeria, Ghana, the Portuguese colonies, Vietnam, China, or Latin America—that is, outside the classical centers of Marxist thought in Western Europe or the Soviet Union.[53] This kind of constructive decentring also affected key concepts of Western social sciences and everyday knowledge like "progress," "development," or "modernization," which under the sign of the Third World slowly came to be discussed in a new light.

Conclusion: The Third World in History

So what *was* the Third World? As this chapter has argued, in the "long" 1960s, unequal development, the Cold War, and decolonization came to be conceptualized in the paradigm of the three worlds. Invented within French academia, the Third World became a cornerstone of Western modernization theory, social sciences, and development politics. At the same time, though, the Third World became associated with revolutionary non- or anti-Western politics in the context of the Algerian war and Fanons *Les damnés de la terre*. While depictions of the Third World as distinct from and inferior to the First World lingered on in academic circles, media, and politics of Western societies, the semantic shifts induced by Fanon and others allowed for new imaginations of the world and the self in the First *and* in the Third World. In the process, Third World activists and governments as well as radical leftists in the First World came to see the former as the driving force of a shared project of emancipation. Those ideas had an explicitly global scope and were themselves mediated by a wide array of practices of transnational communication and action. Physical and intellectual mobility, and most of all travel, print-culture, and image-making media, were, as Cynthia A. Young has rightly pointed out, "essential technolog[ies] of time-space-compression" that were "helping to disseminate Third World ideas across the globe."[54] The idea of the Third World itself, in fact, had initially helped to create this global space it was now being disseminated in. While on the one hand preserving essentialist and Eurocentric perspectives, the Third World concept on the other hand was fundamental for decentering claims to the superiority of "the West" over "the Rest."[55] In sum, it was an ambivalent, yet very powerful, discursive reality of the long 1960s.

Whether the term *Third World* still holds any analytical or political value today is more than doubtful.[56] From our point of view, the Third World belongs to days gone by. Advocating the necessary historicization of the concept, as we have done in this chapter, does not, of course, imply that its history is irrelevant for understanding our present day "one world." On the contrary, appreciating the historical dimension of recent processes of "globalization" is hardly possible without accounting for the shared space that the Third World concept had opened up, thus creating and representing global entanglements between seemingly distant worlds.

Notes

1. See Mark T. Berger, "After the Third World? History, Destiny and the Fate of Third Worldism," in Berger (ed.), *After the Third World?* (London: Routledge, 2009), 9–39, 30 (originally published in *Third World Quarterly* Vol. 25, No. 1 (2004)).
2. Frans J. Schuurman, "Paradigms Lost, Paradigms Regained? Development Studies in the Twenty-First Century," *Third World Quarterly* Vol. 21 (2000): 7–20.
3. One of the best articles on the subject is: B. R. Tomlinson, "What Was the Third World?" *Journal of Contemporary History* Vol. 38 (2003): 307–321. See also Vijay Prashad, *The Darker Nations: A People's History of the Third World* (New York: The New Press, 2007).
4. Still the most important starting point: Carl E. Pletsch, "The Three Worlds, or the Division of Social Scientific Labor, circa 1950–1975," *Comparative Studies in Society and History* Vol. 23 (1981): 565–587.
5. On the "long" 1960s, see for example Arthur Marwick, "'1968' and the Cultural Revolution of the Long Sixties (c.1958–c.1974)," in Gerd-Rainer Horn and Padraic Kenney (eds.), *Transnational Moments of Change: Europe 1945, 1968, 1989* (Lanham, MD: Rowman & Littlefield, 2004), 81–94.
6. Despite a general deficiency of scholarly accounts, some authors *have* actually stressed the Third World dimension of "1968"; see for example: Ingo Juchler, *Die Studentenbewegungen in den Vereinigten Staaten und der Bundesrepublik Deutschland der sechziger Jahre: Eine Untersuchung hinsichtlich ihrer Beeinflussung durch Befreiungsbewegungen und -theorienaus der Dritten Welt* (Berlin: Duncker & Humblot, 1996); Arif Dirlik, "The Third World," in Carole Fink, Philipp Gassert, and Detlef Junker (eds.), *1968: The World Transformed* (Cambridge: Cambridge University Press, 1998), 295–317; Kristin Ross, *May '68 and Its Afterlives* (Chicago: University of Chicago Press, 2002); Cynthia A. Young, *Soul Power: Culture, Radicalism and the Making of a U.S. Third World Left* (Durham: Duke University Press 2006); Robert Frank, "Imaginaire politique et figures symboliques internationales," in Geneviève Dreyfus-Armand et al. (eds.), *Les Années 68: Le temps de la contestation* (Bruxelles : Editions Complexe 2000), 31–47; Romain Bertrand, "Mai 68 et l'anticolonialisme," in Dominique Damamme et al.(eds.), *Mai-Juin 68* (Paris : Atelier, 2008), 89–101; several contributions in Janick Marina Schaufelbuehl (ed.), 1968–1978: *Ein bewegtes Jahrzehnt in der Schweiz/Une décennie mouvementée en Suisse*. UnterMitarbeitvon/Avec la collaboration de Nuno Pereira und Renate Schär (Zurich 2009); and numerous contributions in the excellent volume Jens Kastner and David Mayer (eds.), *Weltwende 1968? Ein Jahr aus globalgeschichtlicher Perspektive* (Wien : Mandelbaum, 2008).
7. Reinhart Kößler, *Entwicklung* (Münster 1998), 11–58.
8. Alastair Bonnett, *The Idea of the West: Culture, Politics and History* (New York: Palgrave MacMillan, 2004).
9. Peter Wagner, "Modernity: History of the Concept," in Neil C. Smeilser and Paul B. Baltes (eds.), *International Encyclopedia of the Social & Behavioral Sciences* Vol. 15, (Amsterdam 2001), 9949–9954.

10. Boris Barth and Jürgen Osterhammel (eds.), *Zivilisierungsmissionen: Imperiale Weltverbesserung seit dem 18. Jahrhundert* (Konstanz : UVK Verlagsgesellschaft, 2005).

11. Gilbert Rist, *The History of Development: From Western Origins to Global Faith* (New York: Zed Books, 2002), 47–68.

12. Ibid., 72f.; Arturo Escobar, *Encountering Development: The Making and Unmaking of the Third World* (Princeton, NJ: Princeton University Press 1995); Heide-Irene Schmidt and Helge Pharo, "Introduction: Europe and the First Development Decade: The Foreign Economic Assistance Policy of European Donor Countries, 1958–1972," *Contemporary European History* Vol. 12 (2003), 387–394.

13. Michel Margairaz, "Alfred Sauvy," in Jacques Julliard and Michel Winock (eds.), *Dictionnaire des intellectuels français* (Paris: Éditions du Seuil, 1996), 1032–1034.

14. Alfred Sauvy, "Trois mondes, une planète" [1952], in Elsa Assidon, Sophie Bessis, and Serge Cordellier (eds.), *La fin du tiers monde?* (Paris: Découverte, 1996), 145–147.

15. Strangely enough, the importance of Third World societies for the dynamics of the global Cold War emphasized by Sauvy has received very little attention in historical accounts of the post-war world up to the 1990s. Only recently have historians begun to investigate this aspect, see for example Odd Arne Westad, *The Global Cold War: Third World Interventions and the Making of our Time* (Cambridge: Cambridge University Press, 2005).

16. The most famous citation in Sauvy's article, "Car enfin, ce tiers monde ignoré, exploité, méprisé comme le tiers état, veut, lui aussi, être quelque chose," is a reference to the famous pamphlet *Qu'est-ce que le tiers état?* by Abbé Sieyès in 1789. Revolution, indeed, was to be a central characteristic of Third World societies in the second half of the twentieth century; see the chapter "Third World and Revolution" in Eric Hobsbawm, *The Age of Extremes: A History of the World, 1914–1991* (New York: Pantheon Books, 1994).

17. Georges Balandier (ed.), *Le "tiers monde": Sous-développement et développement*. Préfacé d'Alfred Sauvy (Paris: Presses universitaires de France, 1956).

18. In 1967 it changed its name into *Revue Tiers Monde*, which is still being published today, see http://www.armand-colin.com/revue/30/1/revue-tiers-monde.php (accessed 30 June 2010).

19. The first ones were Robert Descloitres, Jean-Claude Reverdy, and Claudine Descloitres, *L'Algérie des bidonvilles: Le Tiers Monde dans la cité* (Paris: Mouton & Co, 1961); Marc Bonnefous, *Europe et tiers monde* (Leyde: A.W. Sythoff, 1961); H. Chambre, J.-P. Saltiel, and A. Nowicki, *Tiers Monde et Commerce des Pays de l'Est* (Paris: I.S.E.A., 1962); Jean Lacouture and Jean Baumier, *Le poids du Tiers Monde: Un milliard d'hommes* (Paris: Arthaud, 1962).

20. Early Anglophone volumes were Mario Rossi, *The Third World: The Unaligned Countries and the World Revolution* (New York: Funk & Wagnalls, 1963), and Peter Worsley, *The Third World* (London: Weidenfeld & Nicolson, 1964). For a short history of the invention and the first translations of the term see Erik Tängerstad, "'The Third World' as an Element in the Collective Construction of a Post-Colonial European Identity," in Bo Stråth (ed.), *Europe and the Other and Europe as the Other* (Brussels: P.I.E.-Peter Lang, 2000), 157–193.

21. Hermann van der Wee, *Der gebremste Wohlstand. Wiederaufbau, Wachstum und Strukturwandelder Weltwirtschaftseit 1945* (Munich: Deutscher Taschenbuch Verlag, 1984).

22. See the chapter "The Golden Years" in Hobsbawm (1995). For a historical account of consumerism in the last century see Victoria de Grazia, *Irresistible Empire: America's Advance through Twentieth-Century Europe* (Cambridge: Belknap Press of Harvard University Press, 2005).

23. On this process see the chapter "The Problematization of Poverty: The Tale of the Three Worlds and Development" in Escobar (1995).

24. On modernization, see David C. Engerman et al. (eds.), *Staging Growth: Modernization, Development, and the Global Cold War* (Amherst: University of Massachusetts Press, 2003); Michael E. Latham, *Modernization as Ideology: American Social Science and "Nation Building" in the Kennedy Era* (Chapel Hill: University of North Carolina Press, 2000); Andreas Eckert, Stephan Malinowski, and Corinna R. Unger (eds.), *Modernizing Missions* (Munich: Beck, 2010) (originally published in *Journal of Modern European History* Vol. 8 (2010): 1).

25. Bernd Greiner, Christian Th. Müller, and Dierk Walter (eds.), *Heiße Kriege im Kalten Krieg* (Hamburg: Hamburger Editions, 2006).

26. Contemporary awareness of the importance of decolonization was widespread; see for example Geoffrey Barraclough, "The Revolt against the West" [1964], in Prasenjit Duara (ed.) *Decolonization: Perspectives from Now and Then* (London: Routledge, 2003), 118–130.

27. See the contemporary account by Richard Wright, *The Color Curtain: A Report on the Bandung Conference [1956]*. With A Foreword by Gunnar Myrdal and an Afterword by Amritjit Singh (Jackson, MS: Banner Books, 1995). See also Jamie Mackie, *Bandung 1955: Non-Alignment and Afro-Asian Solidarity* (Singapore: Editions Didier Millet, 2005).

28. Yves Lacoste, *Contre les anti-tiers-mondistes et contre certains tiers-mondistes* (Paris : La Découverte, 1985); Tängerstad (2000), 168f.

29. On the Algerian war, see Benjamin Stora and Mohammed Harbi (eds.), *La guerre d'Algérie, 1954–2004: La fin de l'amnésie* (Paris: R. Laffont, 2004).

30. Although the book had for a time been censored by French authorities, in France it sold 150,000 copies until 1968; see Claude Liauzu, "Intellectuels du tiers monde et intellectuels français: Les années algériennes des Éditions Maspero," in Jean-Pierre Rioux and Jean-François Sirinelli (eds.), *La guerre d'Algérie et les intellectuels français* (Paris: Institut d'histoire du Temps Présent, 1988), 105–118, 113. On the publishing house *Éditions Maspero,* see Julien Hage, *L'édition populaire d'extrême gauche en France et en Europe dans les années 1960 et 1970: L'exemple français des éditions Maspero (1959–1983). Mémoire de DEA sous la direction de Jean-Yves Mollier* (Université de Versailles Saint-Quentin-en-Yvelines, 2003).

31. Hans Wehr, *A Dictionary of Modern Written Arabic* (Arabic-English), ed. J. Milton Cowan, 4th ed. (Wiesbaden: Harrassowitz, 1979), 169.

32. On Fanon's life and work, see Alice Cherki, *Frantz Fanon: A Portrait* (Ithaca, NY: Cornell University Press, 2006).

33. "Arise, wretched of the earth" was the beginning of the first stanza of *The Internationale* composed by Eugène Pottier after the Paris Commune in 1871; see Marc Ferro, *L'Internationale: Histoire d'un chant de Pottier et Degeyter* (Paris: Noêsis, 1996). *The Internationale* soon became the most popular anthem of international socialism, thus turning "the wretched of the earth" into a globally recognized representation of the exploited, revolutionary industrial workers.

34. On this aspect, see Christoph Kalter, "'Le monde va de l'avant. Et vousêtes en marge': Dekolonisierung, Dezentrierung des Westens und Entdeckung der 'Dritten Welt' in der radikalen Linken in Frankreich in den 1960er-Jahren," *Archiv für Sozialgeschichte* Vol. 48 (2008): 99–132.

35. This is the term used by Berger (2004), 36.

36. For an introduction to the concepts of "neo-colonialism" and "dependency," see for example Robert J.C. Young, *Postcolonialism: An Historical Introduction* (Malden, MA: Blackwell Publishers 2001), 44–56; Ilan Kapoor, "Capitalism, Culture, Agency: Dependency versus Postcolonial Theory," *Third World Quarterly* Vol. 23, No. 4 (2000), 647–664.

37. These alternatives were being discussed by contemporary authors like, for example, Jean Lacouture and Jean Baumier, *Le poids du tiers monde: Un milliard d'hommes* (Paris : Arthaud, 1962), 243–279.

38. OSPAAAL = Organization of Solidarity with the People of Asia, Africa and Latin America.

39. On the conference, see the contemporary accounts by Albert-Paul Lentin, *La lutte tricontinentale: Impérialisme et révolution après la conférence de La Havane* (Paris 1966) and by an anonymous author, "The First Afro-Asian-Latin American Peoples' Solidarity Conference," in *Yearbook on International Communist Affairs* (1967), 451–457.

40. See Ernesto "Che" Guevara, "Create Two, Three … Many Vietnams, that is the Watchword," *Tricontinental* Vol. 14 (1969): 86–95.

41. On the Non-Aligned Movement, the Group 77, and its demand for a NIEO, see for example Mackie (2005); Robert A. Mortimer, *The Third World Coalition in International Politics* (New York: Praeger, 1980); Tomlinson (2003). See also Richard L. Jackson, *The Non-Aligned, the UN and the Superpowers* (New York: Praeger, 1983); Karl P. Sauvant, *The Group of 77: Evolution, Structure, Organization* (New York: Oceana Publications, 1981); and Marc Williams, *Third World Cooperation: The Group of 77 in UNCTAD* (London : Pinter Publishers, 1991).

42. Berger (2004).

43. Jean Daniel and André Burguière (eds.), *Le tiers monde et la gauche* (Paris: Seuil, 1979) marked the beginning of a highly polemical debate on "*tiers-mondisme*" in France. For a critical historicization, see Maxime Szczepanski-Huillery, "'L'idéologie tiers-mondiste': Constructions et usages d'une catégorie intellectuelle en 'crise,'" *Raisons politiques* Vol. 18, No. 2 (2005): 2, 27- 48. An influential historical definition of "*tiers-mondisme*" was given in Pierre Vidal-Naquet, "Une fidélité têtue: La résistance française à la guerre d'Algérie," *Vingtième Siècle: Revue d'histoire* Vol. 10 (1986): 3–18. Historiographical use of the concept has been made, for example, by Robert Malley, *The Call from Algeria: Third Worldism, Revolution, and the Turn to Islam* (Berkeley 1996) or Monica Kalt, *Tiersmondismus in der Schweiz der 1960er und 1970er Jahre: Von der Barmherzigkeitzur Solidarität* (Bern 2010).

44. On Sartre, see Sunil Khilnani, *Arguing Revolution: The Intellectual Left in Post-War France* (New Haven: Yale University Press, 1993); Tony Judt, *Marxism and the French Left: Studies in Labor and Politics in France, 1830–1981* (Oxford and New York: Oxford University Press, 1986) and Michel Winock, "Sartre s' est-iltoujours trompé?" *L'Histoire* Vol. 295 (2005): 34–45.

45. UNEF = Union Nationale des Étudiants de France.

46. UEC = Union des Étudiants Communistes.

47. FUA = Front Universitaire Antifasciste.

48. PSU = Parti Socialiste Unifié.

49. On the cooperation between Guevara and Debray, see Bernhard Gierds, "Che Guevara, Régis Debray und die Focus theorie," in Wolfgang Kraushaar (ed.), *Die RAF und der linke Terrorismus. Bd. 1* (Hamburg: Hamburger Edition, 2006), 182–204; on *Partisans*, see Julien Hage, "Sur les chemins du tiers monde en lutte: *Partisans, Révolution, Tricontinental* (1961–1973)," in Philippe Artières and Michelle Zancarini-Fournel (eds.), *68: Une histoire collective, 1962–1981* (Paris: La Découverte, 2008), 86–93.

50. The most famous examples are the repression of the demonstrations of October 1961 and February 1962; see Jim House and Neil MacMaster, *Paris 1961: Algerians, State Terror, and Memory* (Oxford: Oxford University Press, 2006); Alain Dewerpe, *Charonne, 8 février 1962: Anthropologie historique d'un massacre d'État* (Paris: Gallimard, 2006).

51. *Gaz de guerre* [leaflet], 13 May 1968, BDIC Paris-Nanterre, Fonds Kandel, F delta rés 703/2; "La rue vaincra!" in *L'Action,* 13 May 1968, BDIC Paris-Nanterre, Fonds Kandel, F delta rés 703/2/1.

52. Young (2006), 4.

53. This is one of the central arguments unfolded in Young (2001).

54. Young (2006), 9.

55. Stuart Hall, "The West and the Rest: Discourse and Power," in Stuart Hall and Bram Gieben (eds.), *Formations of Modernity* (Cambridge: Polity Press in association with the Open University, 1992), 118–130.

56. For a discussion of pros and cons see the contributions in Berger (2009).

Chapter 2

China's Great Proletarian Cultural Revolution and the Imagination of the Third World

Zachary A. Scarlett

No event since the Communist Revolution in 1949 had a more significant impact on the Chinese state than did the Great Proletarian Cultural Revolution. This event has garnered tremendous attention from Sinologists; scholars, however, have traditionally approached the Cultural Revolution from the perspective of the nation-state, analyzing the machinations of the Chinese Communist Party (CCP), the causes of student factionalism, and the role of political elites in the movement. Few scholars have considered the Cultural Revolution in a global context.[1] This has led to the perception that the Cultural Revolution was an isolated and insular movement that was generally cut off from the rest of the world. However, many Chinese students, particularly those associated with the Foreign Ministry and Beijing's Foreign Language Institutes, engaged with the political and social movements of the Third World in the 1960s, primarily through national cultural symbols, revolutionary rhetoric, and the image of Mao Zedong.[2] These cultural symbols took on both national and transnational meaning during the Cultural Revolution. Chinese students, who formed into Red Guard units at the beginning of the Cultural Revolution, constructed multiple identities, and envisioned themselves both as the vanguard of revolutionary politics in China, as well as participants in the myriad Third World revolutionary movements of the 1960s.[3] By incorporating the Third World into their movement, Chinese students made the Cultural Revolution both an ultra-nationalist and transnational event.

Chinese students integrated the Third World into the Cultural Revolution in two important ways. The first was by creating a rhetorical bond between the Cultural Revolution and the Third World, specifically by adopting a militant anti-imperialism. Harangues regarding American aggression in Vietnam or Soviet influence in the Middle East, for example, appeared alongside articles sharply criticizing British colonialism in Hong Kong. The Red Guards also used the Third World to castigate their enemies in China, claiming that some officials, such as the head of state, Liu Shaoqi, and the foreign minister, Chen Yi, had betrayed not only the Chinese Communist party, but also the revolution in Asia, Africa, and Latin America. Despite claims of fraternity and solidarity with the Third World, however, the rhetoric of the Cultural Revolution also contained overt strains of paternalism. Unlike in the West, where the Third World inspired radical students,[4] Red Guard newspapers and official state declarations portrayed the Third World as a place where China's revolutionary guidance was imperative. These documents suggest that the only way the Third World revolution could succeed was by following the model established by the Cultural Revolution, and more specifically by Mao Zedong.

The second way in which Chinese students and the state engaged with the Third World was by projecting Mao's image across national borders. Mao became a national and international symbol during the Cultural Revolution. Students published articles and other items in their newspapers asserting Mao's importance in the Third World. Mao appeared in Red Guard newspapers both as the leader of the CCP, as well as a symbol of the Third World revolution. Several newspapers carried a weekly section, entitled "Mao is the Reddest Sun in the Heart of the World's Revolutionary People," which detailed Mao's global importance, and the ways in which his theories were transforming the Third World. Once again a paternalistic tone infused Mao's global image. Mao was often presented as the savior of the Third World, whose revolutionary credentials trumped those of the Soviet Union. There was little difference between Mao as a national hero and Mao as a global symbol. Chinese students used Mao's image as the savior of the CCP and imprinted that perception onto the Third World.

And yet, the representation of the Third World was often imagined rather than based in reality.[5] Students adopted the language, ideology, symbols, codes, and posture of the Chinese state and the Cultural Revolution to compose a Third World devoid of contours and nuance. Some Red Guard groups used the Third World to reinforce their own position in China and reaffirm the necessity and importance of the Cultural Revolution. These students could not escape the rhetoric or images of the Cultural Revolution, and reports of revolutionary movements in the Third World used the same Communist jargon that dominated the Chinese movement. In so doing, the Red Guards mediated the Third World through the means of a Chinese reality. In essence, the Third World came to mirror the Cultural Revolution. Student newspapers made it appear as if many cultural revolutions were taking place throughout the Third World. This representation suggested that the Cultural Revolution had implications that stretched well beyond the borders of the Chinese nation-state.

As with many other events during the Cultural Revolution, that state manipulated and influenced the students' engagement with the Third World. High officials and elite organizations also co-opted the Third World to promote their own agendas during the Cultural Revolution, burnish their revolutionary image, and criticize foreign countries, particularly the United States and the Soviet Union. This had a trickle-down effect; students, who were not privy to the internal machinations of the CCP, adopted the language and the affectation of high officials and approached the Third World in a similar manner. At the beginning of the Cultural Revolution, the Foreign Ministry took the lead in promoting Maoism and the prospect of global revolution. On 17 June 1966, in the first days of the Cultural Revolution, Foreign Minister Chen Yi delivered a speech to students in which he declared that "he [the revolutionary] will strive for the victory of world revolution. ... It is our obligation to internationalism to build up our strength."[6] Ironically, in 1968, the Red Guards accused Chen Yi of subverting global revolution and giving comfort to imperialist enemies.

The Foreign Ministry was not alone in promoting the revolutionary potential of the Third World. At the Eleventh Plenum of the CCP, which took place from 1–12 August1966, the party issued a statement that declared that the world was "in a new era of revolution." Officials at the Plenum also reaffirmed Lin Biao's essay entitled "Long Live the People's Victory," which declared that the Third World had become an important revolutionary area.[7] People's Daily, the official newspaper of the Chinese Communist Party, published several articles proclaiming Mao's importance to the Third World revolution.[8] The newspaper also carried editorials that encouraged students to remain vigilant against imperialism. This became particularly important in the summer of 1967 when Chinese students on the mainland challenged British rule in Hong Kong. The Central Cultural Revolution Committee (CCRG), which became one of the most powerful organizations during the Cultural Revolution, also played a role in shaping the Red Guards' relationship with the Third World. The CCRG promoted a radical approach to foreign affairs and attempted to manipulate China's foreign policy during the Cultural Revolution to support social movements in the Third World.[9] Much of the state's approach to the Third World was also a result of the very negative relationship with both the Soviet Union and the United States. It is the former, however, which is the most important in this discussion. Both China and the Soviet Union claimed to be the global revolutionary authority, and the dispute between the two countries was partially fought over the hearts and minds of the Third World revolution. Indeed, the Sino-Soviet split shaped the state's and the Red Guards' approach to the Third World and set the tone for the internationalism of the Cultural Revolution.

The Sino-Soviet Split and China's Engagement with the Third World

Any ostensible observation of the international situation in the years leading up to the Cultural Revolution would only confirm that China was generally isolated from the rest of the world during the 1960s. After the Sino-Soviet split in 1961, China was unhinged from the Communist world and largely isolated from the international community. However, despite Beijing's antagonistic foreign policy and generally poor relations with the rest of the world, the Third World became extremely important to China in the 1960s. After the breakdown in relations between the Soviet Union and China, the Chinese government began to search for new potential allies. It also increased its support for radical movements in the Third World, bypassing unfriendly state governments and appealing directly to pro-Maoist revolutionary groups.[10] So while the Chinese government may have been isolated from the international community in the 1960s, the Communist party maintained an active campaign to promote Maoism and criticize Soviet revisionism and American imperialism, especially in the Third World.

One of the reasons why China's relationship with the Soviet Union soured was over the issue of how actively communist states should support revolutionary struggles against imperialism in the Third World. Mao and the Communist party were outraged by Khrushchev's claim that the communist and capitalist worlds could peacefully co-exist. Mao strongly believed that imperial powers like the United States would never rest until they had colonized the entire world. Although the relationship between the two countries broke down for myriad reasons, China's approach to the Third World epitomizes the different ideologies that Khrushchev and Mao embraced. The Soviet Union, already regarded cautiously in China because of Khrushchev's commitment to détente with the United States, had traditionally embraced progressive modernization in the Third World that was to be guided by the Comintern.[11] Mao, however, stressed permanent revolution, and the two countries differed over the stability required for modernization and the need for continued revolutionary action in the Third World. After the Sino-Soviet split, China hoped to build a revolutionary consensus in the Third World that would oppose both the United States and the Soviet Union.[12] Many Third World countries, however, were hesitant to turn their back on the more powerful Soviet Union. This created a profoundly precarious situation for China in which international friends were few and far between, and in which solidarity between China and revolutionary groups in the Third World became more important. As Tek Tjeng Lie writes, such a situation must have reminded the Communists of the pre-revolutionary days when the party battled the Nationalist government during the Civil War in the 1940s.[13] Instead of looking to the Chinese peasantry as a place to recruit new members (as they did in the 1940s), the CCP instead looked to the Third World as a powerful ally to fight the United States and the Soviet Union. In 1965, Lin Biao summarized this sentiment by declaring that China's enemies could be defeated only if they were surrounded by a radical Third World, just as the Chinese peasantry surrounded the Nationalist armies from the countryside. Specifically predicting the downfall of the United States, Lin declared that "the peoples of Asia, Africa, Latin America and other regions can destroy [the United States] piece by piece, some striking at its head and others at its feet."[14] Lin's message is clear: only by working together can China and the Third World defeat American imperialism.

Lin's statement was partially the result of years of effort by the Chinese state to build stronger relations in the Third World. In 1960, Beijing celebrated the creation of a Sino-Latin American Friendship Association and a Sino-African People's Friendship Association.[15] After 1962, China also began to push for greater influence in the Afro-Asian People's Solidarity Organization. The party used this organization to argue that the Soviet Union was not interested in solving the Third World's problems.[16] China believed the Third World was its "natural constituency" in the years leading up to the Cultural Revolution.[17] This feeling of solidarity between China and the Third World, precipitated largely by the state's actions, influenced the Red Guards' embrace of revolutionary action in Asia, Africa, and Latin America during the Cultural Revolution.

Many governments in the Third World, however, viewed Chinese motives with suspicion or even outright hostility. And yet, interest in Maoism as an alternative to Soviet Communism grew among radical organizations during the 1960s.[18] Beijing facilitated this increased attention, lauding and support-ing any group that expressed an interest in China. On the other hand, gov-ernments and political parties who voiced opposition or even remained neutral toward Maoism were criticized. China condemned the entire non-alignment movement and its failure to actively combat the United States and the Soviet Union.[19] India's generally cordial relationship with the United States and the Soviet Union also deeply frustrated the Chinese.[20] As an alternative to India's neutralism, China began to actively support pro-Maoist groups in India like the Naxalites. The Chinese government printed countless leaflets in English, Hindi, Bengali, and Nepali that contained different quotations from Chairman Mao, and attempted to distribute these leaflets in areas where the Naxalites convened. They also translated Lin Biao's "Long Live the People's Victory," and dropped copies of the essay from a plane over India.[21] Their efforts paid off at least in the short term—in 1970, students in Calcutta vandalized parts of the city, and the Naxalite leader called on his followers to form into Red Guard units.[22] So while China may have been searching for new allies in the Third World, they were unwilling to compromise their ideals in order to obtain these new friends. This policy made the 1960s and the wave of revolutionary movements that broke out in the Third World extremely important to China. When the Cultural Revolu-tion began, students seized on this growing importance of the Third World in Chinese politics.

Red Guard Rhetoric and the Third World

China's engagement with the Third World during the Cultural Revolution mani-fested itself in the rhetoric of some Red Guard organizations. Ostensibly, any mention of the Third World was meant to show the Red Guards' strong sup-port for revolutionary movements in Asia, Africa, or Latin America. And in some cases, this support signified a genuine feeling of outrage over imperialist abuse in the Third World. However, by reporting on the Third World's support of the Cultural Revolution, students also used the international situation to justify domestic actions and reaffirm their own political campaign. For example, during the foundational meeting of a student group in Beijing called "The World's Revolutionary Proletarians for the Repudiation of Revisionism," a Brazilian and a South African "freedom fighter" both took the stage to laud Mao's revolutionary vision in conceiving the Cultural Revolution.[23] The article reporting this event, published by an organization called the Center to Liberate Foreign Affairs, concluded that even though all of those attending the meeting were speaking a different language, they were able to communicate with one another and "convey the fact that Mao was the reddest sun among the world's revolutionaries."[24] Another Red Guard newspaper published by the Beijing No. 2 Foreign Language Institute reported that the Vietnamese people wanted nothing more than to see "the ultimate victory of the Great Proletarian Cultural Revolution."[25] Chinese students used the Third World as a tool not only to expand their revolution, but also to further its domestic aims. According to these newspapers, the Cultural Revolution's significance stretched around the world.

Chinese students were able to keep abreast of developments in the Third World by reading the "Atlas Fighting Papers," a leaflet published out of Shanghai. This paper denoted exactly where revolutionary struggles (Palestine, Vietnam, Burma) were taking place.[26] Red Guard groups used music to demonstrate their support for the Third World. One song during the Cultural Revolution was entitled "Third World—Let's Unite and Fight."[27] Revolutionary fraternity, however, most clearly manifested itself in the students' staunch anti-imperialist attitude. The Third World's struggle against Western influence was referenced again and again in many student newspapers during the Cultural Revolution. This anti-imperialism was used to project fraternity with the Third World, as well as castigate American aggression, Soviet revisionism, and the ideals of bourgeois capitalism. On the surface, anti-imperialism established a common discourse among the Red Guards and their Third World counterparts.

Antagonism toward American imperialism was particularly acute during the Cultural Revolution, especially regarding the Vietnam War. Some Chinese students attended rallies in order to express their support for the Vietnamese struggle. At one particular rally, Chinese students carried signs that read, "China is behind Vietnam."[28] An article reprinted in the *Peking Review* declared that "the 700 million Chinese people who are armed with Mao Tse-tung Thought most resolutely support their Vietnamese brothers in resisting U.S. aggression to the end."[29] Some Red Guards also used the theater to demonstrate their disdain for American imperialism in Vietnam. In his memoir, Gao Yuan recalls a time during the Cultural Revolution when he and his fellow classmates performed a play in which three students dressed as an American soldier, pilot, and sailor took the stage to "confess their crimes and stupidities in Vietnam."[30] For China, as for the rest of the world, the Vietnam War became one of the central issues of the late 1960s. It also placed some Red Guard organizations in league with many Third World revolutionaries.

However, while the students' support for the Vietnamese struggle was often meant to express solidarity, backing from the government held a strategic purpose.[31] China wanted to position itself as the savior of the Vietnamese people, especially in comparison to the Soviet Union. To this end, they denied the Soviets permission to use Chinese airspace in order to deliver military equipment to the Sino-Vietnamese border.[32] This decision colored the way that students saw not only the Vietnam War, but also the entire Third World. Chinese students' feelings of solidarity with Third World revolutionaries often intermingled with the state's tactical battle against foreign enemies. These students were never able to actually escape the state's foreign policy, and any condemnation of imperialism was also a tacit rejection of the Soviet Union's revisionism and a reaffirmation of Mao Zedong Thought.

Rhetorical support for anti-imperialist struggles went beyond Vietnam. In June of 1967, for example, the Center to Liberate Foreign Affairs lamented the invasion of Arab countries by Israeli forces, and claimed that this invasion was the work of surging imperialists. According to an article published in the organization's newspaper, "if Israel did not have American backing, it could not conduct the invasion of Arab countries." The article went on to blame the predicament in the Middle East on "the armed invasion of the American imperialists and their running dogs."[33] The Mexican authorities' slaughter of students in October of 1968 also garnered attention, but was again placed in an imperialist context. One article, entitled "A Storm is Shaking the Backyard of U.S. Imperialism," notes that "young Mexican students have recently unfolded torrential waves of struggle against persecution and slaughter."[34] While expressing support for revolutionary causes abroad, these reports also reminded the Red Guards that the counterrevolutionary enemies of the Communist state were everywhere, and that vigilance was the only antidote to these omnipotent forces. This in turn reinforced the need for the Cultural Revolution, and furthered the belief that the Third World revolution and the Chinese student movement were one in the same. Victory in the latter would insure the ultimate success of the former.

At times, the Red Guards' anti-imperialism did move beyond rhetoric, but only when specific Chinese issues were at hand. In June 1967, during some of the most chaotic and radical days of the Cultural Revolution, British ownership of Hong Kong became a major issue. When a demonstration was held in Hong Kong against English rule, a Red Guard newspaper lauded the "patriotic acts of our fellow countrymen in the struggle to resist the English invaders." The same article went on to mention that demonstrators in Hong Kong were looking to the Cultural Revolution to emulate as a form of protest, even planning to "hold a Beijing style march."[35] When, in August 1967, it became clear that the

Chinese government would not support protesters in Hong Kong with anything beyond words, Chinese students and workers began to hold mass demonstrations in front of the British mission in Beijing. These protesters formed into the "Liaison Station of Capital Revolutionary Rebels against Imperialism and Revisionism," and continued to place pressure on the British government to abdicate rule in Hong Kong. The protest became frenetic and took on a "fanatic revolutionary fervor."[36] Both Zhou Enlai, the vice-chairman of the CCP, and Chen Boda, the head of the CCRG, tried to intervene and disperse the students, but they would not listen to these high officials. Partly motivated by an editorial that appeared in *People's Daily* on 3 June 1967 that urged all Chinese to support protests in Hong Kong against the British government, many of the workers and students were convinced that their protest represented a truly revolutionary action.[37]

The protest lasted through the summer, until finally on 20 August 1967 students and workers stormed the British embassy and burned part of the building to the ground. These events embody the chasm between rhetorical denunciations of imperialism in the Third World and tangible action on the part of the Red Guards. During the Cultural Revolution, students used their own newspapers to vociferously condemn imperial aggression in the Third World. And yet the greatest show of revolutionary force against imperialism during the Cultural Revolution involved British colonialism in Hong Kong. It took a purely Chinese issue to transform the Red Guards' anti-imperialist rhetoric into action. The Chinese government's anti-imperialism and support for the people of Hong Kong also proved to be ostensible—Zhou Enlai and Chen Boda were both furious with the students and workers who took part in the burning of the British missions. Zhou and Chen held a meeting on 22 August that excoriated the students' actions. Zhou declared that burning the embassy was tantamount to anarchy, and that the students and workers were out of control. He also downplayed China's future support for Hong Kong and pledged that diplomacy rather than militancy would guide foreign affairs for the time being.[38] Even Mao did not approve of the burning of the embassy, and arrested several members of the CCRG that he believed were behind the students' actions.[39]

The above examples demonstrate how the Third World became a means through which the Red Guards could target foreign enemies, particularly the United States and the Soviet Union, as well as legitimate their own actions. The Third World, however, was also sometimes used to criticize enemies in the CCP, who certain Red Guard organizations declared were not only responsible for suppressing the masses at home, but indeed had conspired to stifle revolutionary people throughout the world. Red Guard groups cast their opponents as enemies of the world's revolutionary people. Much of this criticism, however, was dictated by officials in the CCP. For example, in the campaign against Liu Shaoqi, the CCRG ordered officials in the Foreign Ministry to hand over their archives concerning Liu's attitudes toward global revolution. The propaganda team of the CCRG was to look through this archive and ascertain if Liu had suppressed foreign revolutionaries, as he (supposedly) had done in China.[40] Meanwhile, students in China followed the lead of the CCRG. In September 1967 Red Guards from the No. 2 Foreign Language Institute reported with a certain amount of disgust that in 1965 Liu Shaoqi told the people of Latin America "if American imperialists interfere with you, we cannot go to help you because it is too far."[41] The article concluded that this statement proved that Liu Shaoqi had a highly revisionist and anti-revolutionary attitude.

The case against Chen Yi relied even more heavily on global narratives, mainly because Chen Yi was the foreign minister. Chen Yi was one of the more moderate high officials during the Cultural Revolution, and he was eventually criticized by members of the CCRG and the Chinese students. Chen Yi's downfall came from his involvement in the "February Adverse Current," a campaign conducted by radical officials in the CCP who believed that the Cultural Revolution was being subverted by moderate voices. In a meeting among leading government officials on 16 February 1967, Chen Yi and several others criticized the radicalism of the Cultural Revolution and the actions of the CCRG, claiming that they were the true revisionists in China. After the meeting, Mao learned of Chen's statement and quickly reprimanded the foreign minister.[42] Once again, the students followed suit. A new organization called the "Liaison Station to Criticize Chen Yi" was formed, which attracted members from more than 35 different Red Guard units.[43] Chen Yi was accused of being a "flunky of imperialism" and of proposing less hostile relations with the United States. Any mention of Chen Yi's domestic crimes was almost immediately followed by a criticism of his willingness to capitulate to the enemy and tolerate American imperialism.[44] Although the students' actions were approved by the CCRG, some in the government moved to protect Chen Yi.[45] Zhou Enlai particularly criticized the phrase "Down with Chen Yi," which the radical "Liaison Station to Criticize Chen Yi" began to write on big character posters and chant at rallies. In February 1969, Chen Yi was sentenced to hard labor in a factory along with the other officials involved in the February Adverse Current. His supposed crimes, both foreign and domestic, were used to justify his removal from any position of authority.

The fact that these students used domestic issues as well as the Third World to disgrace Liu Shaoqi and Chen Yi suggests that many Chinese students looked to the global revolutionary movement of the 1960s as another means to attack their enemies. The Third World played a complex and contradictory role in many criticism campaigns. The passion displayed in these articles suggests that many did actually believe that Liu and Chen had hindered the Third World revolution, and were disgusted by their actions. On the other hand, the Third World was co-opted by the Chinese students and used for purposes that furthered their own chaotic and violent revolution at home. Finally, the cases against Liu and Chen demonstrate the pervasive influence of the state. Officials in the CCP initiated criticisms of Liu and Chen, and dictated the direction of the campaigns against these two officials.

Whether used to establish solidarity, castigate their enemies, or reinforce their own actions, what came to characterize the students' rhetorical engagement with the Third World was an overwhelming feeling of paternalism. Student newspapers often suggested that the Red Guards were solely responsible for the Third World's revolutionary education. Paternalism manifested itself in the depiction of the Third World, which was often described as fawning and eager to consume whatever it could from China. For example, a newspaper reported that one student from West Pakistan followed Chinese students around all day begging them for a book on Mao Zedong Thought.[46] Paternalism also manifested itself in such a way as to suggest that Chinese students were the vanguard of the global revolution of the 1960s. One headline, in a newspaper published by Beijing No. 2 Railroad Middle School Red Guard Unit, declared, "we are the hope for the liberation of all mankind."[47] Another piece printed at the end of a Red Guard newspaper includes the phrase "we proletarian revolutionaries are the owners of the new world."[48] This paternalism, however, was not entirely the students' own doing; such feelings of superiority were often fostered by the state. From the beginning, the Communist party had promoted the idea that the Cultural Revolution was more important that any campaign yet undertaken by other leftist organizations. Pronouncements from the party stressed that unlike the Soviet Union, China was one of the few countries that was moving forward with its revolutionary struggle.[49] This furthered the idea that misguided radicals in the Third World needed to be saved from the torpor of revisionist countries. Chinese students embraced this, and believed that the Cultural Revolution represented the pinnacle of global radicalism. Overall, the state's influence and the Red Guards' own feelings of revolutionary grandeur created a paternalism that often mixed with genuine feelings of solidarity between China and the Third World, and made global narratives vital to how Chinese students imaged their own movement.

The Savior of the Third World: Projecting Maoism across National Borders

The Third World's role in the Cultural Revolution was multi-directional. Not only was the Third World present in the Cultural Revolution, but Chinese students and the CCP also promoted the idea that the Third World was eager to consume China's brand of revolution. This was often facilitated by the image of Mao Zedong. During the Cultural Revolution, Mao's meaning in Chinese society embodied both national and international significance. Mao not only became a savior of the Chinese state, but also a transnational symbol of revolutionary change, one whose popularity peaked in the 1960s. This was represented in the propaganda from the Cultural Revolution. In many posters, the symbol of the red sun was used to demonstrate Mao's awesome presence. All of the qualities of the sun—its consistency, its power, and its place in the sky—were embodied in the figure of Mao Zedong. Like the sun itself, Mao's light did not only shine on China, it also illuminated the Third World. One propaganda poster, for example, urged Chinese students to "resolutely support the anti-imperialist struggle of the Asian, African, and Latin American people."[50] The poster itself is a montage of determined people, some of them armed, who appear to come from several different areas of the world. Behind them in the corner is a red sun, a symbolic reminder of the ubiquity of Mao Zedong. Another poster read, "American imperialists, get out of South Vietnam."[51] Standing right above this caption is a Vietnamese family, all armed with rifles and grenades. Again a red sun burns over their heads. This image of the red sun demonstrates how the propaganda from the Cultural Revolution projected Maoism across borders and promoted the idea that Mao was the leader of the global revolution of the 1960s. The sun, however, was not limited to propaganda posters or even to Mao Zedong. Many Chinese students, in fact, described themselves literally as "the red sun at 9 o'clock in the morning."[52] That the students saw themselves as the morning sun suggests that the Red Guards believed that the Cultural Revolution was a means to prove their revolutionary credentials and to fetter out an older generation of officials that had impeded the progress of the Communist state. Such a sentiment was shared throughout the world during the 1960s, and came to embody the radical spirit of the decade. For the Red Guards, once the older generation of Communist leaders was gone, they would inherit not only Mao's revolution, but also the global revolution of the 1960s. In fact, in the article in which students called themselves the morning sun, they also exhorted their fellow Red Guards not to "leave to others what we should do ourselves."[53] Mao's light may have stood at the center of the Third World and the Cultural Revolution, but the students presented themselves as the inheritors of the global revolution.

During the Cultural Revolution, students suggested that the Third World was willing and eager to consume Mao's theories and ideology. This again manifested itself in several different student newspapers, and often came in reports from Third World revolutionaries themselves. One student in Tanzania, for example, wrote a Red Guard newspaper to say that after receiving and reading *The Quotations of Chairman Mao,* he rushed right over to the local library and demanded that the book be included in their collection.[54] A student from Zanzibar wrote to a Red Guard publication to inform Chinese students that "in Africa, Chairman Mao's works are becoming the spiritual food of the revolutionary people."[55] Another writer from Morocco informed students that he "studied Mao's work for almost two months," after which he realized that the problems of the Moroccan peasantry was the same as the problems of the Chinese peasantry.[56] Reading Mao's work was furthermore described as a revelation for many revolutionaries of the Third World. A Brazilian "friend" who traveled to China in 1968 claimed, "for decades I have been seeking for a road that will lead Brazil to liberation. Today I have found it in China."[57]

For China's students, the way that the Third World was going to realize its revolutionary aspirations was the same way that the Red Guards would ultimately triumph: by using Mao Zedong Thought as a weapon. A headline in one student newspaper declared that "Mao Zedong Thought is the beacon of the world's revolutionary people."[58] In the same article about the Moroccan revolutionary, a Syrian writer reported that he saved his money every day so that he could come to China to see Mao. The writer declared that it "would be great if Chairman Mao would come to Syria."[59] Pictures were also a useful way of portraying Mao's importance in the Third World. One such picture showed a group of "Latin American friends" reading Mao's little red book with a caption that read, "Latin American friends wholeheartedly study the treasured red book *Quotations of Chairman Mao Tse-tung*."[60] Another picture captured a group of Congolese students in front of Mao's portrait with their guns raised above their heads.[61]

Red Guard newspapers also suggested that Mao provided these revolutionaries with much-needed encouragement during the low points of their revolution. One newspaper noted that even though revolutionaries in Angola, South Africa, and Zimbabwe have "encountered numerous problems and hardships, they are still using Mao Zedong Thought to arm themselves."[62] For their part, foreign diplomats, at the behest of the Foreign Ministry, also attempted to spread Maoist ideology. Chinese officials serving in Africa took to reciting Mao's sayings on public buses. One Chinese embassy even attempted to put up a sign affirming Mao's revolutionary superiority.[63] Things got so bad in Kenya that in 1967, Chinese diplomats were expelled from the country for distributing Maoist propaganda.[64]

Like the movement's rhetoric, the students' transformation of Mao into a global symbol of resistance presents a muddled picture of the Cultural Revolution. In many ways, promoting Maoism abroad represented an authentic concern for the Third World. Students wanted to share Mao's radical message with other revolutionaries. One must also keep in mind, however, the singular position that Mao occupied in Chinese society during the Cultural Revolution. The only way that the Chinese students could assist the Third World during the Cultural Revolution was to offer them the hegemonic symbol of the Cultural Revolution. They simply did not have access to any alternatives. Projecting Maoism into the Third World also furthered the idea among the Red Guards that the Cultural Revolution lay at the absolute center of the global student movement, and that Maoism was its predominate ideology. Finally, Mao's transformation demonstrates that the Red Guards framed the Third World in terms of the Cultural Revolution and envisioned that the political and cultural symbols of their movement were similarly being utilized in revolutionary movements around the world.

Conclusion

That China used the Third World as a prop during the Cultural Revolution is not unique. The Third World became a major symbol of the global student movement during the 1960s, employed in various countries and contexts as a means to promote revolution. This was particularly true in the West, where the Third World acted as a type of inspirational model of revolution for European and American students. Although the Third World played a major role in China during the 1960s, it did not function in the same way as it did in the West. In fact, China's relationship with the Third World was inverted; Chinese students were going to inspire and educate the Third World, not vice versa. What Chinese and Western students did share, however, was a somewhat reductionist attitude toward the Third World. National realities impeded Chinese and Western understanding of the Third World. Struggles in the Third World were co-opted, distorted, and manipulated so as to fit into the framework of the Cultural Revolution. Many Chinese students viewed the Third World as a place without a true revolutionary identity, where those who were committed to radical change shared the ideals and the goals of the Cultural Revolution.

Two scholars who have studied the relationship between China and the Third World have stated that "the Cultural Revolution had very little to do with the Third World" and that one of the goals of the Cultural Revolution was to demonstrate to foreign radicals that they could not rely on China for help.[65] While this may be true in some official circles, Red Guard newspapers indicate that the Third World played a major role in the construction of the students' identities during the Cultural Revolution. Articles detailing the Third World's reliance on China and on Mao reinforced the Red Guards' actions and expanded the implications of their movement beyond the borders of the Chinese state. By projecting national cultural symbols—namely language and Mao's image—into the global arena, the Red Guards were also able to maintain a national as well as an imagined transnational identity that imbued a sense of importance in their actions and affirmed their own revolutionary grandiosity. In order to maintain these identities, the Red Guards needed to construct a Third World whose revolutionary mission was nearly identical to the Cultural Revolution. This profoundly altered the students' worldview. For many Red Guard organizations, the 1960s was not a period in which students exercised their own freedoms and spontaneity to challenge authority and the status quo, as is often remembered in the West, but a time in which the Cultural Revolution was being repeated over and over again throughout the rest of the world.

Sonya Rose has stated that when cultural symbols are repeated in different temporalities, they often take on new resonances and new meanings.[66] Such was certainly true during the Cultural Revolution. That Chinese students were promoting Mao's revolutionary ideology or criticizing imperialism during the Cultural Revolution was not novel. In fact, the cultural symbols that were used during the Cultural Revolution had appeared in several other campaigns enacted by the Communist party.[67] What was new, however, was that the Cultural Revolution occurred during the ascendancy of the international left, not only in the Third World, but also around the globe. This created the appearance that what lay before the Chinese students was a revolutionary audience eager to consume Mao's radical ideology. Not only were cultural symbols repeated in a new temporality, but their meanings were also expanded and applied to a global discourse of revolution. This gave the Cultural Revolution a new significance, one that could not be contained by the borders of the Chinese state. It also reinforced the importance of the Cultural Revolution, suggesting to eager young students in China that their campaign was a movement to reshape the entire world. And although the violence and the chaos of the Cultural Revolution cannot be reduced to one cause, understanding the Third World's role in the movement offers a deeper insight into the Red Guards' mentality. The Red Guards were, in many ways, modeling revolution for a world that seemed on the brink of radical social, cultural, and political change. In the minds of many Chinese students, victory in the Cultural Revolution would have freed the Third World and made China the ultimate revolutionary authority around the world during a decade when revolution was very much en vogue.

Notes

1. Two notable exceptions are: Ma Jisen, *The Cultural Revolution in the Foreign Ministry* (Hong Kong: The Chinese University Press, 2004); and Cheng Yinghong, "Xiang shijie shuchu geming: 'Wenge' zai Ya, Fei, Li de yingxiang chutan" ("Exporting Revolution to the World: Initial Research on the Influence of the Cultural Revolution in Asia, Africa, and Latin America"), *Contemporary Chinese Studies* No. 3 (2006).
2. This chapter is both temporally and geographically bounded. In the following pages I primarily discuss the years 1966 to 1968 when students operated with a modicum of autonomy before they were sent to the countryside. This study is also mostly limited to the city of Beijing, where the Cultural Revolution began, and where students exerted the most influence on the movement.
3. For the purposes of this chapter and this volume, I use the term *Third World* as a short-hand for Asia, Africa, and Latin America, particularly those countries who were struggling against colonialism and imperialism. Although there was repeated reference to these anti-imperialist movements in China during the 1960s, the term *Third World* was not actually formalized into CCP doctrine until 1974, when Mao articulated his theories of the "Three Worlds." This new policy, which separated the globe into a developed, developing, and underdeveloped world, was precipitated

by the defection and death of Lin Biao and China's new policy of détente with the United States. Before the development of this theory, the Third World was seen in terms of anti-imperialism rather than economic development. The term *Third World* therefore rarely appeared in official or Red Guard newspapers, although China's conceptualization of Asia, Africa, and Latin America aligned itself with the general understanding of anti-imperial and anti-colonial movements of the Third World in the 1960s. For a longer discussion of Mao's Theory of the Three Worlds, see Alexander C. Cook, "Third World Maoism," in Timothy Cheek (ed.), *A Critical Introduction to Maoism* (New York: Cambridge University Press, 2010), 296–299.

4. For examples of this, see Max Elbaum, *Revolution in the Air: Sixties Radicals Turn to Lenin, Mao and Che* (New York: Verso, 2002) and Jeremy Varon, *Bringing the War Home: The Weather Underground. The Red Army Faction, and Revolutionary Violence in the Sixties and Seventies* (Berkeley: University of California Press, 2004).

5. In one of the most complete studies of the Cultural Revolution, Roderick MacFarquhar and Michael Schoenhals write that they have purposefully minimized their use of Red Guard tabloids, preferring other sources that lead to a more accurate picture of the Cultural Revolution. This study takes the opposite approach, not necessarily because it disagrees with MacFarquhar and Schoenhals's analysis, but because it has a different purpose than their study. The goal here is to gain a better understanding of who the Red Guards were and what they were trying to accomplish during the Cultural Revolution by placing certain cultural signifiers in a global context. While this may not necessarily lead to an exact replication of the events of the Cultural Revolution, it does offer a deeper insight in the Red Guards' identity and mentality. See MacFarquhar and Schoenhals, *Mao's Last Revolution* (Cambridge, MA: Harvard University Press, 2006), 481.

6. Quoted in Ma (2004), 13.

7. Cheng (2006).

8. Ma (2004), 153.

9. For example, in 1967 Qi Benyu and Guan Feng, two members of the CCRG, encouraged members of the Foreign Ministry to break with Chen Yi and to take a more radical stance toward Burma and Mongolia. See Ma (2004), 191.

10. The Naxalites in India are one example of this type of approach to the Third World. See Sreemati Chakrabarti, *China and the Naxalites* (New Delhi: Radiant Books, 1990).

11. Odd Arne Westad, *The Global Cold War: Third World Interventions and the Making of Our Time* (New York: Cambridge University Press, 2005), 6.

12. George T. Yu, "China and the Third World," *Asian Survey* Vol. 17, No. 11 (November 1977): 1038.

13. Tek Tjeng Lie, *An Indonesian View: The Great Proletarian Cultural Revolution* (Djakarta: Lembaga Ilmu Pengetahuan Indonesia, 1970), 14.

14. Lin Biao, "Long Live the Victory of the People's War," *Renmin Ribao* (3 September 1965).

15. Roderick MacFarquhar, *The Origins of the Cultural Revolution* (New York: The East Asian Institute of Columbia University, 1974), 271.

16. Charles Neuhauser, *Third World Politics: China and the Afro-Asian People's Solidarity Organization, 1957–1967* (Cambridge, MA: Harvard East Asian Monographs, 1968), 41–43.

17. Ibid., 286.

18. See Elbaum (2002)
19. Gopal Chaudhuri, *China and Nonalignment* (New Delhi: ABC Publishing House, 1986), 17–27.
20. Barbara Barnouin and Yu Changgen, *Chinese Foreign Policy during the Cultural Revolution* (New York: Kegan Paul International, 1998), 73.
21. Chakrabarti (1990), 61.
22. Cook (2010), 295.
23. The race of this South African freedom fighter was not mentioned. While Chinese students during the Cultural Revolution were keenly aware of the Civil Rights movement in the United States, there is little mention in student newspapers of the oppressive South African regime. Usually, when South African revolutionaries are mentioned, they are positioned as fighting for communism, and not necessarily to end apartheid.
24. "Chedi suqing li shi 'xiu qi' zai guoji gongdong zhong de liu du zai jing guoji you ren jihui fennu pipan hei xiu qi," *Wai shi hongqi* (17 May 1967) in Song Yongyi, *Xin bian hong wei bing xi liao* (Oakton, VA: Center for Chinese Research Materials, 2001), 11848.
25. "Mao zhuxi shi shijie renmin xin zhong de hong taiyang," *Wai shi zhanbao* (9 October 1967) in Song (2001), 11890.
26. Lincoln Cushing and Ann Tompkins, *Chinese Posters: Art from the Great Proletarian Revolution* (Chronicle Books: San Francisco, 2007), 97.
27. Lei Ouyang Bryant, "Music, Memory, and Nostalgia: Collective Memories of Cultural Revolution Songs in Contemporary China," *The China Review* Vol. 5, No. 2 (Fall 2005), 154.
28. Yang Kelin, *Wenhua dageming bowuguan* (Hong Kong: Dongfang chubanshi, 1995), 502.
29. "Statement of the Chinese Foreign Ministry on the New Developments in the Vietnam Situation," *Peking Review* Vol. 10, No. 11 (10 March 1967), 12.
30. Gao Yuan, *Born Red: A Chronicle of the Cultural Revolution* (Stanford, CA: Stanford University Press, 1987), 66.
31. Shu Guang Zhang, "Beijing's Aid to Hanoi and the United States: China Confrontations, 1964–1968," in Priscilla Roberts (ed.), *Beyond the Bamboo Curtain: China, Vietnam and the World beyond Asia* (Stanford, CA: Stanford University Press, 2006), 273.
32. Ibid., 274.
33. "Jianjue zhichi alibo renmin de fan qinlue zhengdou," *Wai shi hongqi* (14 June 1967) in Song (2001), 11860.
34. "A Storm is Shaking the Backyard of U.S. Imperialism," *Peking Review* Vol. 11, No. 42 (18 October 1968), 21.
35. "Yao jiefang, na qi qiang," *Wai shi zhan bao* (18 September 1967) in Song (2001), 11881.
36. Barnouin and Yu (1998), 71.
37. Ma (2004), 183–188.
38. Ibid., 205–207.
39. The burning of the British enemy led to the arrest of Guan Feng, Wang Li, and eventually Qi Benyu, all members of the CCRG. Guan, Feng, and Qi were each accused of being "ultra-leftists." Moreover, this incident dealt a severe blow to the

radical leftists in the CCP, many of whom shifted their course after learning of Mao's anger. See MacFarquhar and Schoenhals (2006), 224–238.

40. Ibid., 212.

41. "Yao jiefang, na qi qiang," *Wai shi zhanbao* (18 September 1967) in Song (2001), 11881.

42. MacFarquhar and Schoenhals (2006), 191–197.

43. Ma (2004), 117.

44. "Chen Yi she 'san xiang yi mei' de chuigushou," *Wai shi hongqi* (30 June 1967) in Song (2001), 11864.

45. Ma (2004), 118.

46. "Mao zhuxi shi shijie geming renmin xin zhong de hong taiyang," *Wai shi hongqi* (26 May 1967) in Song (2001), 11855.

47. "Women shi ren lei jiefang de xiwang," *Women shi xiwang* (December 1967) in Song (2001), 12375

48. *Bei Ying Zhan Bao* (1 January 1967) in Song (2001), 1041.

49. Such sentiments can be found in the Communist party's early pronouncements, such as the Sixteen Points and the May 16th Notification. Both reinforce the impression that the Cultural Revolution was the pinnacle of revolutionary thinking during the 1960s. For more on these two pronouncements, See MacFarquhar and Schoenhals (2006), 40, 92–94.

50. Cushing and Tompkins (2007), 100.

51. Ibid., 99.

52. "Women shi ren lei jiefang de xiwang," *Women shi xiwang* (December, 1967) in Song (2001), 12375

53. Ibid., 12375. One of the common themes among many students during the 1960s was the feeling that the previous generation of leaders had failed. In the Third World, this feeling often manifested itself in the sense that many leaders had not properly coped with the difficulties of post-colonial society, or that they were unsuccessful in ending colonial domination itself. In China, many students were upset about the adulteration of the Communist Revolution and of the potential that the students themselves may never have the opportunity to make their revolutionary mark on China. Despite the different motivations for their rebellion, what remained constant across state borders was the sense that the stultifying policies of the older generation had to be abandoned for the revolutionary fervor of the youth.

54. "Jingen Mao Zedong shijie yi pian hong," *Beijing gongshe* (15 September 1967) in Song (2001), 836.

55. "Mao zhuxi de shu shi shijie renmin zui ai du," *Dui wai wenhua zhanbao* (5 August 1967) Song (2001), 4227.

56. "Mao Zhuxi shi shijie geming renmin xin zhong de hong taiyang," *Wai shi hongqi* (5 May 1967) in Song (2001), 11855.

57. "The Asian, African and Latin American Revolutions must take the road of the Chinese Revolution and Win Victory," *Peking Review* Vol. 10, No. 46 (10 November 1967), 34.

58. "Mao Zedong sixiang shi shijie renmin geming de dengta," *Dui wai maoyi* (14 June 1966) in Song (2001), 4186.

59. "Mao Zhuxi shi shijie geming renmin xin zhong de hong taiyang," *Wai shi hongqi* (5 May 1967) in Song (2001), 11855.

60. *Peking Review* (12 April 1968), 18.

61. *Peking Review* Vol. 11, No. 19 (10 May 1968), 16.

62. "Mao Zedong sixiang shi quan shijie geming remin de zhilu mingdeng," *Dui wai maoyi* (21 July 1966) in Song (2001), 4209.

63. Yan Jiaqi and Gao Gao, *Turbulent Decade: A History of the Cultural Revolution* (Honolulu: University of Hawaii Press, 1996), 74.

64. Ma (2004), 167.

65. Lillian Craig Harris and Robert L. Worden, "China's Third World Role" in Craig Harris and Worden (eds.), *China and the Third World: Champion or Challenger* (Dover, MA: Auburn House Publishing Company, 1986), 3.

66. Sonya Rose, "Cultural Analysis and Moral Discourses," in Lynn Hunt and Victoria Bonnell (eds.), *Beyond the Cultural Turn: New Directions in the Study of Society and Culture* (Berkeley: University of California Press, 1999), 229.

67. In fact, the cult of Mao was employed during the Socialist Education Plan in the 1960s. Despite the ferocity with which the students worshipped Mao, the Cultural Revolution was not the first campaign in which his image played a major role. See Maurice Meisner, *Mao's China and After: A History of the People's Republic* (New York: The Free Press, 1986), 295.

Chapter 3

Politics and Periodicals in the 1960s
Readings around the "Naxalite Movement"

Avishek Ganguly

A study of 1968 and the "Third World" can proceed in at least two directions. First, through a literal attempt to trace the different protest movements that happened around the Third World during the course of that year, taking the events in France, and perhaps the United States, as the implicit model that seeks to produce "1968" as a valorized historical marker in the first place. Such a heuristic, however, can raise questions about its widespread relevance and applicability, not the least of which is due to the fact that "the year of global crisis halfway between the end of World War II and the end of the Cold War, has yet to establish a solid position in contemporary history."[1] A second, somewhat less literal attempt on the other hand can theorize 1968 only as a synecdoche, a rhetorical figure that may be understood as a placeholder for all the diverse social and political movements taking place around that time throughout the world. However, the post–World War II years witnessed long and continuous histories of protest movements in the Third World—often in the form of anti-colonial struggles against various European powers—that were taking place prior to 1968 or even the 1960s. At the risk of going against the grain of this volume, it might be then possible to argue that a Euro-American 1968 probably needs to organize a Third World in order to claim a global relevance for itself. Recent arguments about the specifically European provenance (leaving out even North America) of the events of that year on the one hand, and the absence of too many studies on the non-Western careers of 1968 on the other would also seem to support this view.[2] Nevertheless, a synecdochal reading that problematizes the privileging of 1968 as a singular marker within a seemingly continuous narrative of protest and social movements can also productively supplement our understanding of the Third World-ism specific to the 1960s movements that currently derives from two prominent moments of revolution in Asia: the Cultural Revolution in China and the war in Vietnam. In place of a singular *annusmirabilis,* then, I would like to propose "the long 1960s."[3] I would argue for an understanding of the diversified antiquity and discursive construction of 1968 in terms of the 1960s that will hopefully open up interesting comparativist perspectives that go beyond simplistic models of influences and connections. My attempt is to move beyond the critical conundrum of either accusing the temporal category of 1968 of being Eurocentric and therefore a false universal, or excusing its (European) provincialism from a corresponding nativist impulse that might unproblematically claim the Third World (China, Vietnam) for its beginnings.

In the first section of the essay, I will explore the origins of the radical Naxalite movement in India that had peaked between 1967 and 1972 in order to stage the complex articulation of such protests.[4] In the second section, I will use the occasion of the Naxalite movement and related larger political developments to segue into a brief discussion of a remarkable yet relatively understudied textual archive of the 1960s in India: a group of influential English language periodicals that started appearing between the years 1959 and 1968—*Seminar, Economic and Political Weekly, Mainstream* and *Frontier*—emerging as the pre-eminent forum for debates and discussion about politics, society, and economics within national and international contexts. A comprehensive study of the influence of these periodicals on informed debate and decision making in the post-independence Indian polity and public, all of which continue to be published even if some have lost their erstwhile prestige (and circulation figures), falls outside the scope of this essay.[5] I will therefore focus specifically on *Frontier,* the Calcutta-based weekly, since it had the most sustained engagement with the Naxalite movement in particular, and developments in international left politics in general.

The Politics: The Naxalite Movement

The beginnings of the Naxalite movement can be traced to the outbreak of armed resistance by a group of peasants, "tribals," and local communist revolutionaries at Naxalbari, a village near Darjeeling in northern Bengal (from which the movement took its name) on 24–25 May 1967. Their protest was aimed most immediately at the local oppressive landlord-police nexus, and by extension, as sympathetic accounts have argued, at the post-colonial bourgeois Indian state and its systemic structures of inequality and repression.[6] The Naxalite movement, like many other social protests of the 1960s, appeared to be a spontaneous, popular uprising. However, unlike many of these movements, it had largely institutional beginnings in so far as it took its place within the history of communist parties and politics in India. In order to develop an understanding of the origins, if not the spread, of the protests it is therefore instructive to revisit the ideological milieu that had incubated the movement.

The Naxalites, as the adherents of this radical politics came to be known, strained loyalties within the two existing communist parties in India—the Communist Party of India (CPI) and the CPI (Marxist), or CPI (M)—and precipitated a second decisive split to form the CPI (Marxist-Leninist), or CPI (M-L), the party most closely identified with their cause. The split mirrored the erstwhile Sino-Soviet dispute in international communism that led to a realignment of communist parties and politics in most places. Ideological tension within the CPI, the first and undivided communist party of India formed in the 1920s, had already become evident during the Indo-China conflict in 1962. Differences about "the characterization of the stage of the Indian revolution," and the problems of taking a unified stand on the China-Soviet Union confrontation eventually triggered its first split—between the 'pro-Soviet' CPI and the 'pro-China' CPI (M) in 1964. In spite of the split, a common element of the tactical lines of both the parties, however, retained the emphasis on "peaceful means" for achieving either a "national democratic revolution" or a "people's democracy" in the country, a stance that would eventually constitute a rift between the more radical, pro-militancy factions—the future sympathizers of the Naxalite movement—and the rest of the party. The newly formed CPI (M), however, soon started distancing itself from "the Chinese line" in international communism following certain disagreeable actions including the latter's support for Pakistan during the Indo-Pakistan conflict in 1965, and, along with the CPI, also decided to participate in the West Bengal state legislative assembly elections in February 1967. This move constituted a second strategic point of difference with the political methods of the Naxalites who advocated "seizure of power through an armed agrarian revolution."

Addressing the extreme agrarian inequality present in most parts of the region, the CPI (M) had campaigned on the promise of major land reforms benefiting landless peasants and sharecroppers famously using slogans like "Land to the Tiller." However, since no party had a clear majority in the 1967 election, a coalition "United Front" government was formed and led by a chief minister who belonged to the other constituent party—the short-lived Bangla Congress—but heavily backed by the CPI (M). The minister for land revenue in the new government, Hare Krishna Konar, a member of the CPI (M), immediately made an announcement toward making good on the party's electoral promise of redistributing surplus land and ending the eviction of sharecroppers. Newly empowered by their party coming to power, CPI (M) cadres and activists enthusiastically carried on with the task of organizing the peasantry in many districts of the state, preparing them to take back the ownership of huge tracts of agricultural land often illegally maintained by big landlords and to which the latter believed they had a rightful claim.On the other hand, newly entrusted with the responsibility of governing within a parliamentary process, the party leadership quickly realized the difficulty of overcoming legal and bureaucratic constraints in the way of such large-scale land redistribution, and started betraying signs of going back ontheir electoral promise. This move, perceived as inaction and ideological compromise, sparked off widespread disillusionment among the party members. Revisiting the gestures of the earlier split within the communists, the more radical members within the CPI (M) gradually started gravitating toward prominent dissidents like Charu Mazumdar, who openly criticized the party's "revisionist" tendencies while simultaneously advocating a strategy of "seizure of state power through armed struggle" modeled on the revolutionary ideas of Mao Zedong.[7] Mao's approval of Lin Biao's call for a people's war based on guerilla tactics and rural bases in the Third World, during the Eleventh Plenary Session of the Central Committee of the Chinese Communist Party in August 1966 probably served as the most immediate precedent for making such an argument.[8] This political tendency of dissident Indian communists acquires further significance within the larger history of a global reception of Maoist thought at the height of the Cultural Revolution in China.[9]

In keeping with the professed aims of the CPI (M), Mazumdar, along with some like-minded dissident leaders of the party's Darjeeling district committee like Kanu Sanyal and Jangal Santhal, had been active in organizing the local peasantry since the late 1950s, and this mobilization had already "attained a new level of organization and militancy when it was programmatically linked with the struggles of tea plantation workers in the neighbouring gardens."[10] Emboldened by the new developments, Mazumdar and his cohorts now led the peasants and tribals, armed with not much more than bows and arrows, to occupy and symbolically establish their claim over small tracts of land that were owned—illegally in the eyes of the peasants—by local *jotedars* (landlords).[11] A series of such low-intensity incidents happened between March and May 1967, while both the strength of the peasant resistance and the consequent police reprisal in aid of the landlords became more intensified. The decisive confrontation came on 25 May, when, following the ambush and death of a local police inspector on the previous day, a huge police contingent clashed with a large group of armed tribals and peasants resulting in the death of some tribal Santal women and children, among others, and sparking off an insurgency that would continue for several weeks. The longer build-up and grassroots constituency of the first moment of the Naxalite movement, and its overtly violent confrontation with state power—characteristics shared by some other Third World protest movements as well—thus gives it a character of a full-fledged social revolt, which then complicates the dominant narrative of 1968 as a series of spontaneous, urban, youth-based protests around the world.

The deployment of a massive police and para-military force enabled the government authorities to successfully quell the uprising in the Naxalbari region by August 1967, resulting in large-scale arrests and surrenders. However, it was scarcely anticipated at that time that the collapse of what was clearly the first stage of a militant movement would soon give rise to a series of similar violent confrontations not only in different parts of the state of West Bengal, but also in many other parts of the country. By November 1967, the Naxalites, as they had come to be known by then, had already established two periodicals to articulate their views: *Deshabrati,* a Bengali weekly, and *Liberation,* a monthly English publication; they had also formed an All India Coordination Committee of Communist Revolutionaries (AICCCR) to channelize increasing dissent from pro-Naxalite, Maoist members within CPI (M) party units all over the country. One such prominent dissenting faction outside West Bengal was formed in Andhra Pradesh under the leadership of T. Nagi Reddy, who led a mass exodus of radicalized members from the state's CPI (M) party unit to form their own "Coordination Committee" that briefly became a part of the AICCCR. The AICCCR eventually broke with the party in 1968, and a formal announcement of the formation of India's third communist party, the CPI (Marxist-Leninist), was made on 22 April 1969. Factionalism seemed to plague the new party from inception as well—the Andhra Pradesh group, for instance, separated within a few months over differences about the correct strategic line to be pursued for the success of the Indian revolution—but the CPI (M-L) emerged as the communist party most closely affiliated with the Naxalite movement as it took its course in the following years. At its peak, the movement enjoyed widespread support among students and youth not only in West Bengal but also in Bihar, Andhra Pradesh, Orissa, Punjab, and some other states, only to degenerate into a campaign of unorganized violence that called forth severe repressive measures from the state. By the mid 1970s, the Naxalite movement that had started in the foothills of northern Bengal and spread to college campuses in Calcutta and Delhi was more or less over.[12]

A unique aspect of the Naxalite movement was that it was constituted by the mobilization of sections of the autochthonous peoples in the region—mostly Santals and Oraons, but also ethnic minorities like Rajbangshis. As Sumanta Banerjee, author of one of the better-known accounts of the movement, observes in an article in *Frontier:*

> The Naxalbari movement has also rescued from the abyss of oblivion and negligence another aspect of our socio-economic life—the fate of the tribal population—and has drawn attention to their revolutionary potential … the primitive custom of bonded labour is still a practice among them. As pointed out earlier the question of organizing the landless has been neglected so long. The tribals who form a major part of them naturally shared the same neglect.[13]

Whether understood as an extension of a rural-based Asian revolution argued by Mao Zedong Thought as opposed to an urban proletariat-based European model, or as a direct contrast with the solidarity between students and intellectuals observed on the streets of cities elsewhere in the world, the participation of autochthonous peoples with histories of older and deeper struggles into this protest formation can provoke new ways of thinking about the category of the collective subject of these social movements.

The Periodicals: *Frontier*

I have deliberately restricted the discussion of the Naxalite movement to what can be termed its ideological rather than material or social origins so far in this chapter. I will now attempt to explore some of the concrete sites where these ideological discussions could materialize by focusing on a significant although understudied development—the emergence, within a decade (1959–1968), of a set of English-language journals in India that came to exert a shaping influence on academic and informed discourse on contemporary issues.[14] *Seminar,* founded by Raj and Romesh Thapar in 1959 in Bombay, and later started coming out from New Delhi; as was *Mainstream,* edited and published by Nikhil Chakravartty since 1962; *Economic and Political Weekly* (EPW), formerly *Economic Weekly,* started appearing from Bombay in 1966 with Sachin Chowdhury as its editor; and *Frontier,* founded in 1968 by Samar Sen in Calcutta, the youngest entrant to this remarkable cohort of periodicals.[15] All of them had similar aims of building vital connections between academia and the broader reading public while producing superior analytical journalism, but each maintained its unique style and organizational format: for instance, longer, analytical articles would more often find their place in *EPW* and *Seminar,* with the latter planning every monthly issue around opposing viewpoints in approaching a "problem," while *Mainstream* and *Frontier* opted for a combination of strong editorials and opinion pieces on contemporary affairs. These periodicals appeared at a time in the history of newly independent India when the post-colonial state was grappling with a host of issues critical to its survival like modernization and development on the one hand and nascent separatist movements on the other. Taken together, they also presented, and this is most relevant to our purpose in this essay, a discursive site for discussing and debating a theoretically informed and globally situated left critique of the Indian left.

Topics of international relevance, from the politics of the Cold War and Non-Alignment to the rise of the New Left and Nuclear Non-Proliferation, were also vigorously discussed and meticulously analyzed in the pages of these publications. All of these periodicals were interested in the changing configurations of left politics in India and abroad; however, it can be argued that *Frontier,* perhaps due to the proximity of Calcutta to the events in Naxalbari, devoted more editorial attention to discussions of the Naxalite Movement than its peer publications. In my reading of these extensive reports, debates, and discussions in the pages of the early issues of *Frontier* (1968–1972), I attempt to locate an important and influential discourse on the imagination of a global and Third World 1960s.

The first issue of *Frontier* was published on 1 April 1968, less than a year after the uprising at Naxalbari, and only a month before the events of May '68 in France. It was founded, with the initial monetary help of friends and admirers, by Samar Sen, a noted Bengali poet, intellectual, journalist, and translator. Sen had started *Frontier* after losing his job at *Now,* another weekly and arguably the predecessor of *Frontier* that had been thriving during his tenure as editor but where he was accused of being overtly leftist. Like Sen, the founding editors of all the other journals were prominent journalists if not public intellectuals in their own right, and have become legendary figures in contemporary Indian magazine publishing, not the least for variously standing up against the curbs on the freedom of press imposed by the "Emergency" declared by Prime Minister Indira Gandhi from 1975–1977. All of them had leftist political sympathies, but found themselves at different stages of disillusionment with the official communist parties in India when they started their publications. Between themselves, Raj and Romesh Thapar (*Seminar*), Sachin Chowdhury (*Economic Weekly*, later *EPW*), Nikhil Chakravartty (*Mainstream*), and, of course, Samar Sen (*Frontier*) also mentored generations of scholars, intellectuals, and journalists by opening up the pages of their journals for publishing their initial research and findings. Sen continued to edit the weekly till his death in 1987, after which the work was taken over by Timir Basu. Given its self-positioning as a leftist critique of the left, *Frontier* was enthusiastic about the revolutionary developments at Naxalbari and critical of the police repression unleashed by the state. The Naxalite leadership, however, was initially skeptical of *Frontier*'s editorial positions, mostly due to the latter's support of the CPI (M) in the state assembly elections in 1969, and its critique of the movement's rhetorical and practical excesses. Adversity, however, brought them closer when, after the government ban on Naxalite publications like *Deshabrati* and *Liberation, Frontier* offered a sympathetic forum for keeping the discussion alive and the communication going between the scattered leadership and its followers.

Several pages in every issue of *Frontier* were devoted to analyses of the ongoing debates within Indian and international left politics—some of which I have outlined above—but May '68 proved to be an editorial windfall for initiating a discussion of contemporary global protest movements. Observations and commentary from *Frontier* correspondents in France and the United States published during those years provide an interesting glimpse of the internationalist imagination of a "global sixties" at work in the pages of the weekly. I provide below an extended quote from a piece entitled "Letter from France—'Naxalite International'" written by Ashok Rudra, a regular contributor, in order to illustrate this better:

> What is happening in Calcutta and elsewhere in India by way of attacks on apparently trivial or meaningless targets by extremist youths is no isolated phenomenon. A wind is blowing all the world over, at least in all parts of the world outside Eastern Europe, where alone conformism reigns supreme. Everywhere else in the world increasing numbers of young people are not only rejecting the values of their elders, which include not only the institutions of the State but also institutions of the traditional left parties, but are also paying heavier and heavier prices:

ruining their studies, their careers, and clashing more and more often with the forces of law and order, resulting in deaths and injuries. This phenomenon has been there with us for the last four or five years: with West German students fighting the police over Vietnam; with American youth marching on to the White House, keeping a nervous President Nixon awake a whole night; with this anti-imperialist movement of American youth getting more and more militant by its tactical alliance with the anti-racialist struggle of the American Negroes; with students of even the staid British universities resorting to the unprecedented action of taking over universities under the leadership of extremist leaders; above all, with the revolution in France in May 1968, which started with students taking over universities and developed into young workers taking over factories, and a general strike paralyzing the whole country.[16]

The argument that a proper understanding of the extremist protests by young people in India can be best understood only if it is considered in a comparative context that takes on board the French, the German, and the American contexts becomes evident in the author's discussion of the states' responses as well:

This phenomenon has been with us for some time. But what is new in these countries is the adoption by the extremists of a tactic of what is being called urban guerillas. In France the practitioners of this form of warfare are called "les casseurs"—the breakers. The news these "breakers" have been making *read exactly like* those one has been reading about the Naxalite rampages in Calcutta. ... The news the upholders of law and order are making in France also read exactly the same as in India. Those who are forging special laws for West Bengal to allow preventive detention could have learnt a few lessons by studying the type of "anti-casseur" legislation the French Government has been preparing.[17]

Since armed resistance had rarely been a feature of social protests in post–World War II Western Europe and North America until groups like the German Baader-Meinhof Gang (or Red Army Faction) and the Weathermen in the United States were formed in the 1960s, the debates on the legitimacy of violence as a means of revolution had mostly remained marginal to their domestic political discourse. In contrast, social movements in the Third World before, during, and beyond the 1960s have often been characterized by armed struggle; a study of the Third World careers of 1968 will necessarily need to engage with this significant development. These concerns were being formulated even as the events were unfolding, as evidenced by the following extract from "Armed Struggle in America," an article on the Black Panthers and the Weathermen published in the *Frontier* issue dated 5 December 1970:

By and large Western leftists have viewed armed struggle rather benevo-lently and patronizingly as the revolutionary tool of the oppressed colo-nies, but armed struggle in the oppressor mother country has always been viewed from the safe distance of a lyrical romanticism. ... As the prospects of armed revolution in the Third World developed in the last decade, all that the white Western left was prepared for, ideologically and practically, was to stand on the sidelines and cheer—sounding even militant at times. ... The most pathetic unfolding of this theme was the spectacle during the May revolt in France, when the tottering bour-geoisie summoned and received the aid of the "old left" to re-establish the power of a bankrupt capitalist regime. ... Today, in the U.S. there are signs that the ideological and political groundwork is being laid for armed struggle, for the first time in an advanced capitalist country.

In an interesting negotiation between the global and the local, most of these *Frontier* articles reporting on and analyzing revolutionary situations in other countries would often end with a section that would elaborate its "relevance to India." For instance, a review of *Warwick University Ltd.* (edited by leftwing historian E.P. Thompson, Penguin, 1970)—a book that chronicled the contro-versial issue of secret political files on leftist students and staff being maintained by the university that was revealed during a student occupation of university buildings—asks at the end, "How does all this relate to Indian universities and students?" and provides an answer as follows:

Our universities are supposedly modeled after the British pattern. ... Definitely there are significant differences in the subjective conditions prevailing in India. University education is less guarded by liberal tenets and more prone to open identification with the ruling class structure. ... [Here] mere academic exposes will not be enough. Students are re-quired to stimulate direct action not to expose but to demolish.

A series of books that had been published during the 1960s and variously commented on the ongoing or recently concluded protest movements all around the world were discussed in the well-known book review section of *Frontier.* Some of the titles reviewed included *Obsolete Communism: The Left-Wing Al-ternative* by Daniel Cohn-Bendit and Gabriel Cohn-Bendit, *Intellectual Origins of American Radicalism* by Straughton Lynd (New York, 1968), *Confrontation: Student Revolt & The Universities* by Daniel Bell and Irving Kristol (New York: 1969), *Long March, Short Spring: The Student Uprising at Home and Abroad* by Barbara Ehrenreich and John Ehrenreich (New York, 1969), and so on. The following extract from the review of *Obsolete Communism* also reveals the com-parative approach that was espoused by Third World commentators on the Third World revolutionary situation:

Cohn-Bendit's criticism and condemnation of the French Communist Party and his search for the roots of its betrayal in the history of the Bolshevik Party of the Soviet Union are important. Especially for those of us in India who are shocked and stupefied by the spectacle of E.M.S. Namboodiripad using the hated and ill-reputed Malabar police to hunt down Ajitha and her comrades and trying them as *criminals* for attacking some police outposts, and Jyoti Basu launching a police campaign to disarm the Naxalites.[18]

Contemporary discussions of torture, prisoner abuse, and human rights violations have a disturbing prehistory in the 1960s when these methods were systematically implemented both in colonial situations like Algeria and postcolonial countries like India. Ranajit Guha's "On Torture and Culture," published in *Frontier*, 23 January 1971, straddles Fanon and *Frontier* in an attempt to drive home a central argument about the problem of "When a regime takes to the use of torture as a part of its normal routine of political 'pacification,' [the state's response to the Naxalite movement being the immediate referent] it must end up by producing a high incidence of mental disorder both among the torturers and the tortured."

What I have attempted to do in this essay is to introduce an alternative archive from the Third World into the study of the global 1960s. I have restricted myself to a brief reception history of only one significant journal, which should, however, take its place in a larger reception history of all these publications. It would also enable a new insight into the 1960s, this time as a point of departure for a history of contemporary print and magazine publishing in India, and perhaps even the Third World. My reading of the ideological origins of the Naxalite movement and the larger discursive formation of which it was arguably a part seeks to pluralize ways of thinking about the events of the 1960s, and also complicate a straightforward narrative of influences and connections on the West/North–East/South geopolitical axes. It can perhaps be argued that journals like *TelQuel* in France have performed similar functions at the peak of their influence in offering creative literary responses to sociopolitical events taking place around them. However, the dominant imagination of the global and the transnational that is necessarily routed through the "West" often remains undisturbed on such a reading. In reading the textual archive of *Frontier* and its sister periodicals, this chapter attempts to imagine the Third World imagining the global 60s. As I have tried to show with the diverse examples from the pages of *Frontier,* this imagination of the global by and in the Third World is characterized by a comparativist approach already existing in that moment, which I submit, can productively supplement the histories of really existing networks of solidarity between the different protest movements all over the world.

Notes

1. Carole Fink, Philipp Gassert, and Detlef Junker (eds.), *1968: The World Transformed* (Cambridge and New York: Cambridge University Press, 1998), 1.

2. For an argument about why even a "transnational" study of 1968 should confine itself to the boundaries of Europe, see Gerd-Rainer Horn and Padraic Kenney (eds.), *Transnational Moments of Change: Europe 1945, 1968, 1989* (Lanham, MD: Rowman & Littlefield, 2004), especially "Introduction: Approaches to the Transnational."

3. "The long 1960s" as a category for studying that influential decade has already been theorized, most notably by Fredric Jameson in his essay "Periodizing the Sixties" in Sohnya Sayres et al.(eds.), *The Sixties Without Apologies* (Minneapolis: University of Minnesota Press, 1984), 178–209. It is also mobilized in their respective accounts of the decade written by Arthur Marwick, *The Sixties: Cultural Revolution in Britain, France, Italy, and the United States, c.1958–c.1974* (Oxford and New York: Oxford University Press, 1998) and Gerd-Rainer Horn, *The Spirit of '68: Rebellion in Western Europe and North America, 1956–1976* (Oxford and New York: Oxford University Press, 2007). While Marwick and Horn have used the "long 60s" as a temporal category to include the pre-history and aftermath of the protest movements in Western Europe and North America, my usage here has a slightly different purpose. As I attempt to show in the rest of the chapter, for any understanding of a "global" 60s/"1968" to be meaningful and relevant, we will need to extend the spatial reach, the geography of the protest movements beyond Euro-America, to places where the presence of longer and continuing struggles might outweigh the uniqueness of a single year of far away, miraculous events.

4. My usage in this essay follows the established convention of referring to the movement by different names like the Naxalbari movement, the Naxalite movement, etc.

5. As part of a history of print and magazine publishing in post-independence India, I am beginning to work on a larger, more detailed study of the reception and influence of these periodicals.

6. See, for instance, Sumanta Banerjee, *In the wake of Naxalbari* (Calcutta: Subarnarekha, 1980).

7. By some accounts, the events of the communist-led armed peasant rebellion in Telengana, in the erstwhile princely state of Hyderabad in southern India in 1946–1951, was the earliest example of the application of Maoist revolutionary strategies and even predated the final victory of Maoism in China itself, thereby leaving a precedent in Indian Maoism.

8. For Lin Biao's thesis, see "Long Live the Victory of People's War," *Peking Review* Vol. 3 (September 1965). The Naxalbari uprising also received immediate recognition from the Chinese Communist Party, with the latter hailing them as the truly revolutionary faction in India. The message was put out through Peking Radio broadcasts and editorials in the *People's Daily* and *Peking Review*. See, for example, *Peking Review* Vol. 29 (14 July 1967), *Peking Review* Vol. 33 (11 August 1967), and *Peking Review* Vol. 39 (22 September 1967).

9. For a study of the global spread of Maoist thought during the 60s, see Arif Dirlik, Paul Healey, and Nick Knight (eds.), *Critical Perspectives on Mao Zedong's Thought* (Atlantic Highlands, NJ: Humanities Press, 1997).

10. Partha Chatterjee, *The Present History of West Bengal* (Delhi: Oxford University Press, 1997), 87.

11. Although there is an ongoing debate on their proper self-identification, "tribals" is still the accepted usage in India for the country's huge indigenous/autochthonous population.

12. Naxalite militancy has recently been on the rise in many states in India, particularly those with significant tribal populations, prompting the government to identify it as a major domestic, terrorist threat to law and order.

13. Sumanta Banerjee, "Naxalbari: Between Yesterday and Tomorrow—II," *Frontier* (24 May 1969), 10.

14. It should be noted here that I am not looking at the literature published by the Naxalite groups themselves since it generally functioned as little more than the programmatic, official mouthpiece of the party. These periodicals, in contrast, were not affiliated to any political party and had a larger, national circulation and influence.

15. I was unable to locate any systematic history of these periodicals except for isolated reminiscences that were mostly published on the occasions of commemorative anniversary issues.

16. Ashok Rudra, "Letter from France—'Naxalite International,'" *Frontier* (13 June 1970), 7–8.

17. Ibid.

18. Ashok Rudra, "The Anti-Leader," *Frontier* (14 June 1969), 14–16; Daniel Cohn-Bendit, Gabriel Cohn-Bendit, and Andre Deutsch (eds.), *Review of Obsolete Communism: The Left-Wing Alternative*.

Chapter 4

Liberation Struggle and Humanitarian Aid

International Solidarity Movements and the "Third World" in the 1960s

Konrad J. Kuhn

The war in 1968 between Nigeria and its secessionist province Biafra and the start of the construction of a gigantic hydroelectric dam on the Zambezi river in 1969 in the Portuguese east African colony had extraordinary resonance beyond the country's borders and generated a wide range of transnational solidarity efforts and humanitarian aid engagement in Europe and North America. Both events in the southern hemisphere allow a close look at the ideological and physical connections and transfers between protest movements in the North and liberation movements in Africa. The severe famine in Biafra due to the ongoing war evoked the largest humanitarian aid action since the Second World War and the first in the Third World. The images of children dying of hunger were the stimulus for a broad range of people to become engaged with Third World issues for the first time. It was therefore a key event for mobilizing protest groups, humanitarian aid workers, and thousands of donors. For the churches and their aid agencies, Biafra was a turning point with strong implications for future humanitarian aid work. Although Biafra as an African conflict had many political interlinkages, these issues were not widely discussed. Nevertheless, Biafra emphasized the broader public's consciousness of decolonization and Third World issues, raised by collective actors beyond formal politics.

The Cabora Bassa dam, on the other hand, represented much more than a hydroelectric power plant in a remote, underdeveloped area of northern Mozambique. The dam allowed the protest groups to denounce the involvement of major European corporations, revealing the support of colonial power in Africa and the apartheid policy in southern Africa. Thus, the dam bridged the different contexts and connected the liberation movements in Africa with emerging solidarity movements in West Germany, Switzerland, the Netherlands, Sweden, Italy, and Great Britain. Furthermore, as an ideal symbol or the denunciation of injustice, Cabora Bassa served as a linking element for political students and church actors. With both Biafra and Cabora Bassa it became obvious for solidarity movement activists that humanitarian approaches to solidarity were not sufficient. Rather, for equitable development, the influence of corporations and European governments and the support and stability given to colonial rulers through the industrialized nations had to be criticized. In this way Biafra and Cabora Bassa led to important transnational actions of solidarity, but they are rarely mentioned in existing literature.

In the first part of this chapter, I will give a brief overview of the phenomena and the history of solidarity movements regarding issues of the Third World. Second, I will show how Biafra functioned as a formative event for a new kind of humanitarian aid that strongly shaped the view of the aid-receiving "Third World" within Western societies. Third, I will use as an example the actions against the Cabora Bassa dam to look at the transnational dimension of protest activities and the reciprocal references and implications of this formation of solidarity. I will generally argue that the discussion of issues regarding the inequitable relationships between the Third World and Europe is part of a general search for new forms of politics by the movements around 1968, that Northern protest and Southern topics were closely related to each other and that, in this way, 1968 as a global phenomenon opened windows for agency and opportunity for actors from the Third World that had not existed before.

Solidarity Movements: An Attempt at an Overview

The critical issue of injustice in the world and of solidarity with the people of the so-called Third World was raised by the student protest movements in the late 1960s in Europe and the US, with their commitment to international solidarity, anti-colonialism, and anti-imperialism. Conditions in the southern hemisphere and their wars of independence interested, inspired, and radicalized movement activists. At the same time, the earlier engagement of church actors and missionaries for the people in former colonies in Latin America, Africa, and Asia changed from an apolitical and paternalistic approach to foreign development aid into an attitude of solidarity with the peoples of the Third World.[1] The student groups formed heterogeneous and various solidarity movements, together with activists from the peace movement and from critical theology circles. Intellectuals and theorists from the Third World were well received in these new groups and their texts were studiously read. The armed struggles of liberation movements were taken as inspiration for general resistance against the capitalist system, not only by members of radical leftist groups but also by the newly emerging broad student and church solidarity groups. The church itself was increasingly concerned with political-ethical issues through the ecumenical conferences in Geneva (1966) and Uppsala (1968) and the pontifical development encyclical "Populorum progressio" in 1967. Development thus became a priority issue in the church and was understood as a means for structural changes with the target of social justice and social liberation. For this the churches—influenced by liberation theology—were an important foundation for the formation of solidarity movements. These new development policy and solidarity groups, characterized by dependency theoretical analysis, demanded structural changes in the relationships between the rich North and the poor South, and therefore viewed existing development aid critically. These new actors in Europe and North America encountered the world universally and retained equality, freedom from hunger, and oppression as motives for their engagement. Via publicity campaigns in Northern countries, they attempted to create an awareness for the problems of the Third World. National protagonists in sectors such as banking, international trade, consumer policy, and cultural relations were confronted with intense scrutiny and publicly articulated critique, with Biafra and Cabora Bassa as two early campaigns. Through the demands of the social awakening of the 1960s for a new definition of solidarity, development aid policy became a contentious transnational field of discussion that occupied a considerable segment of the European and the North American public.

Famine and Airlift in Biafra: Humanitarian Aid in the Third World

After the declaration of independence in Nigeria, severe internal conflicts resulted in a military coup in July 1967, and the secession of the eastern provinces, known as Biafra.[2] The outbreak of violent and brutal civil war was conducted with cruelty, resulting in countless casualties among the civilian population. The reasons for the war included the economic interests in rich oil wells in the delta of the Niger River as well as the ethnic frictions that had been kept in check during British colonial rule. The Ibos, traditionally resident in the Biafra region and Christianized early on by British and Irish missionaries, were favored by the colonial administration, which caused the envy of the Haussas and the Yorubas. The Ibos had hardly any influence in the newly emerging state after the independence of Nigeria in 1960. The encirclement of secessionist Biafra in a landlocked circle of rain forest surrounded by Nigerian troops caused a severe famine, affecting mainly children. Nigeria used this blockade policy and thus starvation as a weapon of war to defeat Biafra. There had long been almost no information on the ongoing catastrophe available to the world public, while Biafra gained only minimal support from governments of other states. On the other hand, Great Britain and the Soviet Union provided arms as well as military and diplomatic support to Nigeria.[3]

In the spring of 1968, the International Committee of the Red Cross (ICRC) and a number of Christian churches sounded the alarm, which did not awaken public interest. It was only when images of children dying of starvation were increasingly shown in print and especially on television during the summer that interest in Western Europe and North America increased. Strong emotions were evoked and the desperate fight for survival of the locked-in Republic of Biafra stirred up public opinion and had an extraordinary impact on the mobilization of donations and solidarity. The images showed starving children, reduced to walking skeletons with distended bellies and faded hair due to undernourishment. Estimates on the body count are around 2 million.[4] The militarily defeated leadership of Biafra soon began to distribute these images of famine caused by the blockade internationally. It hired the advertising agency *MarkPress* in Geneva, which waged Biafra's war in press releases on arms deliveries, designed to embarrass European governments with stark warnings about starvation. The advertising agency also arranged flights to Biafra for newsmen from Western Europe and North America, who provided eyewitness reports in their publications.[5]

Soon churches as well as the ICRC were engaged in transportation of relief material and food aid to Biafra, which resulted in the establishment of an airlift with regular flights from Sao Tomé.[6] The Catholic Caritas organizations were working closely together with Protestant humanitarian organizations and the World Council of Churches. In October 1968, the ecumenical Joint Church Aid was founded by 33 church aid organizations from 21 countries as an ad-hoc coordination for humanitarian aid in Biafra. By December 1969 it had transported over 57,000 tons of aid material on 5310 flights to Biafra, while the ICRC airlifted 22,000 tons, mostly food aid in the form of stockfish, milk powder, and flour. Besides the enormous amount of donations there were several governments contributing for airlift support: the United States provided $57 million, West Germany $10 million, Great Britain $5 million, the Netherlands $5.3 million, Switzerland $4.5 million, and Canada $2.8 million.[7] Biafra was for all involved organizations the largest humanitarian aid action since the end of the Second World War.

The war in Biafra strongly influenced public opinion in Western countries—in the view of one West German diplomat, even more than the Vietnam war or the Soviet invasion in Prague: "Neither Vietnam nor the events in Czechoslovakia have moved people so strongly as the starvation of the Ibos."[8] An additional factor for this intense solidarity can be found in the Christianity of the secessionist Biafrans, the Ibos. Church aid agencies did not shy away from discriminatory and racist calls for donations characterized by elements of a religious war, recreating the colonial favor of the Ibos, as the example of Swiss Catholic aid agency Caritas clearly shows: "The Ibos are characterized by their intelligence, energy and efficiency, while the mostly Muslim Haussas are not capable of the same achievements. Thus, jealousy leads in Africa to war and murder, especially because 60 percent of the Ibos are Catholic. This is reason enough for the Muslims to use the opportunity to get rid of as many Ibos as possible."[9] Both the admiration for the Christian, independence-loving Ibos and the horror evoked by pictures of starving children led to a unilateral form of solidarity and commitment for Biafra in public opinion and perception in Western Europe and North America.

Biafra as an African conflict had various implications and reverse effects for the humanitarian organizations in the North. The huge amount of donations, the logistical challenge and rapid growth, caused structural problems and confusion among the operating aid agencies. Best known is the case of ICRC physician and former French Foreign Minister Bernhard Kouchner, who was disgusted by the organization's political neutrality and founded *Médecins sans frontières* in 1971 to be able to conduct humanitarian aid under a new "morality of urgency" without the restrictions of state or legal obligations.[10] The aid actions for Biafra caused major upheavals and led to reorganizations in the ICRC, Caritas Internationalis, and even Caritas Switzerland. The structures of these aid agencies, having originated from the reconstruction work in war-torn Europe, were reshaped for their new mission in foreign aid in the Third World due to the events in Biafra. Biafra was thus a crucial focal point for humanitarian aid, evoking a political consciousness among the volunteers in Biafra and strongly adding to previously existing feelings in the European and North American public.

Donations and Solidarity Efforts: Biafra Action Groups Arise

On the local level, the Biafran conflict resulted in the creation of a multitude of action groups. For example, Aktion Pro Biafra (Frankfurt and Zurich), Joint Biafra Famine Appeal (Dublin), Biafra Actie Comité (Amsterdam), American Committee to Keep Biafra Alive (New York), and Aktion Biafra-Hilfe (Hamburg) were all founded in May or June 1968.[11] Most of these groups consisted of students, workers, physicians, and priests, and were active in the collection of donations on the streets, in churches, and in public relations campaigns to "make the public aware of the urgency of aid by using press, television, radio, posters" as stated by Aktion Pro Biafra.[12] Motivation came both from a general wish to be active—"to make a bit of a hustle," as Swiss Biafran activist Urs Emmenegger puts it—and by an attempt to combine political action with humanitarian aid, as in the case of West German Ruth Bowert.[13] The donations collected were used to support the airlift established by Joint Church Aid and some of the young activists managed to visit the war-stricken region themselves. These activist groups were very well received in the public sphere at the time and publicly supported by scholars, politicians, writers, business leaders, and editors-in-chief. Aktion Pro Biafra even had a high-ranking (although purely male) patronage committee and was officially supported by the mayors of Frankfurt and Zurich. This support led the way to close cooperation with established aid agencies and common calls for donations.[14]

Clearly, the sympathies of all activists were always on the Biafran side. Explicit political critique of neo-colonial structures and of the involvement of the former colonial power Great Britain was indeed articulated in demonstrations, but never gained greater success due to weak support of the heterogeneous supporting donors and action groups concerned with Biafra.[15] This was true as well with the critique of the practice of arms exportation to the Nigerian troops or the seldom-broached issue of the involvement of multinational oil corporations in the Biafran delta. The strong support for Biafra was mostly humanitarian and not explicitly political. The Biafran cause was thus never supported by the more political student movement organizations of the 1960s, for example the Sozialistischer Deutscher Studentenbund (SDS), although the West German Aktion Biafra-Hilfe tried to involve them but was rejected because Biafra did not match the suggested leftist and socialist concept of power, as student leader Daniel Cohn-Bendit puts it in retrospect.[16] It was only after the downing of an ICRC aircraft in June 1969 by the Nigerian army, illegally equipped with anti-aircraft guns built by Swiss arms company Oerlikon-Bührle, that the issue of arms exportation was articulated in a broad campaign and led to the so-called Bührle scandal in Switzerland. This resulted in a political initiative to ban arms exportation, started in 1969 by peace movement activists and voted on in 1972, but defeated by a mere 50.3 percent.[17] It was this campaign that moved rather theologically informed groups to a political position. Thus, Swiss Protestant pastors wrote about the antagonism between humanitarian aid and arms originating from the same country: "We have been collecting money for Biafra in our parish for several months. Coin by coin, sums have been accumulated to ease the war suffering. At the same time our country's arms factory has been earning a huge amount on the same war. The credibility of our humanitarian effort is thus at risk. This is a cause for great concern."[18] Biafra was thus an activating "key event" for some of the younger generation of students in critical church and university circles interested in development issues, and it motivated them on an emotional level to participate in Third World issues, development policy, and critical solidarity work, although Christian paternalism toward African suffering remained.[19] Biafra furthermore enabled a general public in Europe and North America to show solidarity with the suffering population and to engage in humanitarian aid in Africa for the first time.

Cabora Bassa: Mammoth Dam and Protest Catalyst

The gigantic Cabora Bassa dam, with an output of 2000 megawatts, a retaining wall 160 meters high and 30 meters wide, and a reservoir of 2700 square kilometers surface area, was built between 1969 and 1979. It remains one of the largest hydroelectric plants in the world. The primary benefactor of the generated electricity was to be the highly industrialized apartheid regime in South Africa, illustrated by the fact that transmission lines were only planned to the neighboring country and not to regions of Mozambique.[20] Planned by Portugal, largely financed by South Africa and supported by Rhodesia, the Cabora Bassa scheme was a strategic undertaking in defense of the white minority regimes in southern Africa, as well as an area of growth, and thus a symbol for the theory of modernization. Starting in 1961, Portugal, as the last colonial power in Europe, was challenged militarily by the independence movement, which required enormous government expenditures. Only with the support of its NATO partners could Portugal sustain the war at all. At this point, Portugal, still poor by Western European standards and a developing country itself, was oppressing other developing countries—its colonies—with the support of industrialized countries. With the dam and its irrigation projects as a white development zone, Portugal hoped to attract settlers and investors to exploit its plentiful mineral deposits in the Zambezi valley, thus halting the advance of the Frente de Libertação de Moçambique (FRELIMO) liberation movement into southern Mozambique. Thus, Cabora Bassa was, in the sense of "social engineering," a part of a larger development plan, in which colonial power Portugal was promised an economic and political strengthening of its colonial rule. Already early on, opposition to the power plant stirred in the ranks of FRELIMO, both politically as well as militarily, via guerilla attacks on the construction site. FRELIMO's struggle against Cabora Bassa was supported by the independent African states, the Organization of African Unity, and the World Council of Churches.[21] Through multiple UN resolutions against the dam, the international public was made aware of the situation.[22] In various European countries the newly emerging solidarity movements, consisting principally of church youth groups, some of them already active on the Biafra issue, responded positively by denouncing Portuguese colonialism in Africa and condemning the participation of European corporations in the consortium that built Cabora Bassa. This consortium brought together numerous German, French, South African, and Portuguese corporations. The Swedish electricity firm ASEA, originally involved in project planning, withdrew in September 1969 shortly before signing a contract. This was due to pressure from an intensive campaign that had sympathizers in the social democratic government of Olof Palme, despite resistance from trade unions. More than any other single issue, the campaign against Cabora Bassa mobilized and radicalized Swedish opinion, contributing both to the development of the reorganized solidarity movement and to the decision to extend official Swedish government support to the liberation movements in the region.[23] The Italian firm Società Anonima Elettrificazione also withdrew from the project in May 1970, after the Italian government cancelled interest subsidies for the export credit, due to great pressure from the Italian Communist Party.[24] The British corporations GEC (or English Electric) and Barclays Bank were also interested in the project, but similarly withdrew based on pressure from resolutions of the ruling Labour Party and from the action group Dambusters Mobilizing Committee in London including the Anti-Apartheid Movement, the Liberation Committees of Angola, Mozambique, and Guinea (Bissau), and the Movement for the Liberation of Angola.[25]

Campaigns and Protest Networks of Solidarity

In West Germany, the Cabora Bassa issue was taken up in January 1969 via the publications of the Sozialistischer Deutscher Studentenbund (SDS), with a discussion of Portuguese colonial rule and its support by West Germany.[26] These links between the government and the colonial war allowed the student solidarity movement to tie the "common struggle against imperialism" to concrete starting points. The struggle against "one's own government and economy" gave the theoretical debate on imperialism a specific ground for confrontation, and gave the respective solidarity movements a specific form of "responsibility." It was only the support within NATO and the delivery of materials from European corporations that created the necessary connection for a concept of assumed links of solidarity originating in a common adversary in an imaginary struggle. The Cabora Bassa public campaign in Germany began with an appeal in early 1970, signed by numerous well-known personalities such as Alexander Mitscherlich and Ernst von Weizäcker, calling on the participating German corporations Siemens, AEG-Telefunken, BBC Mannheim, Hochtief, and Voith to withdraw from the project.[27] The foundation of the campaign spread quickly to established organizations such as trade unions, religious youth groups and church working groups, peace movement organizations, and the Young Socialists. In addition, numerous action groups and local Cabora Bassa groups formed, all active against the dam via intensive public relations. These groups also sent boycott postcards to consortium members,[28] and disrupted shareholder meetings.[29] FRELIMO itself endeavored to act directly in Europe against the dam and wrote an open letter to West German Chancellor Willy Brandt accusing West Germany of actively supporting Portuguese colonial rule and promoting the construction of the dam.[30] The Brandt government remained firm in its stance and announced in July 1970 that it would stand by the issuance of state guarantees to the export companies.[31]

In Switzerland, opposition to Cabora Bassa first became evident on the occasion of a private visit of the South African prime minister and finance minister to the Swiss Federal Council and Zurich-based banks in June 1970, which raised the possibility of negotiations for Swiss equity participation for the power plant.[32] There were no Swiss corporations directly represented in the construction consortium; however, consortium member Brown Boveri & Cie (BBC) Mannheim was a German subsidiary of a Swiss corporation, of which the parent company held a 56.6 percent stake.[33] Swiss critics of the dam project focused on this indirect participation, because it was assumed that the Swiss BBC Baden was involved in supplying electrotechnical equipment, or it at least hoped to take over portions of the project freed up by the withdrawal of the Swedish, British, and Italian corporations. Regarding the UN resolutions and the international opposition to Cabora Bassa, Jean Ziegler,[34] member of the Swiss National Assembly, broached the subject in a parliamentary inquiry to the Swiss Federal Council on the construction of the dam, and called for action to be taken against the participating Swiss corporations.[35] This interest in Cabora Bassa was quickly adopted by the still-young solidarity movement in Switzerland, some of them church youth groups already involved in the relief efforts for Biafra. The activities of these Cabora Bassa working groups included the publication of articles and letters to the editor, organizing informational meetings, and research and data analysis.[36] Opposition was directed mainly toward BBC Baden and the Swiss banks, which were called on to not participate in Cabora Bassa, neither in supplying equipment nor with equity participation.[37] Furthermore, the Federal Council was advised not to award export risk guarantees for equipment, warning of "an affair that contains all the elements of an international scandal."[38] Swiss industry occupied itself intensively with the project. The delivery by the Swiss BBC of electrical equipment for the power plant with a value of approximately 25 million Swiss francs is a case in point. This situation was not known at the time, but the claims of Swiss industry involvement by the solidarity movement later proved to be accurate.[39] The fact that a Swiss export risk guarantee was never requested might be attributable to the intensive public relations work of the student solidarity movement groups. It might also be because the share of Swiss supplier BBC Baden was partially covered by the German corporations Hermes and Kreditanstalt für Wiederaufbau.[40]

The central mobilization brochure for the broad and diversified solidarity movements active in national and transnational networks against the Cabora Bassa dam was the widely distributed Dutch booklet "*Cabora Bassa—Een dam tegen de Afrikanen,*" published by student activists, translated into German and English, and containing background information and addresses of organizations in the solidarity movement.[41] The Cabora Bassa groups were also in direct contact with the liberation movements in the Portuguese colonies, via information offices in exile and English language newspapers, and found recognition as Northern contacts and feedback groups for an imaginary common concern. At this point the campaign against Cabora Bassa was beginning to offer direct material support of African liberation movements through the solidarity movements. From this direct involvement, country-specific and often distinctly Maoist or communist-oriented solidarity committees arose providing ideological and material support for the liberation movements, especially in southern Africa.[42]

Involvement in the campaign declined noticeably around 1973. Solidarity work focused on new issues, and with the election victory and accession to power of FRELIMO in 1975, the topic disappeared completely from the focus of solidarity movements. The complexity of the situation was apparently too confusing and it completely mismatched the worldview of the activists, who often had romanticized projections and dreams of simplicity in the liberation movement.[43] After independence, the new FRELIMO government was in urgent need of foreign currency from energy exports to apartheid South Africa, and therefore allowed the power plant to be completed by the original consortium, after being repackaged as a Portuguese entity. Notable is the complete absence of ecological criticism of the project. Apparently the anti-imperialistic point of view allowed one to overlook these connections and problem areas.[44]

Concluding Remarks

Over the course of 1968, the Third World became a major topic of interest for the students in the protest movements. Thus, actors of existing development aid policy were seemingly challenged by the new emerging development policy groups in the church and student environments. But also the wider public focused on the decolonized parts of the world, and with mass media there soon was a distinct public image of the Third World.

The Biafra operation was the first of a new kind of humanitarian aid. Support and participation via aid donors became truly global and is an early example of the Third World as a field of operation for humanitarian aid agencies. Thus humanitarian aid in today's well-known form emerged: European– or North American–based aid agencies providing food and development aid, funded by public donations raised using modern communication and media channels. The Biafra operation was furthermore a crucial event for humanitarian interventions as well as a general turning point toward secular activities of church actors in the field of emancipatory development aid. The political implications and interlinkages of this conflict were not widely debated and the action groups remained generally quiet on such issues. In addition, the difference between the vast popular support for secessionist Biafra and their governments' backing of Nigeria was not criticized. Nevertheless, the solidarity and aid for Biafra fostered the emergence of a multitude of groups, some of them with student's involvement, that were engaged in practical solidarity work and transnational campaigns for Third World issues. Via the direct aid work in Biafra, the humanitarian organizations served as an important performative tool for the view of Africa and the shaping of how the war was perceived in Europe and North America. Starvation and famine had an emotional impact on action activists as well as donors, while the mass media played a central role in mobilizing public opinion with the production of images and information on this African conflict. These images of Africa as aid receiving, starving from hunger, and struck by war are long lasting and remain today. The events in Biafra and the humanitarian aid provided are in this sense a persistent burden on efforts to emancipate Africa to the point of a self-reliant continent.

For the church organizations and part of the leftist student action groups, the debate over the Cabora Bassa dam in distant Mozambique was a central starting point for the practical discussion of imperialism and the dependency theory analysis of the global economy. Third World conditions were concentrated on the dam, ideally: the construction of a technocratic mega-project in an African colony with direct participation of European corporations, guaranteed by European states, supporting both white domination in southern Africa in general as well as the Portuguese colonial rule through the sale of electricity to the apartheid regime. With the dam, the protest movements were able to illustrate the globally effective connections of oppression with a concrete example, and effectively identify the participation of one's own corporations at the national political level. In this way, the regional pragmatic and activist connection of Cabora Bassa led many of the young development policy groups in Europe to politicize their formerly Christian humanitarian objectives. The opposition to Cabora Bassa caused a change in the political structure of the solidarity movements, in that for issues of development policy, the gap between church actors and the new student groups could be bridged. In addition, through the existence of militarily active, anti-colonial liberation movements, solidarity, a sense of identity, and even support of the armed liberation struggle in the Portuguese colonies became possible.

Generally, there are three observations I would like to make with this brief analysis of the historical factors of two events that motivated and structured expressions of solidarity:

First, we encounter transnational networks, shared concerns, border-crossing transfers, personal encounters, synchronized mobilizations, and reciprocal references in different locations of the world playing a crucial role in the development of a global 1968. Northern protest events and issues were often closely linked to Southern topics and struggles. This is not only true for Vietnam and Cuba, but also for development in southern Africa or in Nigeria/Biafra, as this chapter has shown. The close cooperation with additional national groups on a concrete campaign presented options of transnational interaction both with similar groups in other countries as well as with liberation movements in the Third World. Here one could think of a national scope in which to base campaigns, criticisms, and political activities, closely linked to a comprehensive transnational network. Both theoretical analyses and concrete examples arose out of this scope; the development policy advocates built a sort of resonance network in the North that picked up these issues and translated them for their respective national situation. Thus, we encounter a transnational perspective combined with national identities as primary contexts and key aims of engagement. The 1960s opened in this way the views of perception for experiences out of Europe or North America. The Third World thus became the central focus of the protest movements of the 1960s. It was the events in the Third World that enabled protest movements to address their criticism and demand new forms of politics, both in their national contexts as well as on a transnational level. Thus, it is important that we examine how various groups in Europe and Northern America—student groups, church actors, state policy makers, business actors—analyzed, constructed, and contested the links, images, arguments, and themes that flowed between the Third World and their world. The Third World shaped and constructed not only the solidarity movement but also humanitarian organizations, the media, and a general public in a highly effective way. For further research we need to ask, therefore, how the Third World generated and reformulated development policy, political systems, and mass culture in transnational contexts and thus served as a performative tool for the distribution of ideas of global justice and responsibility.

Second, the agency of Southern activists and their performative role in a "politics of action" in the North had rarely been put in a research focus so far. Through the emerging interest of protest movements of the 1960s the actors in the often recently decolonized countries—or those still in a struggle for independence—had a unique chance to bring their issues into a transnational context. In this area the new or the future elites encountered broad response and resonance and their issues were taken up by various groups and heard by a broad public. It was they who commanded symbolic resources such as communication and knowledge, and who gained political support by mobilizing solidarity groups, church actors, and a broad mass of donors for their cause. Thus, the year 1968 was formed as much by the liberation movements and the young independent governments in Africa as by the protest movements in Europe and North America. This said, the direct connections between the solidarity movements and groups in the North and the Third World liberation movement actors are equally important and deserve further historical research.

Third, we encounter several problematic dimensions in these new solidarity relationships, created on the basis of compatible elements. The solidarity movements and their political activists identified themselves with struggles for liberation in the southern hemisphere and perceived themselves as part of a global campaign against imperialism. This led to situations of misunderstanding and accentuated the difficulties of addressing solidarity. This chapter has focused especially on these problems emerging from a concept of solidarity relationships, which often had more of a one-way character and in which there were distinctions between providers and beneficiaries. Thus, we find this international orientation of solidarity made use of simple binary opposites in the sense that not only a common enemy—imperialism—but also a common goal were projected onto liberation movements worldwide. There is the essential role of the transitory nature of the unequal connection as well as the effect of the complexity-reducing force of the enduring colonial projections on the solidarity movements. Identification with the liberated parties first became possible when the ambiguous positions became assumingly clear. Thus, solidarity movements self-empowered themselves in their desires for authenticity and their search for a fixed and unchanging "other" in the Third World.

Notes

Research for this chapter was supported by grants from the AVINA Foundation and the Gottfried R. Friedli Foundation. I am grateful to Daniel Speich and Jim Rudolf for helpful comments on earlier drafts. All quotations are translations by the author.

1. Therefore I do not agree with the distinction between "charitable" and "political" from a political sciences view when it comes to solidarity movements; see Marco Guigni, "Concluding Remarks: Conceptual Distinctions for the Study of Political Altruism," in M. Guigni and F. Passy (eds.), *Political Altruism? Solidarity Movements in International Perspective* (Lanham, MD: Rowman & Littlefield, 2001), 235–244.

2. H. Ekwe-Ekwe, *The Biafra War: Nigeria and the Aftermath* (Lewiston, NY: Edwin Mellen, 1990); and A. Harneit-Sievers, J. O. Ahazuem, and S. Emezue, *A Social History of the Nigerian Civil War: Perspectives from Below* (Hamburg: Lit, 1997).

3. The US intervened in favor of Nigeria in the Biafra conflict but supported the Biafran independency by heavy humanitarian aid due to public pressure; see L. A. Nwachuku, "The United States and Nigeria 1960–1987: Anatomy of a Pragmatic Relationship," *Journal of Black Studies* Vol. 5 (1998): 575–593; and J. E. Thompson, *American Policy and African Famine: The Nigeria-Biafra War 1966–1970* (New York: Greenwood Press, 1990). See also H. Ekwe-Ekwe, *Conflict and Intervention in Africa: Nigeria, Angola, Zaire* (Hampshire: Macmillan, 1990), 11–68. For China, France, and African states, see N. Obiaga, *The Politics of Humanitarian Organizations Intervention* (Landham, MD: University Press of America, 2004).

4. Cf. R. Boutet, *L'effroyable guerre du Biafra* (Paris: Editions Chaka, 1992).

5. R. Braumann, *L'action humanitaire* (Evreux: Flammarion, 2000), 59. See, for Nigeria's civil war, "Hate, Hunger and the Will to Survive," *Time Magazine,* 23 August 1968.

6. For this airlift, see the memories of one of the key actors, T. Byrne, *Airlift to Biafra: Breaching the Blockade* (Dublin: Columbia Press, 1997). See also J. A. Daly and A. G. Saville, *The History of Joint Church Aid,* 3 vols. (Copenhagen, 1971). For the ICRC, see T. Hentsch, *Face au blocus: Histoire de l'intervention du Comité international de la Croix-Rouge dans le conflit de Nigéria 1967–1970* (Geneva: Droz, 1973).

7. The total amount of aid given is $166.3 million (until May 1970); see Thompson (1990), 130 and 167. For Caritas and Biafra, see M. Schmidhalter, "Die Hilfsaktionfür Biafra: Wendepunkt in der Auslandshilfe des Schweizerischen Caritasverbandes," *Schweizerische Zeitschrift für Religions- und Kulturgeschichte* Vol. 98 (2003): 171–182; and Nicholas Omenka, "Hilfefür Biafra. Die Feuerprobefür die Katastrophenhilfe des Deutschen Caritasverbandes," *caritas '97/Jahrbuch des Deutschen Caritasverbandes* (Freiburg, 1996), 69–76.

8. Graf Posadowski-Wehner, Leader of the "Afrika-Referat" in the Foreign Office (Auswärtiges Amt) of West Germany in Bonn, cit. "Rettungdurch die Stockfisch-Bomber," *Der Spiegel* Vol. 25 (1969): 104–116, here 113.

9. Spendenaufruf Caritas 1968, cit. Urs Altermatt, "Caritas Schweiz: Von der katholischen Milieu organization zum sozialen Hilfswerk 1901–2001," *Von der katholischen*

Milieuorganisation zum sozialen Hilfswerk: 100 Jahre Caritas Schweiz (Lucerne: Caritas, 2002), 15–42, here 29. For a religious discourse, see Protokoll der Kommission für internationale Angelegenheiten des SEK, 11. März 1968, in: Swiss Federal Archives Berne (hereafter BAR), SEK-Archive, J 2.257, 2001/124, Bd. 10, Doss. 151.

10. For Biafra as a starting point for "Doctors without borders," see P. Aeberhard, "A Historical Survey of Humanitarian Action," *Health and Human Rights* Vol. 2 (1996): 30–44; and J.-C. Rufin, *Le piege humanitaire* (Paris: J.C. Lattes, 1986), 60. A critical perspective on humanitarian aid is provided in F. Broche, *Au bon chic humanitaire* (Paris: Première Ligne, 1994), 50–54 for Biafra.

11. For "Aktion Biafra-Hilfe" (with a foreword by Golo Mann as a critic of the West German student's movement), see T. Zülch and K. Guercke, *Biafra: Eine Dokumentation* (Berlin: Lettner, 1968). The Archive of the "Biafra Actie Comité" 1968–1971 can be found in the International Institute of Social History Amsterdam. For the "American Committee to Keep Biafra Alive," see Thompson (1990), 75–79.

12. Aktion Pro Biafra, Leaflet 1968, in: Swiss Social Archives Zurich (hereafter SozArch), SWN QS.

13. "Rettungdurch die Stockfisch-Bomber," *Der Spiegel* Vol. 25 (1969): 104–116, here 114.

14. See "Communiqué der Caritas, HEKS, SAH und der Aktion Pro Biafra," 29 June 1968, in: SozArch, SAH-Archive, Ar 20.971.115.

15. For example, in Basel with around 5,000 participants shouting anti-British slogans, cf. BAR, SEK-Archive, J 2.257, 2001/124, Bd. 10, Doss. 156. See also F. Forsyth, *The Biafra Story: The Making of an African Legend* (Barnsley: Leo Cooper, 2001), 274.

16. Cf. T. Zülch, "Die anderen 68-er: Von der Protestbewegung zur Menschenrechtsorganisation, 40 Jahre Gesellschaft für bedrohte Völker," Medienmitteilung, 5 July 2007, http://www.gfbv.de/pressemit.php?id=979&highlight=biafra (accessed 4 March 2009); D. Cohn-Bendit et al., "Kopfschrott oder Gefühlsheu? Eine Diskussion über Internationalismus," *Kursbuch* Vol. 57 (1979): 199–221. For an SDS perspective on Biafra, see P. Antonello et al., *Nigeria gegen Biafra? Falsche Alternativen oder über die Verschärfung der Widersprüche im Neokolonialismus* (West-Berlin: Wagenbach, 1969).

17. Ruedi Tobler, "Wenn Schweizer Kanonen auf IKRK-Flugzeugeschiessen: Der Bührle-Skandal,"H. Looser et al. (eds.), *Die Schweiz und ihre Skandale* (Zurich: Limmat, 1995), 93–104.

18. Resolution by pastors of canton Aargau, 26 December 1968, in: BAR, SEK-Archive, J 2.257, 2001/124, Bd. 10, Doss. 156.

19. As Swiss activists put it in their memoirs, cf. A.-M. Holenstein, R. Renschler, and R. Strahm, *Entwicklung heist Befreiung: Erinnerungen an die Pionierzeit der Erklärung von Bern* (Zurich: Chronos, 2008), 90–93.

20. Essential K. Middlemas, *Cabora Bassa: Engineering and Politics in Southern Africa* (London: Weidenfeld and Nicolson, 1975). See also A. Isaacman, "Displaced People, Displaced Energy, and Displaced Memories: The Case of Cabora Bassa, 1970–2004," *International Journal of African Historical Studies* Vol. 38, No. 2 (2005): 201–238; and A. Isaacman and C. Sneddon, "Portuguese Colonial Intervention, Regional Conflict and Post-Colonial Amnesia: Cabora Bassa Dam, Mozambique 1965–2002," *Portuguese Studies Review* Vol. 11, No. 1 (2003): 207–236.

21. The World Council of Churches provided direct financial aid to FRELIMO and other liberation movements and gained a wider audience through the issuing of a pamphlet on Cabora Bassa in 1971, cf. *Cabora Bassa & the Struggle for Southern Africa,* ed. World Council of Churches (Geneva: World Council of Churches, 1971).

22. The building of Cabora Bassa was condemned in UN Resolution 2507, XXIV (21 November 1969), by the colonial commission of the UN General Assembly in document A/73-20 (November 1970) and in UN Resolution A 8022, XXV (December 16, 1971). The 26th General Assembly finally condemned Cabora Bassa on 20 December 1971 in UN Resolution 2873, XXVI.

23. The protest in Sweden, starting in 1968, is covered in T. Sellström, *Sweden and National Liberation in Southern Africa: Formation of a Popular Opinion* Vol. 1 (Uppsala: Nordiska Afrikainstitutet, 1999), 473–504.

24. *Der Spiegel* Vol. 24 (1970): 96. See also letter by the Swiss Embassy in Portugal to the Swiss Federal Political Department, 5 January 1971, in: BAR, EPD, Abteilung für Politische Angelegenheiten, E 2001 (E-01), 1982/58, 440, AZ C.41.111.Uch.

25. The British government itself was not putting pressure on the companies; it was only the ruling Labour Party; see for example "Bericht der schweizerischen Botschaft in Grossbritannien (Keller) zu Cabora Bassa" (24 June 1970), in: BAR, EPD, Abteilung für Politische Angelegenheiten, E 2001 (E), 1980/83, 536, AZ C.41.111.0.Uch. Evidence for the British Dam Busters Committee is given in UN-Reports, see for example *Cabora Bassa and the future of Mozambique: Report to the Special Committee on the situation with regard to the implementation of the Declaration on the granting of Independence to colonial countries and peoples (A/8148/Add.1),* eds. United Nations (New York, 1972). The campaign against Cabora Bassa in Great Britain is not covered in the literature on British protest and social movements.

26. The SDS-Info dating from January 1969 addressed the Portuguese colonies. The issue from 20 May 1969 dealt with the imperialism of the Federal Republic of Germany and starting in February 1969 there were presentations on colonialism and the struggle for independence in the Portuguese colonies in Africa, which were released under the title "Der revolutionäre Befreiungskrieg in Angola, Guinea-Bissao und Mozambique," cf. thereto R. Müller, "Überlegungenzum Verhältnis von Wissenschaft und politischer Basisarbeit," *Friedensforschung und Entwicklungspolitik* (Düsseldorf: Bertelsmann Universitätsverlag, 1975), 157–162.

27. Aufruf der "Kampagne Cabora Bassa," 1970, cit. Georg Schreyögg and Horst Steinmann, "Legitimationsprobleme im internationalen Projektgeschäft—Cabora Bassa und die Siemens AG," J. Zentes et al. (eds.), *Fallstudien zum Internationalen Management: Grundlagen- Praxiserfahrungen- Perspektiven* (Wiesbaden: Gabler Verlag, 2004), 503–520, here 511.

28. Siemens alone received over 2,000 protest postcards by April 1971; cf. G. Schreyögg and H. Steinmann, "Corporate Morality Called in Question: The Case of Cabora Bassa", *Journal of Business Ethics* Vol. 8 (1989): 680.

29. R. Tetzlaff, "Transnationale Unternehmen, der Staat und der Bürger—Zwerge gegen Giganten: Hat es Zweck, gegen 'Multis' zu protestieren?" Entwicklungspolitische Korrespondenz (ed.), *Siemens: Vom Dritten Reich zur Dritten Welt* (Hamburg: Gesellschaft für Entwicklungspolitische Bildungsarbeit, 1983), 107–119.

30. This open letter from Marcelino dos Santos (vice president of FRELIMO) to the chancellor of the Federal Republic of Germany, dated 19 March 1970 (Bundesar-

chiv Berlin, DZ 8/7302-002) was printed on 17 June 1970 in *Frankfurter Rundschau* and is reproduced in W. Balsen and K. Rössel, *Hoch die internationale Solidarität: Zur Geschichte der Dritte Welt-Bewegung in der Bundesrepublik* (Köln: Kölner Volksblatt Verlag, 1986), 286–288.

31. Doc. 293, notes 16 and 17, in: *Akten zur Auswärtigen Politik der Bundesrepublik 1970* Vol. 2 (Munich: Oldenbourg, 2001), 1096.

32. "Was sucht der südafrikanische Ministerpräsident in der Schweiz? Schweizer-Geld für Rassen-Bau?" *Zürcher AZ*, 15 June 1970, 1.

33. The files of the BBC's communication department in the archive of (what is today) ABB Switzerland indicate clearly that the campaign against Cabora Bassa was very well documented; cf. Corporate Archive ABB Group Baden (hereafter ArABB), B 0.8.100.539 Kommunikationsabteilung/Cabora Bassa 1970–1979.

34. Jean Ziegler (born 1934), senior professor of sociology (Geneva), member of Parliament for the Social Democrats in the Swiss National Assembly (1967–1983 and 1987–1999), United Nations special rapporteur on the right to food (2000–2008), and since March 2008 advisor to the UN Human Rights Council.

35. Kleine dringliche Anfrage Jean Ziegler, 10 June 1970, in: BAR, EPD, Abteilung für Politische Angelegenheiten, E 2001 (E), 1980/83, 536, AZ C.41.111.0.Uch.

36. Thus it is incorrect when it is declared that "empathy and support (for the liberation movements) were completely absent, for example, in neutral Switzerland" (329); see P. Gleijeses "Scandinavia and the Liberation of Southern Africa," *The International History Review* No. 2 (2005): 324–331.

37. Cf. For example *Was geschieht in Cabora Bassa? Dokumentation,* eds. Arbeitsgruppe für Kirche und Gesellschaft der evangelischen und römisch-katholischen Universitätsgemeinden Bern und Arbeitsgruppe Angola (Berne, 1970), 2.

38. Open letter from the Arbeitsgruppe Angola and the Arbeitsgruppe für Kirche und Gesellschaft Bernetothe Swiss government, 13 June 1970, in: SozArch, Ar 430.25.3.

39. There were rectifying transformers, valves, and devices for high-tension direct current transmission lines delivered; seeArABB, B 0.8.100.539, Information über Cabora Bassa, Hr. Bernhardt und Dr. Rinderknecht, 7 January 1971, 11. During the debates, although, Eric Bernhardt (Sales Director) stated the amount of BBC Baden only with a value of 11 million Swiss francs, see "Cabora Bassa im Meinungsstreit," *Der Bund,* 1 February 1971. This is the amount covered by Hermes-Exportrisikogarantie.

40. *Oekumene Rundbrief* 2, ed. Evangelische Studentengemeinden Berlin, 15 July 1970, quoted in M. Stähli, H. K. Schmocker, and R. H. Strahm (eds.), *Cabora Bassa: Modellfall westlicher Entwicklungspolitik* (Berne: Kandelaber Verlag, 1971), 69–70. The coverage (decided on 21 April 1970) included approximately 11 million Swiss francs; see ArABB, B 0.8.100.539, Information über Cabora Bassa, Hr. Bernhardt und Dr. Rinderknecht, 7 January 1971, 11.

41. The German versions were edited in 1971 and 1972; see S. Bosgra, *Cabora Bassa: Ein Dammgegen die Afrikaner* (Berlin: Cabora Bassa Komitee, 1972). The English pamphlet was edited in Berlin in 1972.

42. For the case of West Germany, see Reinhart Kössler and Henning Melber, "The West German Solidarity Movement with the Liberation Struggles in Southern Africa: A (Self-) Critical Retrospective," in U. Engel and R. Kappel (eds.), *Germany's Africa Policy Revisited. Interests, Images and Incrementalism* (Münster: Lit Verlag, 2002), 103–126.

43. Cf. Bahman Nirumand, "Sehnsuchtsräume: Warum die Revolution ausblieb,"in D. Cohn-Bendit and R. Dammann (eds.), *1968: Die Revolte* (Frankfurt: A.S.A Fischer, 2007), 223–234.

44. A. Isaacman and C. Sneddon, "Toward a Social and Environmental History of the Building of Cabora Bassa Dam," *Journal of Southern African Studies* Vol. 26, No. 4 (2000): 597–632. See also P. McCully, *Silenced Rivers: The Ecology and Politics of Large Dams* (London: Zed, 1996); and B. R. Davies, A. Hall, and P. B. N. Jackson, "Some Ecological Aspects of the Cabora Bassa Dam," *Biological Conservation* Vol. 8 (1975): 189–201.

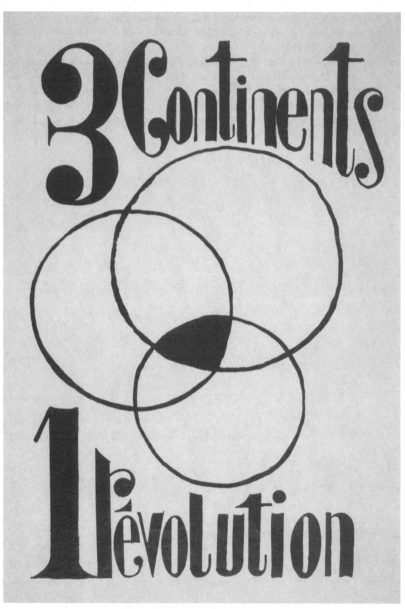

1.1. "Trois continents, une révolution" (Three continents, one revolution), Poster (Serigraph), Paris, 1968. Coll. BDIC, Paris-Nanterre.

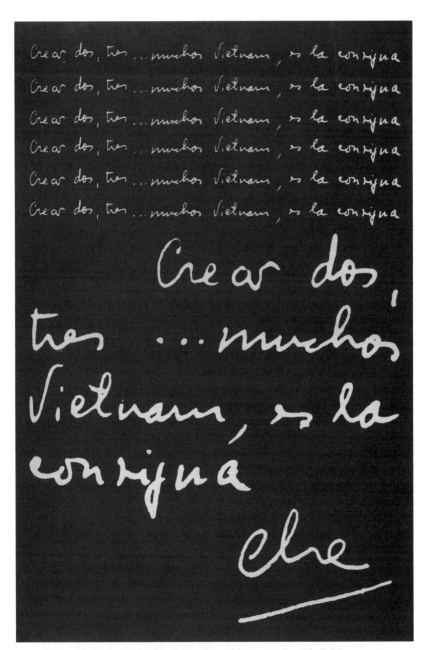

1.2. "Crear dos, tres... muchos Vietnam, es la consigna. Che" (Create two, three … many Vietnams, that is the watchword. Che), Tricontinental Magazine, September-October 1967, n°21. Coll. BDIC, Paris-Nanterre.

1.3. Logo of the Tricontinental, Tricontinental Magazine, January–April 1968, n°4–5. Coll. BDIC, Paris-Nanterre.

2.1. Biafra-Wallpaper during the Student's Protest „Globus Krawall" in Zurich, June 1968. Swiss Social Archives, Zurich, F/Na-0001-040.

2.2. Aktion pro Biafra" poster on Bahnhofstrasse, Zurich 1968. Photography with the kind permission of photographer Luc Chessex, taken from his work "Essai sur la Suisse", 1968–1969.

2.3. Cabora Bassa dam in northern Mozambique under construction, December 1976. Picture taken from: Hydroelectric of Cahora Bassa (Eds.). A Nossa Energia Abraça Moçambique – Our power embraces Mozambique: 25º aniversário da hidroeléctrica de Cahora Bassa, Lisboa 2000.

3.1. "Resolutely support the anti-imperialist struggle of the Asian, African and Latin American people." A poster from the Chinese Cultural Revolution. Image provided courtesy Lincoln Cushing/Docs Populi.

3.2. "Long Live Marxism, Leninism, and Mao Zedong Thought!" Chinese Poster. Image provided courtesy Lincoln Cushing/Docs Populi.

6.1. Students protesting outside of the University of Cape Town, 1968. University of Cape Town Libraries.

6.2. Students stage a sit-in at University of Cape Town, 1968. University of Cape Town Libraries.

8.1. Miriam Makeba in concert at Lovanium University in 1968. Makeba was invited by AGEL, Lovanium's student association. She performed on campus, in front of a huge crowd of students, who were equally galvanized by her artistic talents and political commitments. Image courtesy of Alexandre Luba Ntambo.

8.2. Miriam Makeba in concert at Lovanium University in 1968. Makeba was invited by AGEL, Lovanium's student association. She performed on campus, in front of a huge crowd of students, who were equally galvanized by her artistic talents and political commitments. Image courtesy of Alexandre Luba Ntambo.

8.3. Miriam Makeba in concert at Lovanium University in 1968. Makeba was invited by AGEL, Lovanium's student association. She performed on campus, in front of a huge crowd of students, who were equally galvanized by her artistic talents and political commitments. Image courtesy of Alexandre Luba Ntambo.

8.4. François Kandolo, Lovanium University's student president, released from the Ndolo prison on 14 October 1969. Kandolo had organized the student march of 4 June 1969. He was condemned to serve 20 years in prison. President Mobutu granted him together with the other student organizers an amnesty on his birthday. Image courtesy of Valérien Milimgo.

8.5. The whole group of student organizers on the same day of their release from prison. Image courtesy of Valérien Milimgo.

10.1. Mexican Army troops and tanks enter the Zocalo, in late August 1968 in response to repeated student marches to and rallies in Mexico City's central plaza. Author's archive.

10.2. Thousands of students march through downtown Mexico City on 27 August 1968 to protest President Diaz Ordaz's repression of their movement. Author's archive.

10.3. During their marches, the student protestors organized themselves according to their academic departments. The Facultad de Ciencias Politicas (Political Science Department) from the UNAM was one of the most active delegations in the student movement. Author's archive.

Part 2

Fresh Battles in Old Struggles: New Voices and Modes of Expression

Chapter 5

A More Systemic Fight for Reform

University Reform, Student Movements,
Society, and the State in Brazil, 1957–1968

Colin Snider

> The Brazilian student movement has always had educational com-
> plaints and political struggle present in in its activities.—National
> Student Union, 1963[1]

> Down with Repression! More Funding for Universities!—Banners
> carried at student protests, Rio de Janeiro, 1968[2]

> The well-known qualitative problems of Brazilian education
> continue to manifest themselves.—Governmental Task Force for
> University Reform, 1968[3]

In 1963, the União Nacional de Estudantes (National Student Union, or UNE)
was hopeful of the prospects of reform under progressive President João Goulart heading into 1964. Yet on 1 April 1964, the Brazilian military overthrew
Goulart, putting in place a right wing military dictatorship. Four years after the
coup, students protesting the increasing authoritarianism and repression of the
dictatorship took to the streets, calling for both university reform and the end
of the dictatorship. Even the military leadership under presidents Humberto
Castelo e Branco (1964–1967) and Artur Costa e Silva (1967–1969) was well
aware of the need for university reform, having signed two agreements with the
United States to study the issue in the previous three years. By the end of 1968,
just before instituting the Ato Instucional No. 5 (Institutional Act No. 5, or
AI-5) and ushering in the most repressive phase of the 21 year dictatorship, the
military government issued its *Reforma Universitária* (University Reform). The
Reforma marked the first sweeping university policy any government, military or
civilian, had launched in over 30 years in Brazil,[4] and increased the number of
openings in federal universities, streamlined administration, and provided more
funding for universities with the hope that a new class of university-educated,
white-collar professionals would lead Brazil to its rightful place within the "developed world."

However, as the quotations above make clear, the *Reforma* did not emerge out of the bureaucratic ether. Rather, it marked the culmination of a public debate between the Brazilian state and society that dated back to the late 1950s, before the military had assumed power. While scholars have tended to emphasize the events of 1968 in Brazil in a framework of student resistance and state repression,[5] the debate over the role of universities in Brazil reveals a much more complex process of dialogue between students, the state, and other social actors. These complicated debates over the issue of university reform played a major part in state-society relations in the 1960s and in the events of 1968 in Brazil.

"Developing the Fight for University Reform"[6]: The Debate over University Reform, 1957–1964

The first proposal for university reform originated not with students, but with the government of President Eurico Gaspar Dutra in 1948. That year, the debate over the *Lei deReformas Diretrizes e Bases* (Law of Structural and Basic Reforms, LDB) began.[7] In its original form, the law tackled a broad set of social reforms, including reorganizing agrarian, administrative, and banking policies. It also dealt with educational reform, outlining a plan in which the federal government would expand the university system and increase the number of college-educated students in Brazil in an effort to improve national development.[8] The law was immediately controversial, however, and between other national political struggles like the re-election (in 1950) and suicide (in 1954) of president Getúlio Vargas, the creation of Brasília in the late-1950s, and the election (and resignation six months later) of president Jânio Quadros in 1961, debate over the Lei ebbed and flowed, and it was only passed in 1961.[9]

As the LDB and the issue of university reform stalled among politicians in the 1950s, the student movement picked it up. In 1957, at the First National Seminar for Educational Reform, the leadership of UNE resolved to undertake a "more systemic fight for reform."[10] In the late 1950s and early 1960s, students met annually to debate the infrastructural and pedagogic changes they felt were necessary. Feeling that they were an underrepresented group in the decision-making process in universities, UNE members insisted they should make up one-third of the academic directories of universities. They also demanded an end to the system of "*professores catedráticos,*" who were employed for life or until retirement and who had to meet few academic conditions upon gaining their position. Students complained that this professorial autonomy and job security prevented professors from making "any effort to improve,"[11] and rendered the university system "archaic and authoritarian ... marked by paternalistic and nepotistic professorial relationships, and centered on outdated curricula far removed from the country's social and economic realities."[12] One former professor's assistant even described the system as "medieval."[13] To replace this structure, UNE suggested that Brazilian universities shift to a departmental system.[14] Students also sought more funding from the government for the federal universities, which housed the majority of Brazil's university students into the 1960s.

Another extremely pressing concern for Brazilian students and politicians was the lack of *vagas*, or openings, in the university system. Compared to Spanish America, Brazil's university system was extremely young, with the first university only forming in 1920,[15] just in time for the visit of the Belgian royal family.[16] While only a fraction of Brazil's population attended universities even in the 1960s, the number of students attending universities had grown astronomically in the previous 15 years, increasing from 53,000 students in 1950 to 142,000 in 1964,[17] with some estimates putting 81 percent of that total in the federal universities.[18] Schools were unable to keep pace, and "*excedentes*," the students who passed the entrance exams but could not attend university due to these constraints, began pushing for more openings in the university system.[19] Nor was this a banner that students alone adopted. Pedagogical experts and politicians across the country were increasingly concerned with the rate of growth of university-age students who were not gaining admission for the simple reason that there were not enough openings. President Goulart himself said "the biggest problem facing the Brazilian university" was "the growing number of matriculating students compared to the number of schools."[20]

In order to force the issue of *vagas* and university reform, students, politicians, and pedagogues all appealed to developmentalist thinking in Brazil that had begun in the 1950s under Juscelino Kubitschek, inextricably connecting educational and infrastructural improvements with national development and the need for "constant advances in science, technology, and culture" that only university reform could achieve.[21] Nor were they alone in seeing the quality of higher education and Brazilian development as intertwined. At an address to university rectors from throughout Brazil, one scholar commented that, despite the rapid growth of public and private universities in the 1950s, there had not been a similar growth in "qualified professionals, of scientists and of intellectuals," nor had there been adequate "rapid scientific and technical progress."[22] Another expert noted that "national development" depended upon applied research that could only be accomplished in universities, a task for which Brazilian universities were woefully under equipped.[23] Some even maintained that the perfection of "educational and assistance organs" could only be attained via a "'University-Industry' program" that would create a partnership between public universities and private industries to further Brazilian development.[24]

This proposal was not the only one of its kind, and debate and advocacy were not limited to students or to the political left. In 1961, conservative business leaders, pedagogues, military officials, and middle- and upper-class professionals concerned by the growing "radicalism" of students and workers formed the Instituto de Pesquisas e Estudos Sociais (Institute of Research and Social Studies, or IPÊS).[25] Believing that "the direction of the country can no longer be left only in the hands of politicians," IPÊS's members sought to combat what they feared was mounting leftism in Brazil, threatening Brazil's moral fabric and their own interests.[26] In the 1960s, IPÊS met regularly to discuss issues as diverse as administrative reform, land reform, and development in Brazil, attempting to steer the nature of the discourse away from the left and toward their own politico-economic agenda, with education being a major focus in this matrix.[27] IPÊS sought to mold university students via more contact with businesses in their "Universities in Business" program, which consisted of extra classes for ambitious, entrepreneurial university students.[28] Indeed, with the downfall of Goulart, one of IPÊS's major political concerns prior to 1964 disappeared, giving the organization more time to focus on educational reforms.[29] Thus, by the time the military overthrew João Goulart on 1 April 1964, multiple sectors of society, including students, politicians, business leaders, military officers, and pedagogical experts had all already begun to take firm stances in a broad debate over the role of universities in Brazil and their importance to national development.

"The Urgency of University Reform": The Debate for Reform during the Military Dictatorship, 1964–1968

If the struggle for university reform among the student body began well before the military's coup, Goulart's overthrow gave a new impetus to many student leaders who believed the coup "brought reorganization of student organizations and the mobilization of a new generation of students" with it.[30] The issue of *excedentes,* already simmering, erupted after 1964. The universities simply did not have enough openings for the number of students who passed the entrance exams.[31] A demand for greater governmental spending on higher education accompanied the need for more *vagas.* Students also continued to demand an end to the *catedráticos,* and to seek the most basic infrastructure improvements in universities, including inexpensive student restaurants, clean bathrooms, and functioning drinking fountains, all of which marked a continuation of the demands students had been making prior to 1964.[32]

The new political context of a military government also brought with it new educational and political demands from the students. Responding to the atmosphere of political repression, particularly of progressive leaders, professors, and student leaders, students demanded an end to the military dictatorship both in private publications and correspondences and in public rallies.[33] Additionally, the suspension of all political rights of professors had only left the underequipped universities even more unprepared for the rising number of students. The military government under Castelo Branco also immediately established itself as the students' primary antagonist. First, it burned down the UNE headquarters in Rio de Janeiro on the very day the military assumed power. UNE itself became illegal when the government issued Decree-Law 4464, better known as the *"Lei Suplicy,"* named after Flávio Suplicy de Lacerda, the Minister of Education and Culture at the time. In addition to declaring UNE illegal and creating its own government-supported "apolitical" student organizations—such as the Diretórios Estadual de Estudantes (State Directories of Students, or DEE) and Diretório Nacional de Estudantes (National Directory of Students, or DNE)—the *Lei Suplicy* also attempted to purge the university system of any political activity and criminalized politicization in the classroom. Although it was not strictly enforced, the *Lei Suplicy* became a central part of students' demands for university reform, joining the structural demands that pre-dated the military government.[34] Political opposition leaders joined students in condemning the *Lei Suplicy,* including high-ranking members of the opposition party, the Movimento Democrático Brasileiro (Brazilian Democratic Movement, or MDB).[35]

However, the most polarizing issue that students focused on after 1964 was the collaboration between the Ministério da Educação e Cultura (Ministry of Education and Culture, or MEC) and the United States Agency for International Development (USAID). The MEC-USAID accords, as they came to be known, were to the students as much an ideological as they were an institutional affront. Looking to Cuba, China, and Ché Guevara, students had already become extremely critical of the United States and its role in the Cold War. When the government announced it had entered into the MEC-USAID accords to improve university education, students were immediately critical of the foreign interference, often branding it "imperialism" or "neo-colonialism."[36] In making public their contempt for the MEC-USAID agreements, students felt they were participating in a dialogue that "responded" to the government's own efforts to improve education.[37] They constantly attempted to present their demands to the national government, taking advantage of any opportunity to speak to any member of the government who could address their concerns. Sometimes, these efforts were successful, as when a small number of students gained a hearing with Castelo Branco himself[38]; other times, they were less successful, as governmental officials cancelled the meetings with students at the last minute.[39] Regardless of the relative successes or failures in these individual meetings, however, the student movements went far beyond simple protests and "opposition" to the military government when dealing with educational and political policy. Rather, the student movements' relationship with the state was far more complicated, sometimes involving the "dialogue" created when they took to the streets with their slogans and banners, but just as often using dialogue through petitions and meetings directly with the government.[40]

Not all students opposed the military government or participated in UNE, and some did join the state-sponsored DEEs. Yet even these students acknowledged the need for university reform. For example, the president of the Rio de Janeiro state DEE wrote to the minister of foreign relations, suggesting that students travel to Europe and study the conditions of universities there, so that "there are better conditions for us to offer to President Humberto Castelo Branco a draft of *BRAZILIAN UNIVERSITY REFORM.*[41] Even though those students that supported the dictatorship were nowhere near as vocal or critical of the government as participants in UNE were, education reform remained important to their own state-sponsored student organizations, and they used these organizations to express their own demands and visions for reform.

In spite of students' ongoing demands, they were not the sole voice in the debate on university reform after the military coup. Just as some students participated in the DEEs, many politicians and civilians supported the military government.[42] Some of these supporters and bureaucrats also pushed the military to institute major structural and even ideological reforms in the universities since taking power. Federal Deputy Antonio Carlos Magalhães suggested that, among the "immediate means for combating revolutionary war," the completion "of the University Reform in the shortest time possible" would be as important as the "expulsion of all 'true' agitators among students from their schools."[43] A meeting of members of the Ministry of Education and Culture's Directory of Higher Education sought the immediate "short- and long-term expansion and perfection of Brazilian higher education" via programs like MEC-USAID, which it extended from the original 1965 agreement in 1967.[44]

The military leadership was well aware of the issues students were facing, and it often agreed with students, politicians, and pedagogues on the need for, if not the substance of, university reform. Although Castelo Branco's administration was preoccupied with turning Brazil's economy around and removing "dangerous" political threats via suspension of political rights, arrest, or exile, it also acknowledged the need to begin improving and reforming Brazil's higher education system. Indeed, it often was difficult to ignore the students and their demands, as protests and meetings were regular, and the security apparati, such as the Departamento de Ordem Pública e Segurança (Department of Public Order and Security, or DOPS), were sending in regular reports to the government. Castelo Branco's second minister of education and culture, Raimundo Moniz de Aragão, acknowledged students' dissatisfaction with the university system,[45] and Castelo Branco himself said that Brazil relied on the universities to prepare "technicians and scientists, whose role will necessarily deliver national development."[46] In the Plano Decenal de Desenvolvimento Econômico e Social (Ten-Year Plan for Economic and Social Development), Castelo Branco's government acknowledged the importance of higher education to Brazil's development.[47] The Plan even highlighted the severe enrollment situation facing Brazilian universities, claiming that in 1965 there were 125,406 candidates who had passed the entrance exams, yet there were only 58,929 *vagas* available.[48] And in 1965, Castelo Branco's administration signed the first of the MEC-USAID agreements in an effort to streamline and modernize Brazilian universities.[49]

If Castelo Branco's government acknowledged the specific problems facing Brazilian universities, the students' dissatisfaction, and the need for reform, Arthur Costa e Silva's administration prioritized education. Even before assuming the presidency in March 1967, Costa e Silva had allegedly told the American ambassador John Tuthill that education would be a central part of his administration.[50] Had education reform not been on Costa e Silva's agenda, though, the events of 1968 would have put it there. Students had increasingly begun protesting the dictatorship and taking their demands for university reform to the streets, and protests spread throughout Brazilian society as the military government began cracking down even harder on students and others who voiced dissent.[51] Indeed, part of the pressure to create AI-5 came from high-ranking members of the military who wanted Costa e Silva to do something to reduce the explosion of protests and "subversion" in 1968. Costa e Silva himself was well aware of the students' demands, declaring that "the majority of students clamor for a better quality of education … we respond with the *Reforma Universitária*."[52]

Although the debate over university reform had been growing since 1957 and had become increasingly contentious since 1964, the issue gained even greater urgency in 1968. In March of that year, police confronted students protesting the closing of a student restaurant in Rio de Janeiro. Police opened fire, killing Edson Luís de Lima Souto, a poor high school student who had moved to Rio hoping to attend university and who worked at the restaurant. Students immediately seized upon Edson Luís's death, taking his body to the House of Deputies and displaying it with a Brazilian flag and placards calling the government "assassins."[53] Because Edson Luís had no family in the area, students were able to use his death as a symbol to rally against military repression.[54] Thousands gathered at the mass for Edson Luís in the Candelária Cathedral, where police again attacked the students. While student mobilizations and rallies against the dictatorship had been building since at least 1966,[55] after Edson Luís's death student mobilizations intensified even further, and began to gain support from workers, musicians, and parents of university students.[56]

Although violent police repression sparked many of the protests in the wake of Edson Luís's death in 1968, university reform in no way disappeared from the scene in spite of the increasing opposition to the dictatorship and its repressive measures. If anything, by 1968 university reform and opposition to the dictatorship had grafted to one another. Students from the political left lambasted the "demagogic 'university reforms'" the dictatorship was studying, calling them little more than means for the military government to impose "ideological domination" upon students.[57] They even equated the invasions of university campuses to the military's use of torture and "murder" as part of the military's broader strengthening of the executive branch's power.[58] Students felt that their demands for more openings and more funding would lead to a more "democratic" university system than the one the dictatorship was proposing, and by pushing for a democratic university they were fighting for a democratic society in opposition to the military government.[59] Even students not involved in more radical political groups were increasingly tying the issue of university reform to an end to the dictatorship, as the banners that simultaneously called for university reform and

"*Abaixo a Ditadura!*" ("Down with the Dictatorship!") seen at protests through-out that year made clear.[60] The students were not without a strong argument, either, given that the arrival of the military had led to an increased military pres-ence on campuses and the blackballing of "subversive" professors and student leaders, which had made university education even more precarious.[61] Students assumed that, by opposing the state's interventions in universities and its plans for university reform, they were clearly expressing a "democratic and anti-dicta-torial perspective."[62]

Parents also were increasingly entering into the battle as their children were caught up in the growing violence. Certainly, parents had been involved in the debate on university education previously, such as in 1962, when parents and students alike demanded the federalization of the private Mackenzie University in São Paulo.[63] Still, their involvement was relatively minimal prior to the dic-tatorship. Between 1965 and 1968, though, many were increasingly shocked at the methods the state was employing against their own children. Some parents directly challenged the government's actions, as was the case with one father who went to the local prison and threatened to shoot whoever had arrested his son, only to discover that the arresting officer had been his other son, who had joined the military.[64] Although most parents were nowhere near radical enough to threaten officers with a pistol, many did join their children in the growing public protests like the March of the One-Hundred Thousand in Rio de Janeiro, a march that brought together students, professors, artists, singers, parents, and even some politicians to protest the death of Edson Luís and the increasingly violent crackdowns on students.[65] Even the parents who did not join their chil-dren in the protests were nonetheless concerned about their own children, and actively hoped for a resolution to the growing conflicts of 1968 so that their children would be safe.[66] They too had a vested interest in how the issue of uni-versity reform would play out, as they were among the "hundreds of thousands of fathers and mothers who never finished elementary school" and who hoped that a university degree would help their children enjoy greater material and social gains than the parents had.[67] When these parents began to see the govern-ment increasingly attacking the children of the middle class, they were forced to take sides in the struggle.

By the end of 1968, the issue had reached a turning point of sorts, as the military finally issued its *Reforma Universitária*. The *Reforma Universitária* did in one way or another address many of the issues that had been facing Brazil's university system for over a decade. Among other things, it acknowledged the glaring issue of *vagas*,[68] as well as Brazil's need for more white-collar professionals to lead national development,[69] two issues students had been raising since the 1950s. To address these issues, it proposed expanding the number of federal uni-versities by establishing new schools and federalizing existing schools, thereby creating more openings. It also recommended increasing the number of feder-ally sponsored scholarships for students to attend college. In all, the state would assume control and monitoring the functioning of universities, expanding both the federal funds given to the schools and the number of technicians and bureaucrats who would monitor the schools on the part of the state. Throughout the reform, down to the tiniest detail, the state's control expanded, establishing the model for university education that would dominate Brazil into the 1990s.[70]

Conclusion

When the military government of Costa e Silva issued the *Reforma Universitária* at the end of 1968, in one way it marked the culmination of a decade-long debate on Brazil's universities. Since the late 1950s, university students had been fighting for university reforms, demanding infrastructural and political changes that would give them more opportunities to attend school, a greater voice in the administration of the universities, and better infrastructure. And they were not the sole voices in the debate for university reforms. Both before and after the coup of 1964, pedagogical experts, politicians, white-collar professionals, military leaders, parents, and even artists from all parts of the political spectrum actively engaged in a debate over the future of the Brazilian university system.[71] While this debate could and did lead to direct confrontation between students, professors, leftists, and intellectuals on the one hand, and conservatives, the military government, and business leaders on the other, it also witnessed significant efforts at cooperation, collaboration, and more subtle forms of negotiation in exactly how the universities should be reformed. And the demands did not remain stagnant. Indeed, as the military dictatorship strengthened its control in the 1960s and grew increasingly repressive, students increasingly tied together university reform and the struggle for democracy in the years leading up to 1968. All of this demonstrates how the struggles of 1968 in Brazil were not sudden, and they were not a simple matter of resistance and repression; rather, they were part of much longer processes of contestation and negotiation among and within social sectors and the state.

However, the *Reforma Universitária* did not mark an endpoint in the debate on university reform in Brazil. Although it did address issues that the students had been raising, such as the number of openings in schools and replacing the *catedrático* system with a departmental structure, students maintained their opposition, rejecting the *Reforma* for both ideological and practical reasons. In the 1970s, issues that derived directly from the *Reforma Universitária,* such as annual fees and the functioning of the department system, would be the targets of fierce student criticism, and old issues like the ongoing struggle for openings and federal funding would continue.[72] In the process, 1968 would take on historical meaning as students tried to reconstruct UNE after years of repression.[73] As the 1980s dawned and the dictatorship neared its end, students continued to call for "university reform," and just as it had in 1968, the role of the university in Brazil played a major part in the broader debate on democratization.[74] 1968 stands out in the narrative of Brazil's dictatorship because of the seemingly accelerated pace of events, but 1968 was not an anomalous year. Rather, it was but one eventful year in a decades-long process of struggles and debates between students, society, and the state over the nature of education, development, social justice, and democracy.

Notes

1. Observation from a 1963 study composed by the União Nacional dos Estudantes (National Student Union), *Luta Atual pela Reforma Universitária,* L514, Coleção Livros Aprendidos Pela Polícias Políticas, Arquivo Público do Estado do Rio de Janeiro (APERJ), 5.
2. Banners used in protests in Rio de Janeiro in 1968. Image from the Memória do Movimento Estudantil collection. Online photo archive: http://www.mme.org.br/services/FRM_MME/Album/ImageNavigator.EZTSvc.asp?PhotographUID={EA 79E748-0C20-441F-82CD-8F96A029BD14}&AlbumUID={BBB9B01D-EF89-4724-9660-21F0AD2DB255}&ServiceInstUID={758B8CF2-70C4-4F69-A489-6 441527CBB15}&UserSID={95FF4305-D81B-47C5-AAD3-F8A0E7BC4182}&L anguageID=pt-br.
3. *Reforma Universitária: Expansão do Ensino Superior e Aumento de Recursos Para a Educação,* Relatório da Subcomissão Especial do Grupo de Trabalho da Reforma Universitária, (Brasília: Ministério do Planejamento e Coorenação Geral, Ministério da Fazenda, Ministério da Educação e Cultura, Agosto 1968), 6.
4. Getúlio Vargas's administration was responsible for the previous broad reform, the *Estatuto das Universidades Brasileiras,* in 1931. See Sofia Lerche Vieira, *O (Dis)curso da (Re)forma Universitária* (Fortaleza, Ceará: Edições Universidade Federal do Ceará/ PROED, 1982), 108; and Luiz Antônio Cunha, *A Universidade Temporã: O ensino superior da colônia à era de Vargas* (Rio de Janeiro: Livraria Francisco Alves Editora, 1982), 250–290.
5. See Thomas Skidmore, *The Politics of Military Rule in Brazil: 1964–1985* (New York: Oxford University Press, 1988); and Maria Helena Moreira Alves, *State and Opposition in Military Brazil* (Austin: University of Texas Press, 1985). For Brazilian examples, see Ronaldo Costa Couto, *História indiscreta da ditadura e da aberta—Brasil: 1964–1985* (Rio de Janeiro: Editora Record, 2003); and Élio Gaspari, *A Ditadura Envergonhada* (São Paulo: Editora Schwarcz, Ltda., 2002).
6. *Luta Atual Pela Reforma Universitária,* 9, Coleção Livros Aprendidos Pela Polícias Políticas, APERJ.
7. See, for example, AT c 1960.06.25, Centro de Pesquisa e Documentação de História Contemporânea, Fundação Getúlio Vargas (CPDOC-FGV); CMa pi Mariani, C. 1953.09.17, CPDOC-FGV; CMa pi Mariani, C. 1953.09.17, CPDOC-FGV; CMa pi Mariani, C. 1977.09.01, CPDOC-FGV; GC k 1951.01.10, CPDOC-FGV; and LF c 1929.10.24, CPDOC-FGV.
8. See CMa pi Mariani, C. 1977.09.01, CPDOC-FGV.
9. For the role the discussion had in the 1960s and the various permutations that the law assumed over time, see, for example, "Esboço Inicial do Plano de Restruturação

da Universidade do Brasil," Caixa 46, and "Estudo Sobre Organização Universitá-
ria," Caixa 49, Coleção Paulo de Assis Ribeiro, Arquivo Nacional (AN). See also
"Projeto de Lei da Camara No. 13 de 1960—Fixa as Diretrizes e Bases da Educação
Nacional," Caixa 243, Coleção Paulo de Assis Ribeiro, AN.

10. *Luta Atual pela Reforma Universitária,* 13, Coleção Livros Aprendidos Pela Polícias
Políticas, APERJ.

11. *Luta Atual pela Reforma Universitária,* 29, Coleção Livros Aprendidos Pela Polícias
Políticas, APERJ.

12. Victoria Ann Langland, "Speaking of Flowers: Student Movements and Collective
Memory in Authoritarian Brazil," PhD dissertation, Yale University, 2004, 46–47.

13. Interview conducted with A. P., 26 November 2007.

14. *Luta Atual pela Reforma Universitária,* 30, Coleção Livros Aprendidos Pela Polícias
Políticas, APERJ.

15. Scholars of education in Brazil debate the actual date of formation of Brazil's "first
university." The University of Rio de Janeiro, established in 1920, was little more
than the combination of already-existing schools of law, medicine, and engineering. Some suggest that, since these schools already existed, the first "real" university
was the Universidade de São Paulo, established in 1934. See Luiz Antonio Cunha
(1982), chapter 3; and Raimundo Martin da Silva, "Four Centuries of Struggle: The
Idea of a Brazilian University and Its History," PhD dissertation, Southern Illinois
University at Carbondale, 1982, chapter 5. Here I consider the University of Rio de
Janeiro to be the "first Brazilian university."

16. For more on this visit and its impact on social policy in Rio de Janeiro, see Sueann
Caulfield, *In Defense of Honor* (Durham, NC: Duke University Press, 2000), chapter 2.

17. Luiz Alberto Gómez de Sousa, *A JUC, os estudantes católicos e a política* (Petrópolis:
Editora Vozes, 1984), 75.

18. Maria das Graças M. Ribeiro, "Educação Superior Brasileira: Reforma e Diversifica-
ção Institucional" PhD dissertation, Universidade de São Francisco, 2002, 18.

19. See, for example, *Luta Atual pela Reforma Universitária,* 20, Coleção Livros Aprendidos Pela Polícias Políticas, APERJ.

20. "Discurso pronunciado na cerimônica de abertura dos cursos superiores da Universidade do Brasil," 1–3, AT pi Goulart, J. 1963.00.00, CPDOC-FGV.

21. *Luta Atual pela Reforma Universitária,* 28, Coleção Livros Aprendidos Pela Polícias Políticas, APERJ; *Carta do Paraná,* Anexo II in Maria de Lourdes de A. Fávero, *A UNE em tempos de autoritarismo* (Rio de Janeiro: Editora UFRJ, 1995),
XXXIX–XCIX.

22. "A vitalização da Universidade Brasileira," Discurso instaurador da Reunião de Rei-
tores em Brasília e publicado na *Revista Brasileira de Estudos Pedagógicos,* 1, AT pi
Brito, A.O. 1961.11.29, CPDOC-FGV.

23. See "Comentário, sem assinatura, sobre o artigo de Anísio Teixeira no jornal *Última
Hora,*" AT pi S. Ass. 1964.00.00/3, CPDOC-FGV; "Esbôço de Programa de Go-
vêrno—21 Sept. 1961," RC e ag 1961.09.21 (Pasta I) CPDOC-FGV; and "Plano
Trienal de Desenvolvimento Econômico e Social (Volume 1) (1963/1965), RC e ag
1961.09.21 (Pasta IV), CPDOC-FGV.

24. "Anteprojeto—Campanha Institucional em Favor das Classes Conservadoras do
Brasil," 12, CMa pi S. Ass. 1961.00.00, CPDOC-FGV.

25. Barbara Weinstein offers a great analysis of how, far from remaining passive in the face of workers' organization, business elites formed their own labor organizations in an effort to shape the workers' movement toward the owners' own interests from the 1930s up to and beyond 1964. Although her focus is more on labor policy than education, she also demonstrates how the two could and did overlap, especially in technical education. See Barbara Weinstein, *For Social Peace in Brazil: Industrialists and the Remaking of the Working Class in São Paulo, 1920–1964* (Chapel Hill: The University of North Carolina Press, 1997).

26. Clarence W. Hall, "The Country That Saved Itself," *Reader's Digest* (November 1964): 137. Hall's publication, originally written in the American edition, wound up being retranslated into Portuguese and passed around in IPÊS's publications. For the presence of military leaders, including Golbery Couto e Silva, the future chief of staff to President Ernesto Geisel (1974–1979), see *Instituto de Pesquisas e Estudos Sociais da Guanabara—IPÊS/GB: Relatório Annual Referente a 1968,* 6, Pacote 5, Caixa 37, Coleção IPÊS, AN; and "Discriminação das Contribuições dos Associados em 1969—1° semestre," Pacote 1, Caixa 10, Coleção IPÊS, AN. For more on the association of business leaders and military officers, see also René Armand Dreifuss, *1964: A Conquista do Estado—Ação Política, Poder e Golpe de Classe* (Rio de Janeiro: Editora Vozes, 1981), 174–176. For more on the formation of elites' labor organizations, see Weinstein (1997).

27. "Programa para o 'Forum de Debates' a ser realizado pelo Rotary Club, com cooperação do IPÊS, sobre o Tema: 'Causas da Inquietação Social no Brasil'" and "Seminário do IPÊS," Caixa 317, Coleção Paulo de Assis Ribeiro, AN. See also "Simpósio sôbre a Reforma da Educação—Documento Básico" Caixa 301, Coleção Paulo de Assis Ribeiro, AN.

28. "Universidade na Emprêsa," Caixa 21, Coleção IPÊS, AN.

29. Ofício Secreto no. 377-IPM/CNTI and Ofício Secreto no. 420-IPM/CNTI, Caixa 21, Coleção IPÊS, AN.

30. "Análise do Movimento Estudantil a partir de 1964," 1, Dossie 6, Coleção Fundos Particulares—Jean Marc van der Weid, APERJ.

31. As just one example of this, Luiz Antonio Cunha mentions that, between 1964 and 1968, the number of candidates per *vaga* in medical schools in Brazil wavered between 6.3 and 8.3 candidates. Cunha, *A Universidade Reformanda: O Golpe de 1964 e a modernização do ensino superior* (Rio de Janeiro: Francisco Alves, 1988), 88; see also "No Estado do Rio, A Primeira Cidade Universitária do Brasil—Iniciativa Histórica, 1967/1970," Pasta III, Coleção Ernâni Amaral Peixoto, CPDOC-FGV.

32. *Informação No. 271/DPPS/RJ—Serviço de Cadastro e Documentação (SCD)—23 September 1968,* Pasta 30/31, Coleção DOPS, APERJ. In Bahia, students occupied the rector's office because of the "bad quality of food in the University Restaurant" and the small number of student residential facilities compared to the large student body. See CMa pi Fraga, A. 64.03.04, 7, CPDOC-FGV. For the reference to restrooms and drinking fountains, see "Análise do Movimento Estudantil a partir de 1964," 1, Dossie 6, Fundo Coleções Particulares—Coleção Jean Marc van der Weid, APERJ.

33. See, for example, "Informe S.O.," 14 October 1966, Pasta 5, Coleção DOPS, APERJ; *Revista do DCE Livre Alexandre Vanucci Leme (USP),* Fundo Coleções Particulares—Coleção Jean Marc van der Weid, APERJ; Document 6 (Untitled), Fundo Coleções Particulares—Coleção Jair Ferreira de Sá, APERJ. See also Skidmore

(1988), chapters 2–4; Costa Couto (2003), chapters. 2–3; and Langland (2004), chapter 1.

34. From the standpoint of enforcement, the *Lei Suplicy* was minimally successful. UNE continued to meet illegally well into 1968 and beyond. Additionally, students simultaneously protested the government's attempted control of the Students' Central Directories (DCEs) on campus, even while co-opting them and turning them into just another organ of the student movement. In spite of the difficulty in actually enforcing the *Lei Suplicy*, though, its importance in antagonizing students cannot be overstated. While there were voices of protest against the April coup and support for Goulart remained, many students, as with the rest of Brazilian society, were ambivalent about the military takeover, and were willing to wait and see what happened. With the *Lei Suplicy*, the student movement saw what Luiz Antonio Cunha rightly calls "the first moment of the fight against the student movement's organization in its own arena." Even radical students who were strongly opposed to the military government during the 1960s acknowledged the importance of the *Lei Suplicy* in radicalizing the student movement. See interview conducted with M. D. N., 13 August 2007; interview conducted with F. G., 10 September 2007; and interview conducted with J. A., conducted 27 December 2007. For student mobilizations within university organizations, see "Nota Oficial da UME," Folha 182, Pasta 6, Coleção DOPS, APERJ. For quotation, see Cunha (1988), 60. For evidence of importance of *Lei Suplicy* to radical groups, see "Informe estudantil nacional de política operária," 5 August 1967, Dossie 11 of Fundo Coleções Particulares—Coleção Daniel Aarão Reis, APERJ.

35. "Carta de Augusto do Amaral Peixoto a Derci Gonçalves," AAP algb 66.09.26, CPDOC-FGV.

36. See, for example, "Informe estudantil nacional de política operária," 5 August 1967, Dossie 11, Fundo Coleções Particulares—Coleção Daniel Aarão Reis, APERJ; and "Nota Oficial da UME," Folha 182, Pasta 6, Coleção DOPS, APERJ.

37. *Guerra Popular* No. 1, Ano I, Oct. 1968—Dossie 9, Caixa 5, Doc 245 of Fundo Coleções Particulares—Coleção Daniel Aarão Reis, APERJ.

38. Gaspari (2002), 221.

39. *Estado de Guanabara, Secretária de Segurança Pública, Informes (S.O.-S.A.A.), 22/6/67,* folha 130, Coleção DOPS, APERJ.

40. See Document 6 ("Untitled"), 5, Fundo Coleções Particulares—Coleção Jair Ferreira de Sá, APERJ. See also, Jarbas Passarinho, minister of labor under Costa e Silva and minister of education and culture under General Emílio Garrastazu Médici (1969–1973), *Um híbrido Fértil,* 3rd ed. (Rio de Janeiro: Editora Expressão e Cultura, 1996), 285.

41. "Intercámbio Cultural," Of. No. 36/66, JM c mre 66.03.15, CPDOC-FGV. Original emphasis.

42. See Daniel Aarão Reis, *Ditadura militar, esquerdas e a sociedade* (Rio de Janeiro: Jogre Zahar Editor Ltda, 2005).

43. "Medidas Imediatas de Combate à Guerra Revolucionária," ACM pm 1964.10.00, CPDOC-FGV.

44. "Ministério da Educação e Cultura, Diretoria de Ensino Superior—Convênio de Assessoria ao Planejamento do Ensino Superior," May 1967, AAP rev64 1967.05.09, CPDOC-FGV.

45. *Revista do DCE Livre Alexandre Vanucci Leme,* 97, doc. 10, Fundo Coleções Particulares—Coleção Jean Marc van der Weid, APERJ.
46. Ribeiro (2002), 31. For Castelo Branco's recurring emphasis on the universities' role in Brazilian development, see Humberto de Alencar Castelo Branco, *Discursos,* 3 vols. (Brasília: Secretária da Imprensa, 1965–1967).
47. *Plano Decenal de Desenvolvimento Econômico e Social,* Tomo VI, Volume I, I–II: Educação e Mão-de-Obra (Versão Preliminar), Ministério do Planejamento e Coordenação Econômica, (Brasília, 1967), 16–17.
48. *Plano Decenal de Desenvolvimento Econômico e Social,* Tomo VI, Volume I, I–II, 99.
49. In addition to MEC-USAID agreements in 1965 and 1967, there were a handful of other studies on higher education that the government commissioned prior to 1968. See Sofia Lerche Vieira, *O (Dis)curso da (Re)forma Universitária* (Fortaleza, Ceará: Edições Universidade Federal do Ceará/PROED, 1982), chapter 2.
50. Gaspari (2002), 233.
51. See Langland (2004), chapter 1; Couto (2003), chapter 4; Fávero (1995), 59–72; and Zuenir Ventura, *1968: O Ano que Não Terminou* (Rio de Janeiro: Editora Nova Fronteira S/A, 1988) for just some narratives of these events.
52. Passarinho (1996), 318–319.
53. See Maria Paula Araujo, *Memorias Estudantis: Da Fundação da UNE aos Nossos Dias* (Rio de Janeiro: Ediouro Publicações S.A., 2007), 175
54. For the importance of Edson Luís's death as a symbol and in constructing memory in the student movement, see Langland (2004), chapters 1 and 4.
55. See, for example, "Documento contendo expressões dos sócios da SBPC sobre a 29ª reunião," Dossie 6, Fundo Coleções Particulares—Coleção Jean Marc van der Weid, APERJ.
56. See Flora Süssekind, "Coro, Contrários, Massa: A Experiência Tropicalista e o Brasil de Fins dos Anos 60," in Carlos Basualdo (ed.), *Tropicália: Uma Revolução na Cultura Brasileira* (Rio de Janeiro: Museu de Arte Moderno, 2007), 31–58.
57. *Guerra Popular* No. I, Ano I (October 1968): 3–4. Caixa 5, Doc. 245, Dossie 9, Coleção Fundos Particulares—Coleção Daniel Aarão Reis, APERJ.
58. "Análise do Movimento Estudantil a Partir de 1964," Dossie 6, Fundo Coleções Particulares—Coleção Jean Marc van der Weid, APERJ.
59. *Guerra Popular* No. I, Ano I (October 1968): p. 5. Caixa 5, Doc. 245, Dossie 9, Coleção Fundos Particulares—Coleção Daniel Aarão Reis, APERJ.
60. See the second quotation at the beginning of this chapter. For more photographic evidence of this, see the photo archives of Memória do Movimento Estudantil at http://www.mme.org.br/main.asp?Team=percent7B6CB6B3C4percent2DB6BFp ercent2D4D56 percent2D8B2E percent2D286CD15F2893 percent7D; and Aarujo, *Memória Estudantil,* 160, 178, 181, and 204.
61. "Análise do Movimento Estudantil a Partir de 1964," 3, Dossie 6, Fundo Coleções Particulares—Coleção Jean Marc van der Weid, APERJ. For cases of invasions in Brasília and Minas Gerais, see Antonio Gurgel, *A Rebelião dos Estudantes: Brasília, 1968* (Brasília: Editora Revan, 2004); and Aluísio Pimento, *Universidade: A destruição de uma experiência democrática* (Petrópolis, RJ: Editora Vozes Ltda., 1984), respectively.
62. "Análise do Movimento Estudantil a Partir de 1964," 3, Dossie 6, Fundo Coleções Particulares—Coleção Jean Marc van der Weid, APERJ.

63. "Carta de Paulo de Almeida Salles a Anísio Teixeira, informando-lhe envio de cópia da moção aprovada pelo plenário da assembléia de fundação da associação de pais e alunos na Universidade Mackenzie, São Paulo," photos 159–164, Roll 40, AT c 1960.06.25, CPDOC.

64. Interview conducted with J. F., 19 June 2007.

65. See Gaspari (2002), 296–298.

66. Interview conducted with D. N., 13 August 2007.

67. "Carta de Josio Sales a Artur da Costa e Silva sobre a situação do ensino superior nos EUA," EUG 67.12.16, CPDOC-FGV.

68. *Reforma Universitária*, 8.

69. *Reforma Universitária*, 11.

70. During his administration, Fernando Henrique Cardoso (1994–2002) launched another major university reform that sought to undo many of the changes initiated by the dictatorship, including reducing the number of federal universities in favor of private institutions. See Ribeiro (2002), chapters 4–5.

71. See Süssekind (2007).

72. See, for example, Encaminhamento No. 73/75/DPPS/INT/RJ, Estado do Rio de Janeiro, Secretaria de Segurança Pública/DPPS/INT/RJ, 25 August 1975, 50. Pasta 40, Coleção DOPS, Arquivo Público do Estado do Rio de Janeiro (APERJ); and *Jornal da Engenharia* Ano IV, No. 8 (June 1975): 1; DGIE-DPPS-DO-SB—Seção de Buscas Especiais—Encaminhamento No. 049, 23 June 1975, Pasta 40, Coleção DOPS, APERJ.

73. See Langland (2004), chapter 4.

74. See Colin Snider, "'Uniting to Defend Their Interests': Student Movements, the State, and Educational Policy in Brazil, 1977–1985." Paper presented at the XXVIII International Congress of the Latin American Studies Association, 11 June 2009.

Chapter 6

Speaking the Language of Protest

African Student Rebellions at the Catholic Major Seminary in Colonial Zimbabwe, 1965–1979

Nicholas Creary

> "Their Lordships the Bishops regret that due to the recent events they are obliged to order the temporary closure of the Regional Major Seminary." [This] marked the end of a process which commenced on Monday, [the] 30th September 1974, when the entire student body, with the exception of four students, boycotted lectures and retired to the football pitch.[1]—Kevin Kinnane, secretary general of the Rhodesian Catholic Bishops' Conference, 1974

Between 1965 and 1979 the Catholic Major Seminary of Saints John Fisher and Thomas More at Chishawasha, near Salisbury, Rhodesia, experienced extended periods of rebellion by African students, resulting in the seminary having to be closed on three separate occasions. These dates coincided with the conclusion of the Second Vatican Council (1962–1965), the Rhodesian Front's Unilateral Declaration of Independence (UDI) on 11 November 1965, and African nationalists waging an armed struggle for the liberation of Zimbabwe (1966–1979). Following the student rebellion and seminary closure in 1974, the Rhodesian bishops removed the seminary from the administration of the Jesuit fathers who had run the seminary since its founding in 1936.

A combination of factors contributed to increased student protests, including changes in the canonical administrative structures of the seminary that resulted in ambiguous lines of authority in seminary governance, and the influence of different missionaries' perspectives on the church and African culture in minor seminaries run by different religious orders from the Jesuits. The relatively intellectually open environment in the minor seminaries under the Bethlehem missionaries and the Carmelites, combined with increasing sentiments of African nationalism on the part of the seminarians and an increasingly aging and reactionary Jesuit community, set the stage for the rebellions that would shake the seminary in the 1960s and 1970s. A failed effort to integrate the seminary racially in 1965 ignited African students' frustrations and aspirations into activism and protest.

While the escalating political tensions in colonial Zimbabwe certainly contributed to the seminarians' increasing consciousness of themselves as African Christians, the primary cause of the students' activism in the 1960s and 1970s was the Jesuits' failure to break with the dominant white Rhodesian culture and its paternalistic mindset. This failure on the part of the Jesuits is indicative of their larger failure to inculturate the Catholic Church at their missions in colonial Zimbabwe. As such, African seminarians' expressions of nationalism were part of a broader struggle to decolonize the Catholic Church.

Seminary Beginnings

Two Bantu language–speaking groups populated the territory of contemporary Zimbabwe: the VaShona, who entered southern Africa as early as the ninth century; and the AmaNdebele, who came to western Zimbabwe during the first half of the nineteenth century amid the disturbances associated with the rise of the Zulu state.[2]

Jesuit priests served as chaplains when British settlers financed by Cecil Rhodes' British South Africa Company (BSAC) invaded Mashonaland in 1890 and Matabeleland in 1893. The colonizers seized Africans' land and cattle and established the colony of Rhodesia in 1890. Jesuit superiors received extensive land grants to establish permanent mission stations in and around Salisbury and Bulawayo. BSAC and settlers established large-scale mining and commercial farming operations on lands confiscated from African inhabitants. As in South Africa, the financial success of both systems depended on exploiting cheap African migrant labor.[3]

In 1896, the VaShona and AmaNdebele rebelled against BSAC. African religious leaders played significant roles in planning, organizing, and coordinating armed resistance against BSAC. The rebellion, called *chimurenga* in ChiShona, drastically impeded Christian churches' missionary efforts in colonial Zimbabwe. BSAC suppressed the *chimurenga* in 1897, and after the rebellion, European missionaries began evangelizing aggressively.[4]

Amid growing African nationalism and pressure from London to allow Africans to participate in government, Rhodesian settlers sought to maintain white supremacy by unilaterally declaring independence in 1965. Rhodesia became a pariah state denied official recognition by other countries and subject to international economic sanctions. In 1966, the Zimbabwe African National Union (ZANU) began the second *chimurenga* against the Rhodesian state. The war raged until 1979, and on 18 April 1980, Rhodesia became the Republic of Zimbabwe with a government chosen by the African majority.

The seminary of Saints John Fisher and Thomas More officially opened at Chishawasha Mission on 1 January 1936, with eight candidates for the priesthood and four candidates for the diocesan brotherhood of Saint Peter Claver. The first buildings were made of thatch and mud, and permanent structures were built between 1942 and 1945, largely with the labor of Italian prisoners of war.[5]

By 1940, the first seminarians began their studies in philosophy, and the seminary officially became a major seminary in 1944.[6] Despite the gradual increase in academic standards, the Jesuit staff geared the course of studies at Chishawasha to what they perceived as the low educational level of the students and focused on preparing the seminarians to be mission or parish priests. As was the custom in the pre–Vatican II church, philosophy, and theology courses were taught in Latin. Courses for the major seminarians focused mainly on "theoretical scholastic philosophy and theology … defending theses with three examiners."[7] The first seminarians from the Chishawasha seminary to become priests were ordained in 1947, and were required to spend an additional pastoral year at the seminary.[8]

The Regional Major Seminary and Student Protests

In 1955, the Vatican established the hierarchy in Southern Rhodesia. Salisbury became a metropolitan see and suffragan sees were established in Bulawayo, Gwelo, Umtali, and Wankie.[9] Aston Chichester was installed as archbishop in April.[10] In 1956, Francis Markall succeeded Chichester as archbishop of Salisbury.[11]

The erection of the hierarchy had a significant impact on the seminary. In 1958, Jesuit Father Francis McKeown became seminary rector.[12] Also in 1958, Propaganda Fide decreed Chishawasha a regional seminary.[13] Previously, the superior of the Jesuit community served as the de facto superior of the seminary, reporting to the bishop and de jure superior of a diocesan seminary. As such, the bishop had a canonical right and responsibility to visit the seminary under his jurisdiction, even if he entrusted its administration to a religious institute, such as the Jesuits in this case. As a regional seminary, however, Chishawasha was to serve candidates from all five dioceses in Southern Rhodesia. As such, the seminary became the property of the Vatican and came under the responsibility of Propaganda Fide, which entrusted the administration to the Jesuits. The bishops were free to interact and direct their respective candidates, but did not have the canonical right or responsibility to visit the seminary. Rather, they were required "to meet each year to receive and discuss the report of the Rector on the moral and economic state of the Seminary," and "any observations they may wish to make to the Rector will generally be communicated to him by the local ordinary [the archbishop of Salisbury]."[14]

The change in the seminary's status resulted in confusion concerning the role and authority of the bishops in the seminary's governance and an ambiguous relationship between the seminary rector and the newly established seminary board of bishops.[15] This ambiguity was one of the significant factors that contributed to the rise and expression of student protests at the seminary in the 1960s and 1970s.

The drive to make Chishawasha exclusively a major seminary was another significant contributing factor to the rise of seminarian radicalism. Prior to 1958, there had never been more than seven staff members teaching at the seminary at any time, and after 1940, they were required to teach both minor and major seminarians.[16] By the 1950s, the number of seminarians had increased to the point that Chichester had to solicit funding to expand the seminary physical plant and seek additional money for their support.[17] In 1953, there were 55 students. By 1956, the number had increased to 76.[18]

As rector, Francis McKeown pursued the separation of the minor seminarians vigorously, hoping to ease an increasingly acute staffing problem resulting from the shortage of Jesuits in the Zambezi Mission, the growing number of minor seminarians, and the disparity in ages between incoming minor seminarians and older major seminarians.[19] Beginning with the 1963 academic year, the Seminary of Saints John Fisher and Thomas More at Chishawasha became a regional major seminary.[20] Candidates for the priesthood were then sent to minor seminaries at Chikwingwizha near Gwelo or Melsetter in the Umtali diocese.[21]

As a result of this decision, African candidates for the priesthood were exposed to different perspectives on the church and African culture from those of the Jesuits. The effects of that exposure were significant. The Swiss Bethlehem Mission Fathers, whom Chichester invited to take charge of the southern part of the Salisbury vicariate in 1938, ran the minor seminary at Chikwingwizha. Unlike the Jesuits, the Bethlehem missionaries took a very positive view of African culture, and greatly encouraged the incorporation of African cultural symbols and vocabulary into the corpus of the church's practice.[22] By and throughout the 1970s there were more students from the Gwelo Diocese at Chishawasha Major Seminary than from any other diocese, and in 1977 more than from the dioceses of Salisbury and Bulawayo together. Between 1973 and 1976, nine African priests were ordained for the Gwelo Diocese, compared with six for Bulawayo, four for Umtali, and two each for Wankie and Salisbury.[23] The relatively intellectually open environment in the minor seminaries under the Bethlehem missionaries and the Carmelites, who took charge of the eastern districts of Southern Rhodesia beginning in 1946,[24] combined with increasing sentiments of African nationalism on the part of the seminarians, and an increasingly aging and reactionary Jesuit community set the stage for the rebellions that shook the seminary in the 1960s and 1970s.

By the 1950s, African nationalism in Southern Rhodesia was on the rise with the renaissance of the Industrial and Commercial Workers' Union (ICU), and the founding of the National Democratic Party in 1959. African national-ism began to manifest itself in the seminary during this period as well.[25] Jesuit documents make frequent references to "less visible respect for authority," "chal-lenges to authority," and "lack of respect," including a seminarian proclaiming to a staff member that Rhodesia needed a "Mau Mau," and another incident in which an African deacon struck a Jesuit priest on staff.[26] The rector, Francis McKeown, reported that "the seminarians seem to be far too conscious of their own status and dignity, and too ready to feel slighted and offended."[27] There are frequent references to the seminarians' awareness of the political situation, and that this was causing the problems. African priests who spent their fifth year at Chishawasha were not only becoming less willing to be treated in the same man-ner as seminarians, but "apparently did not consider themselves as seminarians, as was shown by the fact that they tended to ignore notices addressed to seminar-ians," and that the seminarians were "slack" in "raising their hats to priests" and on "a number of similar points."[28]

Francis McKeown noted that "the fifth year has difficulties of its own, the chief being the mental or psychological adjustment necessary to live as a priest and yet one in statu pupillari." According to McKeown, bishops should have withheld fifth year priests' faculties and delayed their attendance at annual dioc-esan clergy conferences "to help remind them that they are still student priests."[29] Another Jesuit priest on staff expressed concern that a fifth year African priest reported that the African workmen at the seminary "were complaining of their wages," and considered it "dangerous if the Seminarians went around enquiring into such matters and sympathising with the workmen."[30] This attitude is indica-tive of the Jesuits' enduring paternalism, and reflective of their growing isolation from the seminarians' concerns.

During his annual visitation to the seminary in 1961, Salisbury Mission superior T. E. Corrigan thought it "incredible" that the seminarians would "talk politics" and found it necessary to suggest means "of controlling this."[31] In 1962, Corrigan noted that the staff was "worried" about "the general discipline," "the contact and knowledge of the staff with regard to the seminarians," and "the cor-responding personal confidence [that] individual seminarians have in the staff." Urging the staff to make "a very positive effort ... to know and be at the disposal of the students," Corrigan observed that it seemed "that the [Jesuit] commu-nity is dangerously isolated from the seminarians, and consequently confidence and discipline are endangered. There is also a very great danger that accurate knowledge of individual seminarians is lacking."[32] By 1963, although Corrigan commended the staff for having decided to take two meals per day with the stu-dents, he also scolded them for not having done anything to improve the lines of communication with the seminarians. In fact, the staff had revised the seminary constitutions and custom book in order "to [impose] a stricter regime." Cor-rigan urged the cooperation of all "to make it reasonable."[33] According to Jesuit Father Patrick Moloney, the staff had established "a little Jesuit enclave at the seminary."[34] As late as 1974, it was common for Jesuit professors to tell African seminarians who asked in-depth philosophical questions in class not to "bother with it" as they were being trained to be "simple parish priests."[35]

1965: An Attempt at Racial Integration

The idyllic enclave came to an abrupt end. In 1964, Francis McKeown proposed and received approval from the bishops to enroll two white students at the seminary for the 1965 academic year.[36] Apparently he did so without either having consulted the other members of the staff or having notified them that he would be stepping down as rector and leaving for sabbatical in 1965. Four students arrived from the segregated seminary of St. John Vianney in Pretoria. Less than a week after the term began, John Diamond, McKeown's successor, noted that the white students had expressed "great dissatisfaction" with the food, accommodations, timetable, and general living conditions. "They have allied themselves quickly with the professional malcontents."[37] They adamantly opposed manual labor, especially laundry.[38] Although two of them—Geoffrey Goodwin and Peter Saunders—left the seminary less than three weeks after the term began, alleging "that they were grossly misled by Fr. McKeown as to conditions here,"[39] their grievances resonated with the African seminarians, who sent an anonymous letter of complaint to the Southern Rhodesian bishops from "the Seminary Group," despite the institution of daily afternoon tea for all the seminarians at the end of February.[40] Additionally, one of the two remaining white students, Anthony Turner, sent a lengthy memorandum on how the seminary should be run to Francis Markall, the archbishop of Salisbury and chairman of the Seminary Board of Bishops, after Turner left the seminary in April.[41]

According to Fr. Christopher Gardiner, the fourth seminarian from St. John Vianney and the only one to stay past the first term of the 1965 academic year, the students were treated "as second class citizens compared to the Jesuits. We began talking with the other students about St. John's, and their eyes opened up: The Jesuits told them this is how it was at other seminaries. We told them that they [the Jesuits] were using and abusing you."[42]

The four "decided to rebel" by not going to manual labor. "We stayed in our rooms and read," said Fr. Gardiner, "There was conflict from the beginning." When they were not punished for their disobedience, many of the African students questioned what they perceived to be differential treatment by the Jesuits, a charge John Diamond denied vehemently in the ensuing imbroglio with the bishops.[43] According to Gardiner, the African students were "disappointed" when Saunders, Goodwin, and Turner left.[44]

Gardiner stated that Saunders, Turner, and Goodwin had approached Markall, their bishop, about transferring to Chishawasha from Pretoria.[45] Gardiner, the only one of the four born in Rhodesia, spoke with Adolph Schmitt, the bishop of Bulawayo. Whereas Markall had some reservations about admitting the white students to Chishawasha, Schmitt was "opposed because the seminary was not ready [for integration]. It would cause problems for the staff and students."[46]

The letter from the Seminary Group written at the end of February and received by the bishops in mid March[47] alleged that the students had been complaining to the seminary authorities for years, yet "nobody hears us." They complained that the books in the library were at least 25 years old, all written by Jesuits, and contained no modern philosophy. The timetable was too rigid, not allowing enough time for study, and they were "merely studying for examinations." As they wanted more time "to read widely," accordingly, they proposed a new timetable. The students also wanted more vacation time and to be allowed to spend vacations away from the seminary. With the money they would save from not being at the seminary during vacations, they requested that it be used to provide morning and afternoon tea. The Seminary Group also asked that ordinations be moved from December to August–September due to the rains limiting access to the event, and that their relatives be allowed to visit, as they "are becoming secular priests and not an order or the like."[48]

In addition to criticizing every aspect of life at the seminary, Turner also accused the Jesuits of being "too paternal" and looking "down on the African clergy and students as second-rate." Consequently, Turner believed, there was an anti-Jesuit feeling among the Africans of Southern Rhodesia.

Despite the tensions that the four white students' presence caused, Christopher Gardiner believed that the Jesuits wanted the experiment to work:

> [On Sundays] Breakfast was prepared around five o'clock in the morning, and those of us who served the mass at Chishawasha [mission] didn't eat until after ten o'clock. [One Sunday in 1966] there were weevils in the porridge [which] had a hard crust on top. I complained to the refectorian, who said he couldn't do anything about it and to complain to Fr. Moloney. I was in my second year, so I picked up porridge and went to show it to Diamond. The other students were afraid of what was going to happen. There was a staff meeting in the rector's office, and I put it on Diamond's desk and said, "Would you eat this?!" Moloney grabbed me, and yelled, "Down to my office!" He read me the riot act. He told me I was "taking advantage of [my] white skin." He told me to tell everyone to be in the refectory in a half an hour. We went back in a half an hour, and at Moloney's order there were eggs and bacon, toast and tea. Diamond then called a meeting and said there would be changes: better food and afternoon tea. And there were. Things radically changed.[49]

This is confirmed by the minutes of the numerous seminary consultors' meetings dealing with the issue of how to keep Christopher Gardiner at Chishawasha.[50]

The Jesuits frequently complained of the poor educational abilities of the African seminarians.[51] Yet by the 1960s, they were becoming aware of the problem of the poor quality of the men that were teaching at the seminary.[52] Diamond did not take the criticisms of either the Seminary Group or Anthony Turner seriously. He thought Turner's memorandum was "really only a heavy joke," and he characterized the anonymous letter as "not typical. … [However] it is a typical example of a certain type of African opportunism and meanness."[53]

Because Turner apparently sent a revised copy of his memorandum to Francis Markall after he left the seminary on 12 April 1965, on 5 May the board of bishops met and decided to ask Propaganda Fide to approve an external investigation of the seminary by "someone experienced in Seminary administration in countries similar to Rhodesia in background," and commissioned Markall as chairman to draft and send the letter of request to Rome.[54]

The bishops' action sparked an immediate and furious response from Diamond and the Jesuit superior of the Salisbury Mission, Edward Ennis. In a flurry of correspondence between Diamond, Markall, and Jesuit superiors in London and Rome, Ennis pressed hard to prevent Markall from sending the letter to Propaganda Fide, and by June had succeeded in making the bishops back down. Ennis and Diamond argued that in 1958 Chishawasha came under Propaganda Fide's control when it became a regional seminary, which entrusted its administration to the Jesuits. Prior to the Rhodesian bishops' decision of 5 May 1965, there had been no criticism of the Jesuits' administration by either the bishops or Propaganda Fide. Thus, calling for an external investigation of the seminary without having previously notified either Diamond or Ennis was not only a gross discourtesy, but an unwarranted drastic measure that would signal a vote of no confidence by the bishops in the seminary administration, the rector in particular; would undermine the authority of the seminary administration and compromise discipline among the students; and would signal to the seminarians that such behavior could achieve results and reward malcontents for inappropriate behavior. This latter reason was particularly unpalatable to the Jesuits given their view that the failed effort at integration had caused such difficulties through no fault of their own, but because the four whites from Pretoria were not the right students with whom to try such an experiment.[55] Evidently, Diamond kept all information of the conflict between the bishops and himself and Ennis not only from the students, but from the seminary staff as well.[56]

Although Diamond had not taken the seminarians' letters seriously, and had intended to let matters at the seminary cool off by themselves, the events of May 1965 were not lost on him. On 22 June, he held a seminary staff meeting and asked his fellow Jesuits to "consider whether any modifications of existing rules and arrangements are desirable."[57]

Resulting from this failed integration experiment, Christopher Gardiner and the African seminarians were allowed to go home for the vacation between the second and third terms, the daily order was changed to include more time for study and less time at manual labor, ordinations were held in August, and washing machines were installed.[58]

The 1967 Crisis

The year 1967 brought another crisis to the seminary.[59] According to Diamond, discipline declined throughout the year, including "representations ... for increased study time and abolition of manual works, culminating in an ultimatum delivered by the beadle, Constantine [Mashonganyika]."[60] Although Diamond noted that study time had been almost doubled to four hours per day since 1965, he decided to close the seminary on 10 October 1967, and send the students home "for further reflection." On 1 November, when all the seminarians except Mashonganyika were allowed to return, they were required to sign an "understanding to abide by seminary rules, manual work, etc."[61]

Given that, unlike the 1965 integration episode, the seminary closed in 1967, there is relatively little documentation of the incident. On 12 October, Diamond sent a letter to the bishops and to Edward Ennis explaining his rationale for closing the seminary: the white students in 1965 "had succeeded in conveying to our seminarians the impression that they were receiving treatment inferior to that of seminarians elsewhere just because they were Africans." Mashonganyika had been away from the seminary on pastoral probation in 1966, and upon returning brought demands for more study time and morning tea, and an end to manual works, culminating in the petition signed by 15 seminarians. According to Diamond, subsequent investigation revealed that Mashonganyika coerced younger seminarians to sign the petition, and the decision to close the seminary was an effort to prevent irreparable damage to the vocations of the younger seminarians as well as to "facilitate getting rid of the unhealthy elements who were at the root of the troubles."[62] Mashonganyika, however, claimed that he was merely bringing the concerns of the majority to the seminary administration in his capacity as prefect, and that "there wasn't any defiance of authority." The petition came from the "majority of students," and there were four or five who "didn't want anything to do with it," of whom three were asked to remain behind to answer staff questions, alleging coercion.[63]

As in 1965, the bishops apparently wanted "to call in an external commission to make a visitation of [the] seminary,"[64] and Diamond responded with the same argument against an external investigation. Unlike 1965, however, there is only one letter from Diamond extant, which appears to be the only evidence of Jesuit resistance to episcopal interference in the seminary administration. There was also no process of self-reflection on the part of the seminary staff or any effort to consider student demands.

There was, however, a confidential two-page summary of comments on seminary training by five recently ordained African priests, which indicated a perception of a condescending, paternalistic attitude on the part of the Jesuits; a narrow focus on scholastic philosophy and "no knowledge of African life" on the part of the staff; and an overemphasis on the seminary constitution and custom book, "too much manual work," and priests having to observe the same rules as seminarians ("[the Jesuits] did not regard you as a priest.") The young priests concluded that

> there was no contact, let alone dialogue, between staff and students. It was a master-servant attitude. ... The trouble in October was not a matter which came suddenly, nor was it instigated by one seminarian, it could and should have come 3 years earlier. It was brewing all the time. Fr. Diamond tried to improve things but was too hesitant and did not have the cooperation of the other staff members.[65]

During the 1960s, although the seminary staffing crisis became more acute, Diamond and his confreres at the seminary flatly refused a suggestion that the Carmelites and Bethlehem missionaries be invited to assist in staffing the seminary.[66] In 1970, Edward Ennis advised the bishops that staffing at the seminary was "minimal" and that the majority of the staff was "of an advanced age." He believed it "a matter of great urgency" that an African priest be appointed to the staff, and that "thought should be given to preparing selected seminarians for future teaching in the Seminary."[67] Although the bishops "agreed" with Ennis's points and sent two African priests for higher studies,[68] they made no effort to appoint an African priest or a priest of a different religious order to the seminary staff until 1975.

The 1974 Strike

By 1974, African seminarians were no longer willing to endure feeling like they were "being trained to be second class priests."[69] Private studies for O- and A-levels were rampant, and lectures "challenged [the seminarians] to want to be liberated not just politically but intellectually, socially, and spiritually. ... We wanted to have the totality of liberation."[70]

The 1974 strike began Saturday, 28 September, when seminary rector John Berrell dismissed Deacon Ernest Mukuwapasi for extended improper conduct.[71] The following day, the theologians met on the football pitch to determine a course of action, and drafted a letter to Berrell in support of Mukuwapasi signed by six recent ordinands.[72] The students were "very disturbed" by the manner in which Berrell tried to remove Mukuwapasi "secretly."[73] They feared that "what has happened to Ernest may be going to happen to many more and, therefore we feel in conscience that things be put right for the good of the Church of God," and asked to meet with the rector following night prayers.[74] The two sides met after afternoon tea, and Berrell refused to discuss the reasons for Mukuwapasi's dismissal. The priests informed their fellow students that "the meeting had been a complete failure"[75]: "One can say that it was here on Sunday evening that the students decided to speak a language that was going to make Fr. Rector see that he was badly understanding the students and that he was underestimating their deep feelings. This language, sorry to say, took the form of a protest."[76]

On Monday, 30 September, the strike began in earnest with the boycotting of classes until Ernest Mukuwapasi returned to the seminary. All but four of the students, including two priests, withdrew to the football pitch, except for meals and spiritual duties.[77] During meals the strikers maintained "a rigid silence." Berrell notified the bishops' secretary general who in turn notified Archbishop Markall. The rector and seminary consultors decided that they could not meet the students' demands.[78] The following day, the priest-organizers tried and failed to meet with Patrick McNamara, the Jesuit superior, and with Archbishop Markall and Bishop Patrick Chakaipa.

Tensions escalated on Wednesday, 2 October. At mass that morning, one of the non-striking priests was the principle celebrant. All the strikers "declined to make the sign of the cross at the beginning of Mass, declined to answer the responses (except those to the Reader) and when [the celebrant] and a deacon were distributing Communion only 12 or 15 came to receive the Sacrament."[79] At meals, those students who were working in the kitchen "were outrageously rude to the Sisters in the kitchen."[80] Berrell and some of the consultors met with the student-priests (strikers and non-strikers) in an effort "to save the seminary from moral and physical ruin and destruction ... if a way could be found." The priests claimed that Mukuwapasi's dismissal was the only issue when Berrell asked if there were "deeper issues," and they asked for "a Kissenger [to] be brought in as a facilitator to take the heat out of the situation: His Grace [Markall] or Bishop Chakaipa was suggested."[81] Neither were available to mediate. Later that night, anonymous threatening letters were placed under the doors of several staff members. On Thursday, 3 October, efforts to secure a mediator failed again, and the incidents of "rude" and "insulting" behavior on the part of the strikers toward the non-strikers and staff increased.[82]

On Friday, 4 October, the students' efforts to contact Bishop Chakaipa failed again. The bishops' secretary general, Fr. Kevin Kinnane, informed the other bishops of the strike, and efforts at negotiation between the seminary staff and the strike leaders also failed. In the afternoon, a reporter from the *Rhodesia Herald* came out to the seminary, and Markall finally arrived to meet with Berrell and the seminary consultors. Markall told the staff that the seminary would have to be closed, and left the details to Berrell.[83]

On the morning of Saturday, 5 October, Berrell gave Fr. Ignatius Mhonda, one of the strike leaders, a letter announcing the closure of the seminary. Mhonda read the letter to his fellow strikers, and they all withdrew to the football pitch. Mhonda and two other priests returned from the football pitch with the notice of closure saying the Rector's signature was not sufficient. They needed a document from Fr. Kinnane to prove that the Bishops really did endorse the closure of the seminary. ... Fr. Kinnane kindly consented to come at once and brought the necessary documents from the Archbishop and the Secretariat, going with these to the football pitch and eventually convincing the strikers that they must pack and go.[84]

The strikers asked if they could stay until the morning of Monday, 7 October, as transportation to their home dioceses would be easier than on Saturday or Sunday. Berrell agreed on the condition that the strikers behave themselves.[85] According to Berrell, "silence and surliness and worse rudeness to the Staff continued. ... Some spent Saturday night annoying and attempting to terrorise members of Staff on the internal telephone system, which had to be disconnected. The same rudeness and surliness continued through Sunday."[86]

On the morning of Monday, 7 October, the seminarians attended mass at 5:30, ate breakfast at 6:00, and then loaded the bus that would take them to Salisbury. "The Seminarians then ascended the terrace steps, formed a group and sang "Ishe komborera Afrika" (God Bless Africa)[87] and a folk hymn about going home after all these wasted years, whilst the Rector and Staff members stood by. The whole group of Seminarians were then solemnly blessed by Fr. Mhonda, entered the bus in silence and departed."[88]

Following the 1974 strike, against Jesuit objections, the bishops appointed an external commission to investigate the causes of the strike and to make recommendations for the long-term restructuring of the seminary. The commission concluded that the situation in the seminary had been tense for some time and Ernest Mukuwapasi's dismissal was the spark that set it off. It recommended that the seminarians not be punished collectively, rather that each bishop deal with each seminarian individually, and that the seminary be reopened for the first term of February 1975 with Berrell as rector through the end of the year and an African priest as vice rector with right of succession in 1976.[89] Thus, after 40 years the seminary's administration passed from the Jesuits to African priests. Approximately 40 of the 107 seminarians returned in 1975. Several of those who did not return joined guerrillas fighting against the Smith regime.[90]

The atmosphere at the seminary under Fr. Tobias Chiginya improved significantly. Chiginya was "quite adept and defused many of the students' concerns," including granting them an elected student representative council.[91] He removed many of the petty rules that had been in force under the Jesuits and "treated us as adults," which was a great "relief" to the students: "It was what we were waiting for all along," reflected Fr. Walter Nyatsanza.

There were, however, tensions between Shona and Ndebele students that generally followed the divisions between the nationalist parties, the Zimbabwe African National Union (ZANU) and the Zimbabwe African Peoples Union

(ZAPU). "Hell broke loose" shortly before the 1979 elections when ZAPU supporters tore down a ZANU poster.[92] Francis Mugadzi, Chiginya's successor as rector, "had very little choice" but to close the seminary, as there was "almost war between the students."[93] The seminary did not reopen until after independence in April 1980.

Conclusion

In a commentary assessing the causes of the 1974 strike, Jesuit W. F. Rea opined that many Africans became Catholics and entered the seminary for "unworthy motives, and mixed ones," alleging that they did so for the only higher educational opportunities available to them at the time. "But when they see their contemporaries in secondary schools and the Universities making more progress than they," he continued, "they cannot face up to the fact that this is due to their own lack of capacity and blame everyone and everything except themselves." He similarly alleged that Africans chose to become priests for the social status that the advanced education that seminary training would bring them, and ultimately absolved the seminary administration of any responsibility for the strike, which, in his view, was the product of African frustration at the lack of status recognition combined with the political situation and bad treatment of the seminary by the bishops.[94]

It seems, however, that Rea himself was determined to place blame for the strike everywhere except with his brother Jesuits. The seminary staff repeatedly refused to change in the face of rising student expectations and demands: they did not heed T. E. Corrigan's admonitions between 1961 and 1963; John Diamond thought the seminarians' complaints to the bishops in 1965 were a joke; nor did the staff take any action on the comments of the young African priests in 1967. While the escalating political tensions in colonial Zimbabwe certainly contributed to the seminarians' increasing consciousness of themselves as African Christians, the primary cause of the students' activism in the 1960s and 1970s was the Jesuits' failure to break with the dominant white Rhodesian culture and its paternalistic mindset. The Jesuits' failure at the seminary is indicative of their larger failure to inculturate the Catholic Church at their missions in colonial Zimbabwe. As such, African seminarians' expressions of nationalism were part of a broader struggle to decolonize the Catholic Church.

Notes

1. Jesuit Archives of Zimbabwe (JAZ hereafter), Box 117/3, Report of Kevin Kinnane, OFM, the Secretary General of the Rhodesian Catholic Bishops' Conference (RCBC hereafter), 5 October 1974.
2. David Beach, *The Shona and their Neighbours* (Oxford: Blackwell, 1994); S. I. G.

Mudenge, *A Political History of Munhumutapa, c.1400–1902* (Harare: Zimbabwe Publishing, 1988); Norman Etherington, *The Great Treks: The Transformation of Southern Africa, 1815–1854* (New York: Pearson, 2001).

3. Charles van Onselen, *Chibaro: African Mine Labour in Southern Rhodesia, 1900–1933* (London: Pluto, 1976); Robin Palmer, *Aspects of Rhodesian Land Policy, 1890–1936* (Salisbury: Central African Historical Association, 1968); David Johnson, "Settler Farmers and Coerced African Labour in Southern Rhodesia, 1936–1946," *Journal of African History* Vol. 33, No. 1 (1992): 111–128.

4. C. J. M. Zvobgo, *A History of Christian Missions in Zimbabwe, 1890–1939* (Gweru: Mambo, 1996).

5. A. J. Dachs and W. F. Rea, *The Catholic Church and Zimbabwe* (Gwelo: Mambo Press, 1979) 136, 138.

6. JAZ, Box 108, Seminary *Historia Domus,* 3 February 1940; 1 February 1944.

7. Interview with Patrick Moloney, S. J., Prestage House Jesuit Community, Harare, 29 May 2000. See also Seminary *Historia Domus,* 30 July 1945.

8. JAZ, Box 108, Seminary *Historia Domus,* 26 October 1947; 22 and 28 December 1948.

9. JAZ, Box 108, Seminary *Historia Domus,* 16 February 1955.

10. Ibid., 24 April 1955.

11. Ibid., 21 May 1956; 8 September 1956.

12. Interview with Francis McKeown, S.J., Canisius House, Harare, 15 May 2000; JAZ, Box 117/8, Constantine Mashonganyika, "The Seminary at Chishawasha," 21.

13. Archives of the Archdiocese of Harare (AAH hereafter), Box 528/E, Sacred Congregation for Propagating the Faith Decree, 25 March 1958.

14. AAH, Box 528/E, "Visitation of Seminaries," 28 August 1959.

15. AAH, 528/F, Francis McKeown to Markall, 21 June 1960.

16. AAH, Box 528/D, Chichester to Hugh Boyle, 17 August 1955; JAZ, Box 116/5, W. F. Rea, "Extracts from the Historia Domus of the Seminary: Chishawasha, 1937–1975," 27–28.

17. AAH, Box 528/C, Governor of Southern Rhodesia to Chichester, 25 May 1950.

18. AAH, Box 528/D, Chichester to Hugh Boyle, 17 August 1955; AAH, Box 528/D, "Seminary Jottings, 1956."

19. AAH, Box 528/E, McKeown to Markall, 23 July 1958; Interview with Francis McKeown, S.J., Canisius House, Harare, 15 May 2000.

20. JAZ, Box 116/5, "Seminary Jottings, 1962"; "Seminary Jottings, 1963"; Box 108, Seminary *Historia Domus,* January 1963.

21. JAZ, Box 116/5, "Seminary Jottings, 1962"; "Seminary Jottings, 1963"; Box 108, Seminary *Historia Domus,* January 1963.

22. Conversation with Rev. Albert Plangger, S.M.B., Mambo House, Harare, 16 May 2000.

23. Dachs and Rea (1979), 148.

24. Ibid., 181–182.

25. See Terence Ranger, *Peasant Consciousness and Guerilla War in Zimbabwe: A Comparative Study* (Berkeley: University of California Press, 1985).

26. JAZ, Box 109, Seminary House Consultations Minutes, 18 August 1958; AAH, Box 528, File E (1958–1959), Markall to McKeown, 18 January 1958.

27. AAH, Box 528, File E (1958–1959), Markall to McKeown, 18 January 1958.

28. JAZ, Box 109, Chishawasha Seminary House Consultors' Minutes Book, 6 March 1961, 2 September 1963.
29. AAH, Box 528, File G (1962–1966), McKeown to Markall, 6 December 1961. See also JAZ, Box 116/3, "Seminary Custom Book, January 1963, nn. 74–79.
30. JAZ, Box 109, Chishawasha Seminary House Consultors' Minutes Book, 6 November 1961.
31. JAZ, Box 108, Memoriale Visitationis, T.E. Corrigan, 27 March 1961.
32. Ibid., 19 September 1962.
33. Ibid., 23 September 1963.
34. Interview with Patrick Moloney, S.J., 29 May 2000.
35. Interview with Rev. Walter Nyatzanza, Africa Synod House, Harare, 15 May 2000.
36. AAH, Box 528, File G (1962–1966), McKeown to Markall, 31 August 1964; Markall to McKeown, 5 September 1964. Interview with Francis McKeown, S.J., Canisius House Jesuit Community, 15 May 2000; Interview with Patrick Moloney, S.J., Prestage House Jesuit Community, 29 May 2000.
37. JAZ, Box 108, Seminary *Historia Domus,* 9 February 1965.
38. Ibid.
39. Ibid, 19 February 1965.
40. JAZ, Box 117/1, Seminary Group to His Lordship, February 1965. See also JAZ, Box 108, Seminary *Historia Domus,* February 1965.
41. JAZ, Box 117/1, Anthony Turner, Memorandum to Reverend Father Rector, 11 March 1965.
42. Interview with Rev. Christopher B. Gardiner, St. Elizabeth Ann Seton Church, Bark River, Michigan, 8 July 2000.
43. See JAZ, Box 117/1 passim.
44. Interview with Rev. Christopher B. Gardiner, St. Elizabeth Ann Seton Church, Bark River, Michigan, 8 July 2000.
45. Ibid.
46. Ibid.
47. JAZ, Box 117/1, Diamond to Edward Ennis, SJ, 29 March 1965.
48. JAZ, Box 117/1, Seminary Group to His Lordship [Francis Markall], February 1965.
49. Interview with Rev. Christopher B. Gardiner, St. Elizabeth Ann Seton Church, Bark River, Michigan, 8 July 2000.
50. JAZ, Box 109, Seminary Consultors' Minutes, 1965–1966; See also, Box 116/7, Diamond to Bishop Adolph Schmitt, 29 October 1965.
51. See JAZ, Box 109, Seminary Consultors' Minutes.
52. JAZ, Box 116/5, McKeown to Fr. Provincial, 16 March, 1960; Francis McKeown, "Some Reflections on matters missionary after a visit to East Africa and the Congo," June 1960; Box 116/7, Diamond to Ennis, 19 April 1966.
53. JAZ, Box 117/1, Diamond to Ennis, 29 March 1965.
54. AAH, Box 528, File G (1962–1966), Markall to Cardinal Sigismondi, Prefect of the Sacred Congregation for Propagating the Faith, n.d., but after 5 May 1965.
55. See JAZ, Box 117/1, Passim. AAH, Box 528, File G (1962–1966), passim.
56. JAZ, Box 117/1, Meeting with Seminary Staff, 22 June 1965; Interview with Rev. Christopher B. Gardiner, St. Elizabeth Ann Seton Church, Bark River, Michigan, 8 July 2000.

57. JAZ, Box 117/1, Minutes of Meeting with Seminary Staff, 22 June 1965.
58. JAZ, Box 108, Seminary *Historia Domus,* 12 April 1965; 24 May 1965; 8, 15, 29 August 1965; 3 September 1965.
59. Christopher Gardiner left Chishawasha to return to St. John Vianney Seminary in Pretoria in 1966 and was ordained for the Diocese of Bulawayo in July 1968. JAZ, Box 108, Seminary *Historia Domus,* 8 December 1966; 13–14 July 1968.
60. Ibid, October, 1967; 1967 "Relatio Annuale to Sacra Congregatio de Propaganda Fide," in JAZ, Box 116/5 "Extracts from the Historia Domus of the Seminary [at] Chishawasha, 1937–1975" [Typescript], 17.
61. JAZ, Box 108, Seminary *Historia Domus,* 10 October and 1 November 1967.
62. JAZ, Box 116/7, Diamond to Father Superior, 12 October 1967; interview with Archbishop Pius Ncube, Archbishop's office, Bulawayo, 10 May 2000; interview with Rev. Constantine Mashonganyika, IMBISA Centre, Harare, 17 May 2000.
63. JAZ, Box 116/7, Diamond to Father Superior, 12 October 1967. Interview with Archbishop Pius Ncube, Archbishop's office, Bulawayo, 10 May 2000. Interview with Rev. Constantine Mashonganyika, IMBISA Centre, Harare, 17 May 2000.
64. JAZ, Box 116/7, Diamond to the Bishops of Rhodesia, 13 December 1967.
65. JAZ, Box 116/7, "Comments on their Seminary Training by 5 African Priests (Frs. Mugadzi, Nhariwa, Chiginya, Marimazhira, Urayai)."
66. JAZ, Box 116/7, Diamond to Ennis, 19 April 1966.
67. JAZ, Box 117/2, Rhodesian Catholic Bishops Conference Minutes, 22 October 1970.
68. Ibid.; Dachs and Rea, *The Catholic Church and Zimbabwe, 1879-1979,* 223.
69. Interview with Rev. Walter Nyatsanza, Africa Synod House, Harare, 15 May 2000.
70. Ibid.
71. JAZ, Box 117/3, John Berrell, S.J., "Rector's Report: The Seminary Strike 30 September to 7 October 1974," 3–4 (Rector's Report hereafter); JAZ, Box 117/4, Rhodesia Catholic Bishops' Conference, "Report of [the] Seminary Commission," 22 December 1974, 2 (Commission Report hereafter). The report does not specify what Mukuwapasi did to anger Berrell, and informants who were present as seminarians did not recall Mukuwapasi's actions either.
72. Commission Report, 2–3.
73. Berrell "[offered] the deacon the opportunity of departing without embarrassment," offering to have him driven from the seminary while the other students were in classes. Rector's Report, 4.
74. Commission Report, 2.
75. Ibid.
76. Rev. Ignatius Mhonda, "A Report to the Bishops concerning the October Events at the Regional Major Seminary of Ss. John Fisher and Thomas More," 25 November 1974, cited in Commission Report, 2.
77. Rector's Report, 6; Commission Report, 4.
78. Rector's Report, 6; Commission Report, 4.
79. Rector's Report, 7.
80. Ibid.
81. Ibid., 7–8.
82. Ibid., 8; Commission Report, 5.
83. Rector's Report, 8–9; Commission Report, 5–6.

84. Rector's Report, 9; see also Commission Report, 6–7.

85. Rector's Report, 10; Commission Report, 7.

86. Rector's Report, 10.

87. Written by Xhosa-speaking South African Enoch Sontonga in 1912. This hymn was associated with the Black South African struggle for equality before and during the Apartheid era, and was adopted as South Africa's national anthem in 1994.

88. Ibid., 10.

89. Commission Report, 10, 17.

90. AAH, Index, "Box 528/O: left after strike, 4 for guerrilla training, 22/10/74 ... Death of Jonathan Dzumbunu and Kenneth Mzilikazi (crossfire?)." Although this file was listed in the AAH Index, access was denied. Interview with Rev. Walter Nyatsanza, 15 May 2000.

91. Interview with Rev. Walter Nyatsanza, African Synod House, Harare, 18 May 2000. This had been one of their demands dating to 1970 when Berrell was first appointed rector.

92. Ibid.

93. Ibid.

94. JAZ, Box 116/5, "Extracts from the Historia Domus of the Seminary [at] Chishawasha, 1937–1975," 26.

Chapter 7

1968 and Apartheid

Race and Politics in South Africa

Chris Saunders

In the now quite extensive literature on 1968 there is all too little discussion of South Africa. Mark Kurlansky, for example, in his well-known book *1968: The Year that Rocked the World,* only mentions the country twice, in passing. While both events he mentions were related to the racial politics of the country, this chapter will argue that he misses the greater significance of 1968 for South Africa.

Kurlansky first records that 1968 was the year in which the surgeon Christiaan Barnard performed the world's first successful heart transplant operation in Cape Town. Barnard had in fact carried out the first such operation at Groote Schuur, Cape Town's leading hospital, on 3 December 1967, but the patient had died 18 days later. That first operation, and the more successful one Barnard carried out on 2 January 1968—this time the patient survived for 19 months—certainly brought South Africa more international media attention than any other single event in 1968. When the operation was performed in January 1968, much was made in both the local and the international media of the fact that Barnard had saved the life of a white man by implanting in him the heart of a black man, for this seemed to show up the absurdity of the country's racial politics, which were dominated by the apartheid idea that races should be kept separate. The apartheid regulations that required Groote Schuur to be racially segregated meant that there were separate wards for white and black patients, but white doctors treated black patients and black nurses attended white patients.[1]

Barnard himself was a critic of apartheid, though he never came out strongly against the system. The second South African–related story that Kurlansky mentions is that the president of the International Olympic Committee spent much of 1968 lobbying to ensure that a South African team could participate in the Olympic Games held that year in Mexico, despite the South African government's insistence that the country's sport be racially segregated.[2] While the president's lobbying was successful and South Africa did not participate in those Olympic Games, the country was then barred from all subsequent games because of the application of apartheid to sport, and the bar was only lifted after the end of apartheid in 1994.

The heart transplant operation and the issue of taking part in the Olympic Games both therefore relate in different ways to the dominant fact of South African life at the time: the obsession with race by the state. They are not, however, the most significant events affecting the country in 1968. More significant in the long run was the resistance that was emerging to the race-based policies of the state, and this chapter focuses on three aspects of that resistance, all of which had transnational dimensions. First, 1968 saw the beginning of a new phase in resistance to apartheid in South Africa, with the birth of the Black Consciousness Movement (BCM). Much influenced by the Black Power movement in the United States, the BCM was to become the dominant resistance movement of the 1970s, one that would pose a serious challenge to the apartheid regime. There was, secondly, a new wave of protest on South Africa's university campuses in 1968, the key event being the sit-in at the University of Cape Town's administration building in protest over the university's failure to confirm the appointment of a black African lecturer. Thirdly, in 1968 the South African government vetoed the selection of a former South African to the cricket team to tour South Africa from England, on the grounds of his race, a veto which, as we shall see, had important consequences in terms of sporting sanctions against the country. Race, and more particularly South Africa's apartheid policy, the most extensive system of racial segregation ever devised anywhere,[3] clearly lay at the center of the significance of 1968 in the southern part of the African continent, and this chapter places the three key events of 1968 in context to show how they relate to apartheid and resistance to it.

South Africa had of course become notorious for the policy of apartheid long before 1968. That policy took many different forms, from the creation of so-called Bantu Homelands, black African areas that were in 1968 in the process of being led toward nominal independence,[4] to the petty restrictions on interracial contact. Resistance to apartheid had largely gone underground after the banning of the African National Congress (ANC) and Pan-Africanist Congress (PAC) in 1960. From its base in exile in Zambia the ANC, working together with the Zimbabwe African People's Union, launched its largest-ever attempt to send guerrilla fighters back into South Africa in 1968. The new president of the ANC, Oliver Tambo, watched as men of the organization's armed wing, Umkhonto we Sizwe (MK), crossed the Zambezi River from Zambia into what was then Rhodesia. But what became known as the Wankie campaign, from the area in Rhodesia that the guerrillas entered, soon failed, for the guerrillas were either killed by the Rhodesian and South African security forces sent against them or were forced to flee into neighboring Botswana. The ANC retained its commitment to the armed struggle after this failure, but from the 1970s was only to send a few individuals at a time back into the country covertly, and the focus was then on attacks on government targets in the urban areas. In the long run it was mass internal resistance, rather than the armed struggle, that would bring apartheid down. Of greater long-term significance than the failed attempt at a guerrilla incursion, then, was the birth of a new internal resistance organization in 1968 inside the country.

The Black Consciousness Movement

As 1968 began, there was little overt resistance to apartheid in South Africa. After going underground, the ANC and the PAC had relatively soon been crushed by the state: by the end of 1963 most PAC activity in the country had been suppressed and in 1964 the main ANC leaders, including Nelson Mandela, the commander-in-chief of MK, which had been engaged in sabotage and planning a campaign of guerrilla war, had been sentenced to life imprisonment. Mandela and his colleagues then languished in prison and in the late 1960s were virtually forgotten figures; it would be over a decade after 1968 before the attention of the world began to be focused on their fate, when a campaign for their release began to gather momentum and was to become known around the world under the slogan "Free Mandela." In 1968 not only were the leading figures in the struggle largely forgotten, but also the apartheid regime seemed all-powerful, and it was willing to use any means, including torture and even the killing of opponents, to suppress any attempt at resistance.[5] That year saw it pass new apartheid legislation through Parliament—the Prohibition of Political Interference Act—to ban multiracial political activity. The first non-racial political organization, the Communist Party of South Africa, had been banned in 1950, at the time of McCarthyism in the United States, and in 1968 there were two political parties that had both white and black members: the small but influential multiracial Liberal Party, which had been formed by a group of whites in 1953 and remained under white leadership but had more black than white members, and the Progressive Party, which had been launched in 1959 by members of the opposition United Party in Parliament fed up by their party's failure to oppose apartheid legislation. In 1968 the Progressive Party had only one member of Parliament, the redoubtable Helen Suzman, who missed no opportunity to speak out against apartheid legislation in the all-white House of Assembly and argue for the introduction of a constitutional democracy. In the face of the new legislation, the Liberal Party, which had put up candidates for elections to Parliament, none of whom had ever been returned, decided to disband.[6] The Progressive Party chose to become a whites-only party in order to continue to exist, meaning that it abandoned such black members as it had, and it would be two decades before the party was once again able to accept black members and again become a non-racial organization. Suzman was able to continue in Parliament until 1989, and from 1974 was joined there by other Progressives, who kept the idea of a non-racial democracy alive, but the party's decision in 1968 to abide by apartheid legislation would forever damn it in the eyes of those who did not believe in any compromise with so evil a system.

Despite the overwhelming strength of the apartheid state in 1968, new re-sistance now came from an unexpected quarter. By 1968 a new generation of black students was emerging at the segregated, apartheid-created universities and the "non-white" section of the Medical School at the University of Natal. Some of these students had read Frantz Fanon and Malcolm X, and knew that the Civil Rights Movement headed by Martin Luther King Jr. in the United States had been followed by the more militant Black Power movement. In July 1968, at the annual conference of the non-racial, but white-dominated, decades-old National Union of Students (NUSAS), to which between 20,000 and 30,000 students were affiliated at the English-speaking, predominantly white universi-ties, the charismatic young Steve Biko and other black students discussed among themselves what they regarded as their second-class status as blacks in NUSAS. After attending another multiracial conference the following month they re-solved to break away from NUSAS and form an all-black student organization. In December 1968, at a meeting at Marianhill, near Durban, they founded the South African Students' Organisation (SASO), which was open only to blacks, whom they defined as all who were oppressed by apartheid, whether black Af-rican or of mixed descent. According to a BCM publication, the *Black Review,* "It was felt that a time had come when blacks had to formulate their own think-ing, unpolluted by ideas emanating from a group with lots at stake in the status quo."[7] Biko believed that most black South Africans had come to accept the idea that they were inferior, and that what was required was psychological liberation: for a people to be free, he said, they had to realize that they had as much right as anyone else to be equal citizens in the land of their birth. This challenge to the mental self-enslavement of blacks by Biko and SASO was a decisive turning point in the long history of resistance politics in South Africa. SASO spawned many other BCM organizations in the early 1970s—organizations that would be banned after the extensive Soweto Uprising of 1976, which the state was to blame on Black Consciousness.[8] After the Soweto Uprising the apartheid state was on the defensive, and many scholars have seen that uprising as beginning the process leading to the final collapse of apartheid in the 1990s.

Student Protest at the University of Cape Town

Of all the events that took place in 1968 in South Africa, the founding of BCM was to have the greatest significance in the long run, but the event in student politics in South Africa that year that received the greatest attention in the media occurred on the almost entirely white campus of the University of Cape Town (UCT). UCT was the leading English-medium university in the country, with many ties to Britain, and its liberal ethos was strongly opposed to the ruling Afrikaner National Party, headed by John Vorster, the dour politician who had succeeded the assassinated H. F. Verwoerd as prime minister of South Africa in

1966. Many students and staff on the UCT campus shared the anti-apartheid views that Helen Suzman of the Progressive Party voiced in Parliament. Though there was no television in South Africa, and strict censorship was meant to prevent the spread of any literature deemed "subversive,"[9] material relating, say, to the Civil Rights Movement in the United States circulated on the UCT campus, including recordings of Martin Luther King Jr.'s "I have a dream" speech. King's assassination in April 1968 sparked a wave of emotion among those who identified with him as the leading black figure of the time, the man more than any other who had been responsible for what seemed a successful challenge to racial segregation in the United States. A few months later came the news that Robert Kennedy had been assassinated. His visit to South Africa in 1966, arranged by NUSAS, had, the country's leading newspaper said at the time, "blown clean air into a dank and closed room." Kennedy had attracted enthusiastic crowds on his visit, and had delivered what many have considered his greatest speech ever in the Jameson Hall at UCT, as the keynote speaker on UCT's annual Day of Affirmation. Kennedy had drawn attention to similarities between the United States and South Africa and had emphasized how any individual could work to help bring about change for the better.[10] It was on that same campus in August 1968, in that very same venue, that students, who had read and heard on the radio of the student revolts that had taken place in Europe and the United States, and especially of the confrontations that had taken place on the streets of Paris in May and June, decided to stage their own protest.

At issue was the decision by the Council of UCT to withdraw an offer of a senior lectureship to Archie Mafeje, a black South African anthropologist who had studied and worked at UCT and had then gone on to Cambridge University in England. The government put pressure on the University Council not to make the appointment, not wanting blacks to teach at what were regarded as white universities. The vice chancellor and Council of UCT feared that if they did not withdraw the offer to Mafeje, the continued employment of one or two other blacks already on the staff of the university would be jeopardized.[11] On 16 August 1968 some 1000 mostly white students condemned the Council's decision at a mass meeting in the Jameson Hall, and then, wanting to do more than merely pass a resolution, 300 students marched down the hill from the upper campus to the university's administration building, entered the building, and refused to leave until the Council had reversed its decision. In the administrative building they set up a virtual "alternative university," at which left wing lecturers spoke on topical issues. Their actions outraged the government, on which the University was dependent for the bulk of its funding, and captured the attention of the local media and of student bodies around the world, many of whom sent messages of solidarity. Some of these messages explicitly linked what was happening in Cape Town to what had happened in Paris and elsewhere, and encouraged the UCT students to see their movement as part of a global challenge to authority, albeit it in a particular environment, where the challenge was to a very explicit and overt form of racial oppression. After 10 days of occupying the administration building, the students, faced with the increasing likelihood of police intervention, were persuaded to abandon their protest and leave the building. The University Council had not backed down and the government's racial policy had not been threatened, but the lives of many of those who took part in the protest were changed by the sit-in.[12] Its leading figure, Raphie Kaplinsky, was one of many who soon left the country, in the face of police harassment. The University's dean of arts resigned from UCT in protest at the Council's action and emigrated. When veterans of the event held a reunion in 2008, 40 years after the event, many of them pointed to the sit-in as shaping their later careers and political involvement. On the UCT campus the sit-in was long remembered as the most important student protest, and the memory of it inspired later generations of students to continue anti-apartheid activity, though there was never to be another sit-in. On the 40th anniversary in August 2008, the University finally made a formal apology for its treatment of Mafeje, and the main venue in the administration building, where the students had held their sit-in, was renamed the Mafeje room.[13]

The D'Oliveira Affair: Cricket, Race, and Apartheid

Later that same month in 1968 what became known as the "D'Oliveira affair" began. Basil D'Oliveira, or "Dolly," as his fans knew him, was a South African of mixed descent who had left the country because of apartheid and become an English citizen and had become one of that country's leading cricket players. In the conservative world of English cricket, the idea that teams should not tour South Africa because of apartheid had won little sympathy by 1968. But when the team was chosen to play in South Africa, D'Oliveira was initially not selected. Many assumed that the selectors had capitulated to the known wishes of the apartheid government, for in terms of South Africa's racial classification system D'Oliveira was "colored" and apartheid's severe segregation meant that he could not be treated in South Africa as an equal member of the English team. Whether or not the selectors had this in mind in their initial selection, when another player dropped out, D'Oliveira was then named as a member of the team to tour South Africa. When he heard this, Prime Minister Vorster announced that his government was "not prepared to receive a team thrust on us by people whose interests are not in the game but to gain political objectives which they do not even attempt to hide."[14] The tour was therefore cancelled. There was then a successful campaign in Britain to stop the South African team, the Springboks, from touring Britain in 1970. After one further Australian tour had taken place, South Africa did not play official test cricket again until the 1990s. It was then too late for D'Oliveira to play for his country in South Africa, for he had by then retired after a long and very successful cricketing career.[15]

In itself the ending of a cricket relationship was not of great significance, and rugby players from Britain were to continue to tour in South Africa for some years,[16] but white South Africans took their sport very seriously, and the ending of cricket tours was a major blow to their identification with the country from which many of them had come, the country's main trading partner, and regarded as one of the most friendly toward South Africa in an increasingly hostile world. The cancellation of the tour in 1968, along with the pressures that year and after against South Africa sending a team to the Olympic Games, was evidence that a major campaign was now underway to isolate South Africa. This campaign would take a long time to gather momentum and to include a ban on the supply of arms and eventually to include financial and other economic sanctions, but eventually, in the late 1980s the isolation of South Africa would contribute significantly to the ending of apartheid. Though South Africa did try to send a multiracial team to the Olympic Games in 1968, sport within South Africa remained highly segregated, and after those Games the Olympic movement decided not to allow any further South African participation while apartheid remained in place.

Conclusion

The events discussed in this chapter are only three among many that took place in South Africa in 1968, but they are emblematic. They show that for South Africa 1968 must be understood in a particular racialized context, even if that local context was inextricably linked to the wider world, whether through intellectual influences, international student contacts, or sporting tours. These three events were not directly related: the government's decision to bar D'Oliveira from playing in South Africa did not have anything to do with student protest; the white students who took part in the sit-in at UCT did not know that black students were about to form an organization that heralded the start of a major new phase in the opposition to apartheid; and for black students elsewhere what happened on the UCT campus was not particularly significant, for they saw white students as privileged and not part of the oppressed masses. But these events were all related in that they arose from the policy of apartheid, and they did not take place in isolation. When black students at the University of Fort Hare began their own sit-in later in the year, to protest the way their leaders had been victimized, police invaded the campus and broke up the protest, and in response white students at other campuses, including UCT, came out in support.[17]

These three events were further evidence of growing resistance to apartheid, and they heralded the build-up of new pressures, pressures that would in time begin to erode the fundamentals on which apartheid rested. At the time, it was difficult to see the significance of these events, though they showed that South Africa was not immune from global influences. It would be another two decades before the end of apartheid was clearly on the horizon, and that was only the case because of the build up of much more overt resistance within the country, increased pressure from abroad, and South African military adventures in neighboring states. These together would eventually destroy the capacity of the apartheid regime to continue its oppression. As the year 1968 came to an end, there was no likelihood that apartheid would end in the near future; it seemed impregnable to most observers. But those opposed to apartheid could hold out more hope for change than when the year began. It would take many years for the consequences of what happened in 1968 to manifest themselves fully. While those consequences could not be anticipated in that year, with hindsight we can see that 1968 was a significant year in the long history of apartheid and its final collapse.

Notes

1. Anne Digby and Howard Phillips, At *the Heart of Healing: Groote Schuur Hospital, 1938 to 2008* (Auckland Park: Jacana, 2008). It was only in April 1969 that a non-white person received a transplanted heart: Ibid., 72. A number of blacks, on being admitted to Groote Schuur, were reported to have said: "Don't give me to Chris [Barnard]!" Barnard retired in 1983, having performed hundreds of heart operations.

2. Mark Kurlansky, *1968: The Year that Rocked the World* (London: Vintage, 2005), 20–21, 328, 348–349. The world's attention was caught by the black power salute given by two African American athletes as the national anthem of the United States was played at the Mexico Olympic Games.

3. Cf. George Fredrickson, *Racism: A Short History* (Princeton, NJ: Princeton University Press, 2002).

4. In 1968 an election took place in the largest of these, the Transkei, a major step toward the "independence" that the South African state bestowed on that "Homeland" in October 1976. No other country was ever to recognize its independence.

5. On continued small-scale acts of resistance, see South African Democracy Education Trust, *The Road to Democracy in South Africa*, Vol. 1 (Cape Town: Zebra Press, 2004), chapter 15.

6. See esp. Randolph Vigne, *Liberals Against Apartheid* (London: Routledge, 1996).

7. *Black Review* (1972): 19, quoted SADET (2004), 684.

8. On the BCM, see especially South African Democracy Education Trust, *The Road to Democracy in South Africa*, Vol. 2 (Pretoria: UNISA Press, 2006), chapter 3; and G. Gerhart, *Black Power in South Africa* (Berkeley: University of California Press, 1978).

9. Christopher Merrett, *A Culture of Censorship* (Cape Town: David Philip, 1994); and Peter Mcdonald, *The Literature Police: Apartheid Censorship and its Cultural Consequences* (Cape Town: Oxford University Press, 2009).

10. See especially Larry Short, "Ripple of Hope in the Land of Apartheid: Robert F. Kennedy in South Africa, June 4th–9th, 1966," *Safundi* Vol. 3, No. 2 (2002); and Dominic Sandbrook, "Robert Kennedy in South Africa," unpublished M.Litt thesis, University of St. Andrews, 1998.

11. One of these was in the Department of African Languages, one in the English Department. The latter had an Afrikaans name, Van der Westhuizen, and the government had not realized, at the time that he was appointed, that he was not white.

12. See esp. Robert Erbmann, "Conservative Revolutionaries: Anti-Apartheid Activism at the University of Cape Town, 1963–1973," History Honours thesis, Oxford University, 2005.

13. The author of this chapter has met many of those involved in these events, and draws upon discussions with them.

14. For an excellent and concise overview, see Martin Williamson, "The D'Oliveira Affair: A Timeline of Events which led to the Cancellation of the 1968–69 England Tour of South Africa," 13 September 2008. http://www.cricinfo.com/magazine/content/story/356092.html.

15. On all this, see esp. C. Murray and C. Merrett, *Caught Behind: Race and Politics in Springbok Cricket* (Johannesburg: Wits University Press, 2004); and "Basil D'Oliveira" in L. Segal and P. Holden, *Great Lives: Pivotal Moments* (Auckland Park: Jacana, 2008). Some rebel tours did take place by cricketers from England. See also Ronald Hyam and Peter Henshaw, *The Lion and the Springbok: Britain and South Africa since the Boer War* (Cambridge: Cambridge University Press, 2003), chapter 13.

16. The Springboks beat the Lions three games to nil in South Africa in 1968.

17. SADET (2004), 682.

Chapter 8

Brother Wally and De Burnin' of Babylon

Walter Rodney's Impact on the Reawakening of Black Power, the Birth of Reggae, and Resistance to Global Imperialism

James Bradford

In October 1968, riots rocked Kingston, Jamaica. The riots were a reaction to the expulsion of black activist and scholar Dr. Walter Rodney from Jamaica by the Jamaican Labor Party. The following weeks massive riots wreaked havoc upon the economic infrastructure of the island. This chapter will explore how Walter Rodney's ideas on imperialism, Black Power, and the Jamaican political system had a profound impact on the politicization of reggae music, Rastafarian culture, and the role of reggae in Jamaican and global politics.

Inspired by the Black Power movement in the United States, Dr. Rodney sought to reawaken black consciousness and empowerment among the poor, black community. He used his academic background to explain the social and political situation of the Jamaican people. In doing so, he helped forge a new self-awareness that had a direct impact on the reshaping of cultural expressions and political representations. Dr. Rodney was a catalyst in the reemergence of the self-consciousness of the Jamaican people, which in turn, affected the change in musical expressions found in the evolution of Jamaican music from ska and rocksteady to reggae. Ultimately, the exploration of Walter Rodney's teachings and his impact on Jamaican culture demonstrates that the rise of reggae music and Rastafarian culture in Jamaica indicate a mass movement, of which reggae plays a key role in substantiating political and cultural self-understanding.

Dr. Rodney and the Riots

The long history of slavery and racial conflict in Jamaica had a profound influence in shaping the political and social foundations from which reggae would eventually emerge. Jamaica gained its independence from Britain in 1962, and prided itself on being one of the only peaceful independence movements. Out of its sovereignty emerged two different political entities: the People's National Party (PNP) and the Jamaica Labor Party (JLP). The JLP appeared the most competent and powerful of the two parties, and was put into power. Many in Jamaica expected radical social and political transformations since for the first time in its history, Jamaicans, and not the British, would make decisions. However, that change never came. Rex Nettleford argued, "Things certainly did not fall apart. In fact, a great many things, like the class structure underlined in color, continued to appear immutable … the political order merely moved from one phase to the next."[1] The JLP demonstrated the authoritarian character of its rule, censoring all oppositional material and violently oppressing the Rastafarian communities, all the while claiming to be the embodiment of peaceful multiracialism.

The JLP created a national motto that would symbolize the direction of the new independent nation: "Out of many, One people." "The motto," writes Nettleford, "targeted social cohesion, political unity, the bliss of multi-racialism, and peaceful, civilized socio-political interaction as goals of independence."[2] The new identity reflected the aims of the government and those in power; however, it contradicted the stark realities on the island. Michael Manley, PNP leader elected president in 1972, stated: "Either one belonged to the great majority who could not escape from the world of manual labor; or one belonged to the minority who enjoyed a privileged status."[3] Jamaica could not escape the intensifying pressure "to address the problems of its identity, or the corresponding emergence of a whole new generation of young radicals anxious to pry the society out of its ostrich-like refusal to face the reality of a black underclass dispossessed in a lop-sided polity structured and operated to enrich a traditional few and strengthen their leverage of power in national decision making."[4] The question of Jamaican identity would serve as the root of political and social grievances later in the decade. Walter Rodney would address this issue directly with his book *The Groundings with My Brothers* and help galvanize the masses into discovering and embracing a new, more realistic Jamaican identity rooted in its African heritage.

Prior to the Rodney Riots, there were a large group of Jamaicans who resisted British colonial culture and also a number of civil disturbances, which foreshadowed the radical change to come. The most obvious element of civil resistance to the British colonial rule and, later, the JLP government were the Rastafarians. The Rastafarian community originated in Jamaica in opposition to the slave trade that displaced millions of Africans. Rastas openly rejected the repressive culture of white supremacy and colonial society. In the 1930s, Rastafarians united under the leadership of Marcus Garvey, who believed that all black people should return to Africa. As Horace Campbell notes, "it is the identification with Africa which laid the foundations for the doctrine of Rastafarian ideology which combined the resistance against oppression with an underlying love for the freedom and emancipation of Africa and African peoples."[5] The Rastafarian community was in perpetual conflict with the authorities on the island and had little to no political representation. Eventually, every aspect of Rastafari culture, from symbols to style to speech, came to represent the support of African heritage and the resistance to cultural norms forced upon them by their colonial oppressors.[6] Both the British government and the JLP did everything in their power to keep the Rastafarian community a silent and powerless entity.

The Chinese riots of 1965, the general elections of 1967, and radical movements on the Univeristy of West Indies campus throughout the 1960s indicated that social unrest was growing in Jamaica prior to the Rodney Riots in 1968. To make matters worse, the PNP and JLP had been fighting an urban war in the slums of Kingston (Trench Town), battling over territory and political hegemony. This decade-long battle was an extreme microcosm of the conflict enveloping the whole island. It was clear the JLP was defending its claim to hegemony and privilege, while the PNP was trying desperately to unify the poor, despondent black majority to confront the JLP. However, as poor, unemployed youth battled over the political territories, Rastafarians struggled to gain any just political and social representation. Though disregarded by the JLP as a cult, the visit of Haile Sellasie[7] in the summer of 1966 to Jamaica demonstrated fully the potential Rastafarians had as a political entity over the misrepresented government, while also signifying the emergence of a black-consciousness and a re-examination of Jamaica's African heritage.[8]

In October 1968, with political tensions running high, the JLP tried desperately to identify the roots of the burgeoning Black Power movement in Jamaica. Immediately, they blamed Dr. Rodney. When he first arrived in Jamaica he noted: "the quality of justice dispensed by the legal system still depends on the color of your skin."[9] Dr. Rodney combined arguments of race and class in a way that attacked the very structure of the Jamaican political system; arguments that had hitherto been prevented from reaching the public forum; arguments that the government was most vulnerable.[10] Dr. Rodney targeted the root of the JLP's political justification—the multiracial myth of Jamaica—and spoke directly to those who lived through the dilemmas he discussed: poor students, the unemployed, and the Rastafarians. Obika Gray comments that "this contact with the urban poor broke new ground, because it was the first time that a member of the radical intelligentsia became directly involved with that sector of the population which was most opposed to the regime."[11] During the latter parts of the summer, the government had pressured the chancellor of the university to fire Dr. Rodney; however, he was unsuccessful. But when Dr. Rodney left for Canada in October, the government took full advantage of the opportunity. He was denied reentry into Jamaica, and cited for instigating violence and treason. That night, hundreds of thousands of students, youths, and Rastafarians took to the streets in protest.

The *New York Times* reported that the Rodney Riots were becoming the most debilitating issue for the Jamaican government. The article states:

Officials and leading citizens had long been annoyed with the concentration here of what they considered radical students and professors,
and the exclusion of one set off last Oct 16 the most destructive rioting
in memory.

The exclusion order was issued against Dr. Walter Rodney, a young
Guyanese lecturer in African History. He advocated a combination of
black power and Castroism and ... he was a subversive danger to the
country.[12]

The Rodney Riots demonstrated that there was a significant threat to the power
of the JLP. Most politicians feared this riot would lead to a revolution, much
like what had occurred in Cuba; however, the riot took on a very different character. "The Rodney Riots were frightening," writes Terry Lacey, "because they
manifested a reservoir of antagonism against the Jamaican government and the
national bourgeoisie, and because they pointed to a source of political strength
... political violence."[13] The authorities noted that the riots were aimed primarily at property, causing more than a million pounds of damage.[14] Though some
would assume that the riots failed to achieve the revolution Dr. Rodney desired,
there were two significant consequences of note. First, the riots demonstrated an
emergent political alliance among students, intellectuals, the unemployed, the
working class, and the Rastas that had been previously nonexistent. Secondly,
the actions of the JLP and the reaction to Dr. Rodney's exile showed the vulnerability of the JLP, and its reliance on force to uphold its rule.[15]

Much of the motivation for the resistance to the JLP can be credited to
the Civil Rights Movement in the United States, especially the Black Power
movement. The Black Power movement inspired Dr. Rodney. He sought ways
to transpose the ideas of activism and change to Jamaica and the West Indies.
He states in his book, *Groundings*: "The present Black Power movement in the
United States is a rejection of hopelessness and the policy of doing nothing to
halt the oppression of blacks by whites. It recognizes the absence of black power,
but is confident of the potential of black power on this globe."[16] Dr. Rodney
further states: "The Black Brothers in Kingston, Jamaica moved against the government of Jamaica ... what has happened in Jamaica is that the black people of
the city of Kingston have seized upon this opportunity to begin their indictment
against the government of Jamaica."[17] Thus, the Rodney Riots came to symbolize the first mass movement of the Jamaican people in resistance to the JLP and,
more importantly, the residue of white colonial society.

In *Groundings*, Dr. Rodney also talks a great deal about his visits to the
slums of Kingston, where he spoke with local youths, students, and Rastas about
Black Power, imperialism, and race. His discussions did not focus on just explaining the current social and political situation—more importantly, he offered
solutions. His belief in Black Power served as a vital tool in creating a new sense
of hope and activism. He states: "Throughout the country, black youths are

becoming aware of their possibilities of unleashing armed struggle in their own interests. For those who have eyes to see, there is already evidence of the beginnings of resistance to the violence of our oppressors."[18] Though most youths and Rastas understood the grievances stated by Dr. Rodney, militancy was a step that invoked violent retribution from the government, and in many ways limited the extent to which many Jamaicans were to express their objections.

Despite Dr. Rodney's call for armed resistance, his ideas on Jamaican heritage and the expression of black unity garnered the most attention. He outlined the three main tenets of the Black Power movement and the escape from oppression: (1) the break with imperialism, which is historically white racist; (2) the assumption of power by the black masses in the islands; and (3) the cultural reconstruction of society in the image of the blacks.[19] These three points would be the staple of his Black Power ideology, and would be reiterated by reggae artists in the future. He also made a call for action to change the interpretation and presentation of Jamaican history that resonated deeply within the black population, who were forlorn with the government's misrepresentation of the past, demanding that the effort must be directed solely toward freeing and mobilizing black minds from knowledge of African history seen as relevant but secondary to the concrete tactics and strategy necessary for black liberation.[20]

Ultimately, Dr. Rodney presented an argument against the JLP government and the need for black unification. He showed the Rastas, youths, and students that "these men (government) serve the interests of a foreign white capitalist system and at home they uphold a social structure which ensures that the black man resides at the bottom of the social ladder."[21] Dr. Rodney presented the black community with a coherent ideology of resistance that both represented the racial problems afflicting Jamaica and the world, but also the social and political contexts that justify and protect the current political system. Dr. Rodney's greatest achievement could well have been that he combined the political and social problems with racial oppression, and in doing so, awakened the sleeping giant that was the black majority.[22]

Dr. Rodney and the Rastafarians

The Rodney Riots are important in showing that Dr. Rodney had a special connection to the people of Jamaica. Though born a Guyanese, he was, like the black population in Jamaica, an African at heart. He had spent his entire life up to this point studying the history of Africa and the cultural affects of colonialism and slavery upon the black populations in the Americas. When he moved to Kingston to teach at the University of the West Indies at Mona, he made a concerted effort to take his teachings outside university walls. In *Groundings*, he laid the groundwork for black academics to become activists: (1) the black intellectual, the academic, within his own discipline, has to attack those distortions that white cultural imperialism has produced in all branches of scholarship; (2) the black intellectual has to move beyond his own discipline to challenge the social myth (the myth about a multiracial Jamaica); and (3) the black intellectual must attach himself to the activity of the black masses.[23]

His meetings with local youths and Rastas, called "groundings" by the Rastas, demonstrated his unique connection to the poor population in Jamaica. He used his intelligence to help educate others about the social and political situation of blacks in modern Jamaica, and what they could do to change their scenario. Rupert Lewis notes that Dr. Rodney used his academic background "to clarify the past and challenge the interpretations of colonial and bourgeois historians" and "many people commented on Rodney's genuineness. To them he became Brother Wally."[24] Unlike other academics, Dr. Rodney felt the need to immerse himself in the ghetto culture of Kingston. His wife, Pat, remarked upon the profound impact he had on her when he took her to the slums and ghettos of Kingston: "Because Walter took me down to Trench town and I met a lot of his friends. I saw the poverty. I saw the other side of Jamaica. It upset me a lot because I saw people rummaging through dustbins. But Walter said he never wanted me to get a false image at any time of wherever we lived, or what life was really like for the majority of the people."[25] By looking at this close connection to the black community, and how his teaching fused previously separate ideologies, we can see his impact on Jamaican history. The people's response to Dr. Rodney's expulsion seen in this context reveals their deep connection to the ideas of Black Power, African liberation, and cultural recreation presented by Dr. Rodney, and the first signs of a burgeoning mass movement of the oppressed majority. But Dr. Rodney also affected the Jamaican community in a way that is less obvious than the riots indicate, for he helped bring in the emergence of a new political and social force, the Rastafarians.

Unlike other social movements of the time, Jamaica had an existing population that represented the black pride and African heritage that Dr. Rodney advocated so eloquently. The Rastafarians had a significant presence on the island since the days of Marcus Garvey.[26] Even after Jamaican independence, Rastafarians remained at the bottom of the social and political ladder. Their lifestyle was grounded in the realities of poverty, and their dreadlocks and their love of marijuana led to a constantly volatile relationship with the Jamaican government. But as a spiritual force, the Rastas represented the African roots of the majority of the Jamaican population. For Dr. Rodney, the Rastas symbolized the distinctly African heritage of the entire West Indies population, and as a result, largely explains why he placed "Groundings" in the title of his book.[27]

During his "groundings," Dr. Rodney discovered the amazing similarities between his teachings and that of the Rastas. Rastafarian teachers like Ras Negus and Ras Planno found common ground with Dr. Rodney on the idea of political liberation in Africa.[28] In many ways Planno and Negus represented the black youths in Jamaica the same way Malcolm X did to the youth of the Black Power movement in America.[29] During Dr. Rodney's time in Jamaica, he had forged a relationship with the Rastas, and it resonated in their involvement in the riots and their growing urge for black liberation. Dr. Rodney viewed the Rasta's as the key to the freeing of black minds.[30] Yet, despite there being a large population of Rasta's on the island, they lacked political representation, and more importantly, had no sympathizers, particularly the politically empowered black middle class. Dr. Rodney, however, would change that. One major impact of his teachings was that he did not alienate, but rather, he captured the attention of the middle-class black population by connecting them to their African heritage found in the Rastafarian community. When students and workers saw Dr. Rodney immerse himself in the culture of Trench Town, they started to acknowledge their own cultural connection with the Rastas and Africa.[31]

The Rise of Reggae

The Rodney Riots showed that the black community in Jamaica was starting to unite. However, their political representation was still long off. With most Jamaicans reluctant to take on the authorities, who were more than willing to fight, Rastas, students, workers, and the middle class embraced alternative mediums to direct action in order to better understand their situation and rediscover their African heritage. Soon elements of Rastafarianism were being adopted by wealthier middle-class blacks: people began wearing African head dresses, growing dreads, smoking ganja, using Rasta phrases such as "I and I," and listening to Rasta music.[32] Of all of the cultural characteristics associated with the Rastafarian faith, it was its music that would inspire Jamaica.

In Jamaica, the social culture, especially for the middle-class black population, was found in the sound systems. Restaurant and club owners purchased enormous amplifiers, and blasted tunes into the open air, resulting in massive dance parties. It was a part of everyday life for most black Jamaicans. The sound systems were also an important factor in substantiating the growth of a purely Jamaican music industry.[33] In the mid 1960s, Jamaican music consisted of rocksteady and ska. Rooted in jazz and Motown, ska and rocksteady gave a mild portrayal of life in Jamaica. They both found happy homes in the sound systems of Jamaica. But the government was also paying close attention to lyrics of the music, strictly censoring any song that commented on the harsh political environment. Rastafarian music—reggae—was very political in nature because it reflected the oppression and poverty that Rastas faced every day. The government did everything in its power to prevent reggae from getting radio play and ruthlessly attacked DJs who played reggae at the sound systems. As Anika Waters writes, "One Rasta respondent told me that whenever he was at a dance and heard the Wailer's song 'Fire, Fire,' he ran. The police would be certain to raid, because they heard only the words 'Babylon burning' and knew well that

Babylon was a Rasta term for police."[34] As reggae surged into the public eye the government worked more aggressively to combat its message, and the prophecy of the lyrics was in many ways fulfilled.[35]

As the political and social climate become more explosive, Jamaicans searched for music with critical political and social messages. Soon reggae was playing at every sound system. Reggae took a giant leap where other music styles would not. Horace Campbell states, "The transition from rock steady to reggae was, like the transition from ska to rock steady, an imperceptible process which was both a response to and a reflection of the changing social condition of the society. Where rock steady had the legacy of singing the sex and romance songs ... reggae laid emphasis on Africa, black deliverance and redemption."[36] Reggae became the voice of political and social distress, and a vehicle for the Rastafarian community to preach African liberation. Soon Rastafarian ideology, which existed in the dredges of Jamaican society for so long, would find itself speaking for an entire population of people through reggae.

Following the Rodney Riots, politics took center stage in the minds of many artists throughout the island. Musicians like Desmond Dekker, the Ethiopians, and Bob Marley and the Wailing Wailers changed not only their musical style from the up beat rocksteady to the slower, more deliberate reggae sound, but also attached lyrics with a more poignant political and spiritual message. The term *reggae* was coined by Toots Hibbert of the Toots and the Maytals, who claims that it meant regular people are suffering and don't have what they want.[37]

Many artists responded directly to the Rodney Riots. The Ethiopians wrote the song "Everything Crash," which talked specifically about the social situation at the time, and became an instant sound system hit:

> Look deh now, Everything Crash / Firemen strike, watermen strike / Telephone pole men, too / down to the policemen, too / What bad by the morning / can't come a good evening / Every day carry a bucket to the well / One day the bucket bottom must drop out / Everything Crash.[38]

The popularity of the song was found in the widespread use of "its opening line, 'look deh now,' which became an oft-repeated phrase during the next election, usually preceding an antagonistic observation about the JLP government."[39] Other songs spoke about the violent aftermath of the Rodney Riots. As the sound systems throughout Jamaica blasted the reggae anthems, the political, social, and Rastafarian elements of the lyrics started to speak to a broader audience.

Jamaicans found solace in the political and social criticisms found in the lyrics, but more importantly were drawn to the African liberation and black conscious elements of the Rastafarian community. As demonstrated earlier, Rastafarians were virtually powerless until they found an effective medium, reggae, to help spread their culture. "The Rastafarian movement, in effect," as Ian Peddle points out, "co-opted reggae music as its chief medium of communication."[40] The best example of Rastafarian ideals embraced by reggae artists, and in turn, embraced by Jamaica as a whole, is the Abyssinians, "Satta Masagna." With lyrics written in Amharic, the Ethiopian dialect, the song spoke of a utopian resting place for the black faithful.[41] David Katz notes that it "has since become one of the most-versioned songs ever recorded in Jamaica, and an all time Rasta anthem."[42] The song portrayed the growing Rastafarian sentiments in the country, and its popularity is a prime example of how Rastafarian ideology found the perfect medium in reggae.

By the late 1960s and early 1970s, reggae artists were using music and the sound systems to comment and reflect on the highly charged political and social environment. Arguably two of the most influential and recognizable reggae artists, Bob Marley and Peter Tosh expanded on the ideas that emerged from the chaos of 1968 and the teachings of Dr. Rodney. They began to attack the JLP and its justification for hegemony, in particular the myth of peaceful multiracialism. In Peter Tosh's, "400 years" he confronts the tarnished past of Jamaica and the terrible misinterpretation by the JLP government:

> 400 years / and it's the same / the same philosophy / I've said it 400 years / Look how long / and the people they still can't see / why do they fight against the poor youth of today? / And without these youths they would be gone / all gone astray.[43]

The domination of reggae music on the sound systems of Jamaica demonstrated the significance reggae played in freeing the minds of youths and openly defying the laws of the government. Reggae and the Rastafarian culture were helping reconstruct Jamaican culture in the eyes of the black majority, just as Walter Rodney had stated.

Reggae artists also expanded upon the ideas of black pride, and the resiliency of the black people in the New World. Dr. Rodney spoke about the amazing cultural impact the black population had in the Americas. He states:

> Now we have all gone through a historical experience through by all accounts we should have been wiped out ... not only have we survived as a people but ... the black people in the West Indies have produced all the culture that we have. ... Black bourgeoisie and white people in the West Indies have produced nothing! Black people who have suffered all these years create. That is amazing.[44]

Bob Marley reiterated the ideas on his last two albums, *Survival* and *Uprising*. *Survival* was a direct response to the statements made by Dr. Rodney about the resiliency and strength of the black people in Jamaica.[45]

These concepts were not just pertinent to Jamaicans though, as they were widely shared by oppressed blacks and minorities all over the world. In many reggae songs, the combination of various social, political, and spiritual elements led to a unique cohesion that broke down nationalist identities and racial boundaries, and contributed to the growing popularity of reggae music around the world. An example of how reggae combined spiritual, political, and social observations can be found in Bob Marley's great song, "War":

> Until that philosophy which hold one race superior / and another / inferior / is finally / and permanently / discredited / and abandoned / everywhere is war / me say war.

> That until there no longer / first class and second class citizens of any nation / until the color of a man's skin / is of no more significance than the color of his eyes / me say war.

> That until the basic human rights / are equally guaranteed to all / without regard to race / dis a war.

> That until the day / the dream of lasting peace / world citizenship / rule of international morality / will remain in but a fleeting illusion to be pursued / but never attained / now everywhere is war / war![46]

The lyrics for "War" were taken from a speech by Haile Selassie during a visit to the United States in 1964. The song addresses the obvious political and social discontent and a sharp criticism to the world order: "that until there no longer first class and second class citizens of any nation." The song also contains Rastafarian influences, since the lyrics are from Haile Selassie himself. But it is the combination of all three elements that make "War" such an important tune, for it not only speaks to the obvious hardships of the people of Jamaica, but also makes connections to oppressed peoples all over the world who identify with the plight of the Jamaican people. As the seventies wore on, and the political and social dilemmas across the globe came to a climax, reggae emerged as an important cultural and political voice of not only Jamaica, but for the much of the Third World as well.

Reggae and Politics

Following the Rodney Riots and reggae's rise in popularity, the country of Jamaica was bound for change. Reggae artists began to recognize the profound impact they were having on the political and social processes of the island. In producing music critical of the social and political structures on the island and the world, combined with the link to African heritage through the Rastafarian community, reggae artists began to recreate the culture of Jamaica, as Dr. Rodney perceived. And with their alliance to the PNP and its leader Michael Manley, the oppressed black majority was finally garnering political clout. Leading up to the 1972 general elections, the JLP and PNP fought for the support of Rastafarians and the endorsements of popular reggae artists. Horace Campbell states: "These artists, who were spearheading the development of a popular culture, were uncompromising in their identification with Africa, such that in 1969 both the ruling party and the opposition leader made pilgrimages to Africa and Ethiopia in an effort to keep abreast of this new pace."[47] Naturally, the PNP found a great deal of support in their promises to change the country.

Songs became focal points of the presidential campaign. For Michael Manley and the PNP, Delroy Wilson's "Better Must Come" became the most famous campaign song. According to PJ Patterson, one of the leaders of the PNP, the song "drove the Michael Manley government from the very first day of its election to do everything possible to improve the social conditions and economic welfare of the people of Jamaica."[48] Michael Manley overwhelmingly won the election of 1972 mainly because his campaign focused on the issues of poverty, racial discrimination, and unemployment, the inspiration for reggae music. But this is nothing new. Politicians in every country around the world use music to garner support. So why is reggae any different?

Reggae influenced politics and social structures so profoundly that it cannot simply "reflect" the Jamaican culture. PJ Patterson explains: "It's fair to say that while the political situation influences music, it also works the other way around and the music influences the political situation. Both the music and the culture interact upon each other and with each other."[49] If reggae acted solely as a "reflection" of society, the desire for change would never be achievable, it would "remain a fleeting illusion to be pursued, but never attained."[50] As much as reggae was a response to the political and social situation of Jamaica in the late sixties, it was also the major force in changing the social and political consciousness of the country and the world in the seventies. Reggae used Rastafarian elements to reconstruct the social and political landscape to acknowledge the African heritage of displaced blacks around the world and demand equal political rights for the oppressed. In doing so, reggae became not just a cultural construct, but also a mass movement embodying the struggles of the politically and socially oppressed peoples of the world (and those in solidarity?).

Reggae is an excellent example of the symbiotic relationship between music and politics, together forging a mass movement of cultural transformation through music. Timothy S. Brown has argued that music does not simply "reflect" society, but actively works to reconstruct it. Brown notes that "the ties between popular music and radical politics become visible: the creation of an alternative sphere of cultural production by the bands themselves."[51] In other words, political music can create a new culture through a mass movement, rather than mirror a pre-existing form. One way to understand how reggae creates a mass movement is to look at how the expression of Rastafarian ideals helped combat the myth of peaceful multiracialism put forth by the JLP. Another is to look at how reggae exposed the social and political injustices, not just of Jamaica, but of the entire world system, in which blacks are overtly disenfranchised and oppressed.

The Rastafarians used race as way to define themselves, but also as a way to resist cultural norms that put them in direct opposition to the myth of a multiracial Jamaican culture. "It was here, quite literally on the 'skin' of the social formation, that the Rastafarian movement made its most startling innovations. Refracting the system of black and white polarities, turning negritude into a positive sign, a loaded essence, a weapon at once deadly and divinely licensed."[52] The Rastas were the incarnation of resistance to the Jamaican and global economic system. They stood as the direct link to Jamaica's African heritage and history, something that the Jamaican government had sought so long to prevent. As Walter Rodney said, "the government of Jamaica recognizes Black Power—it is afraid of the potential wrath of Jamaica's black and largely African population."[53] To Dr. Rodney, the Rastafarians were the vital force in supporting the emergence of black consciousness and African liberation on the island. The music, the speech, and the lifestyle were all ways of confronting the cultural myth while simultaneously, with the help of reggae, creating a new Jamaican culture born from this resistance.

The Rastafarian ideology proved malleable enough to translate to a variety of peoples all around the world. The oppressed minorities and disenchanted youths all over the world looked to reggae as a source of inspiration to resist political and social inequality. In Britain, oppressed blacks immediately identified with the message and aim of reggae music. Dick Hebdige writes: "It was during this period of growing disaffection and joblessness, at a time when conflict between black youths and the police was being openly acknowledged in the press, that imported reggae music began to deal directly with problems of race and class, and to resurrect the African heritage."[54]

However, reggae does not only represent Rastafarian music, as much as its languages and customs permeate the culture of the music. In a broader base, reggae speaks to social and political injustices that billions of people around the world can identify with.[55] Burning Spear, one of the great reggae artists, believes that reggae has become an international phenomenon because people identify with the struggles of oppression and poverty. He states: "The international market people will be listening for music with quality, music with understanding, music wherein they could gain something from, music that could become a help in their life or life style of living."[56] The Rastafarian mythos of the war on Babylon can be easily applied to all peoples who feel as though they are part of the unfortunate oppressed majority. Hebdige explains: "This war had a double nature: it was fought around ambiguous terms of reference which designated both an actual and an imaginary set of relations (race-class nexus / Babylon; economic exploitation / Biblical suffering), a struggle both real and metaphorical, which described a world of forms enmeshed in ideology where appearance and illusion were synonymous."[57]

Bob Marley, the most popular reggae artist ever and considered by many a prophet of Rastafarianism, exploded onto the scene in the 1970s. Bob Marley's message of love and hope in the face of oppression and hatred, while loaded with Rastafarian mythos, made him one of the most universally recognized musical artists in the world.[58] Where Walter Rodney desired a force to recreate Jamaican culture, Bob Marley went further, becoming the voice of the oppressed in the Third World. "The Third World had never produced a global superstar: in his dress code, hairstyle, drug habits, speech patterns, Bob Marley's impact on his audience was in far more ways than merely musical."[59] When the South African government exploded a nuclear device in 1979 to intimidate the freedom fighters, Marley responded. In his last album ever recorded, *Uprising,* he sang, "Have no fear for atomic energy for none dem can stop de time."[60] "Redemption Song" was one of his many attempts to not only chastise the actions of oppressive governments, but to offer hope and encouragement to those still battling for equal rights and justice. In Marley's song "Zimbabwe," from *Survival,* he calls for his brothers and sisters in Zimbabwe to unite and fight for their rights. His career and the body of his work stand in defiance of a global system that could not contain him. Marley, and all other reggae artists who emerged from 1968, brought forth political and social grievances in such a way that people could finally comprehend the causes of their struggles, and more importantly, could themselves be the solution in their act of rebelliousness and resistance. Just by listening to reggae, dancing to reggae, speaking Rasta speech, and smoking ganja people stood in direct defiance of a system that sought to subjugate them and force them into a cultural, political, and social structure substantiated by racial and class segregation. Yet, all of the elements of reggae culture, which Jamaica and the world held so dear, were a product of Walter Rodney's teachings and work in Trench Town.

In so many ways, Bob Marley represents the amazing depth and authenticity of reggae music and reggae culture. For despite selling millions of albums and playing for millions of fans, Bob rarely changed. As Lloyd Bradley says: "Why the world listened to Bob Marley was because he remained unadulterated by the business he chose to operate in … what he delivered was pure Trench Town. Right up until he died."[61] The same can be said of most reggae artists; they represent the struggles of race and class, they live the struggles of oppression and poverty. And by listening to reggae, and confounding in its political and social message, many unite in defiance of a system rooted in privilege and segregation. For many oppressed peoples of the Third World, Reggae embodies a mass movement inspired by the struggles of Third World peoples trying to break themselves from the restraints of an imperialist system rooted in white hegemony. Yet, reggae is not only the embodiment of struggle, poverty, and oppression, it is also the culture of resistance, self-awareness, and hope. And this culture would never have come to pass had Walter Rodney not set foot in the slums of Trench Town.

Notes

1. Rex Nettleford (ed.), *Jamaica in Independence: Essays on the Early Years* (Kingston: Heinemann Caribbean, 1989), 3.
2. Ibid., 4.
3. Michael Manley, *The Politics of Change: A Jamaican Testament* (Washington, DC: Howard University Press, 1975), 158.
4. Nettleford (1989), 4–5.
5. Horace Campbell, *Rasta and Resistance: From Marcus Garvey to Walter Rodney* (Ewing Township, NJ: Africa World Press, Inc., 1987), 19.
6. Ibid., 89.
7. Haile Selassie is the King of Ethiopia and prophet to the Rastafarians. He believed that all blacks should return to Africa and is referred to as "Jah" and "Rastafari."
8. Walter Rodney, *The Groundings with My Brothers* (London: The Bogle-L'Ouverture Publications, 1969), 13.
9. Ibid., 13.
10. Anthony Payne, *Politics in Jamaica* (New York: St. Martin's Press, 1994), 22.
11. Obika Gray, *Radicalism and Social Change in Jamaica: 1960–1972* (Knoxville; Univ. of Tennessee Press, 1991), 153.
12. *New York Times*, 26 November 1968.
13. Terry Lacey, *Violence and Politics in Jamaica: 1960–1970* (Manchester: Manchester University Press, 1977), 98.
14. Ibid., 97.
15. Gray (1991), 160.
16. Rodney (1969), 20.
17. Ibid., 66.
18. Ibid., 15.
19. Ibid., 28.
20. Ibid., 51.
21. Ibid., 60.
22. Gray (1991), 157.
23. Rodney (1969), 63.
24. Rupert C. Lewis, *Walter Rodney's Intellectual and Political Thought* (Detroit, MI: Wayne State University Press, 1998), 86.
25. Ibid., 87.
26. Garvey was a Jamaican who moved to America to unite the Black population and move back to Africa. He is considered one of the fathers and prophets of Rastafarianism.
27. Rodney (1969), 68.
28. Lewis (1998), 99.
29. Ibid., 101.
30. Noel Erskine, *From Garvey to Marley* (Gainesville: University Press of Florida, 2005), 154.
31. Ibid., 156.
32. Ibid., 157.
33. David Katz, *Solid Foundation: An Oral History of Reggae* (London: Bloomsbury, 2003), 3.

34. Anika Waters, *Race, Class, and Political Symbols: Rastafari and Reggae in Jamaican Politics* (Piscataway, NJ: Transaction Publishers, 1985), 102.

35. A great example of this can be found in the legendary cult movie *Rockers* (1978). In the opening of the movie a sound system is broken up by police, and the various characters disperse. The movie cuts to Leroy Wallace and Winston Rodney finding refuge in an old decrepit sugar mill (not a coincidence). It leads to a poetic, vocal version of "Jah No Dead" sung by Rodney, aka Burning Spear. The scene is loaded with political and cultural imagery, as it connects the defiance against the state with the re-emergence of Rasta and African culture in Jamaica.

36. Campbell (1987), 134.

37. Waters (1985), 99.

38. The Ethiopians, "Everything Crash" (1968).

39. Waters (1985), 100.

40. Ian Peddie (ed.), *The Resisting Muse: Popular Music and Social Protest* (Surrey: Ashgate, 2006), 111.

41. Katz (2003), 149.

42. Ibid., 150.

43. Peter Tosh, "400 years." Bob Marley and the Wailing Wailers. *Catch a Fire* (Island Records, 1973).

44. Rodney (1969), 68.

45. Campbell (1987), 144.

46. Bob Marley and the Wailers, "War," *Rastaman Vibration* (Island Records, 1976).

47. Campbell (1987), 135.

48. Lloyd Bradley, *Reggae: The Story of Jamaican Music* (London: BBC Worldwide Ltd., 2002), 71.

49. Ibid.

50. Bob Marley and the Wailers (1976).

51. Tim Brown, "Popular Music / Popular Politics: Some Thoughts on the Role of Rock in West Germany, 1968," paper presented at the forum "Designing a New Life: Aesthetics and Lifestyles of Political and Social Protest," University of Zurich, March 2007.

52. Dick Hebdige, *Subculture: the Meaning of Style* (York: Metheun & Co. Ltd., 1979), 37.

53. Rodney (1969), 28.

54. Hebdige (1979), 36–37.

55. One must only look at the lists of all-time record sales to see that Bob Marley is the only Third World artist represented.

56. Bradley (2002), 64.

57. Hebdige (1979), 38.

58. Marley's album *Exodus* was voted album of the century by *TIME Magazine*.

59. Bradley (2002), 75.

60. Bob Marley and the Wailers, "Redemption Song," *Uprising* (Island Records, 1979).

61. Bradley (2002), 76.

Part 3

Unfinished Business: Challenging the State's Revolution

Chapter 9

The Destruction of the University
Violence, Political Imagination, and the Student Movement in Congo-Zaire, 1969–1971

Pedro Monaville

> Violence: … The emotional power of the word can then be very confusing.
> —Raymond Williams, 1976[1]

On 4 June 1969 soldiers opened fire on a student demonstration in Kinshasa, killing tens of marchers. The exact number of casualties—estimations vary between less than 10 and more than 100 victims—is impossible to establish. After the killing, the army seized the corpses of the dead students and buried them anonymously in a mass grave. These bodies could testify to the scale of the massacre, and identified graves would have constituted material reminders of the event.[2] However, the efforts to make the dead bodies disappear failed to put a closure to the massacre. June 4th remained an unfinished business.[3] The struggle to complete the story of the massacre during the following couple of years—opposing the state to the student movement—ultimately radically transformed the face of Congolese universities.

Violence and Legitimacy

Personally, the moment I became revolted against Mobutu was June 4th 1969. On June 4th 1969, all Congolese students were asked to participate in a pacific demonstration. And we did go and demonstrate. I was here on Rond-Point Victoire. And they fired. I was in the first rows of the demonstration. … I did not realize that they were. … We had seen the soldiers who were there, but we thought: "there are just here to intimidate us." And then suddenly, they started to fire, and everybody yelled: "lie down." And I lied down. And then at the moment when … I noticed that one of my friends did not stand up. And I had blood on me. And then I saw that one of my friends was dead. And this. ... It was the first time I was seeing a dead body. And it changed me completely. And today, this image. ... It is as if it had happened yesterday.[4]

A local group of activists, the Kinshasa Student Circle (C.E.K.), planned the demonstration of June 4th. C.E.K.'s leaders tried to keep their project secret. At Lovanium—the country's most prestigious university, located in the outskirts of Kinshasa—they informed the vast majority of students only on the eve of the march, during an assembly on the so-called Red Square, the center of student politics on the campus. A few hours later, still in the middle of the night, students started to leave their dormitories en masse to get prepared for departure. The turnout was impressive. Nearly all of Lovanium's 3000 students participated in the march. Nevertheless, nearly none among them reached the city center and the Ministry of Education, where C.E.K. had planned to end the demonstration.

Informed of C.E.K.'s project, the authorities intended to stop the demonstration by any means possible before it reached the city center. Soldiers unsuccessfully tried to use tear gas to disperse the marchers. Students seized the grenades and threw them back at the soldiers, as they had been instructed to do by the C.E.K.'s activists. No one, among the students, imagined that the government would allow more violent means of repression to contain the march. However, soldiers started to open fire and targeted marchers a few hundred meters farther away, around what is today called Yolo-Medical, and then around *rond-point* Victoire, in the very populous Matonge district. Hearing the shots, many students thought that soldiers were using white bullets. Once it became obvious that this was not the case, the demonstration broke down. In the memories of many marchers, *rond-point* Victoire marks the end point of the demonstration. Nevertheless, a few did continue to progress in the direction of the Ministry of Education and went as far as Kinshasa's Central Station, where they met students from other schools. Soldiers assaulted female students, and finally opened fire one more time on the marchers. Scores of protesters were arrested and brutally handled in a military camp.[5]

The Congolese government had already used unrestrained violence against its citizens many times during the 1960s. Nevertheless, the events of June 4th marked a rupture with previous massacres. The spirit, if not the techniques, of counterinsurgency, engineered through the help of the Belgian and American governments and tested between 1963 and 1965 in rural areas conquered by the Simba and Mulele rebellions, was for the first time deployed in the space of the capital city.[6] Quite unsurprisingly, Congolese and foreign observers directly associated the events of 1969 with the colonial police operation of January 1959 that had overcame an insurrectional movement in Kinshasa at the expense of more than 100 deaths.[7] Through the repression of the student movement in 1969, the Congolese government adopted a form of violence inescapably reminiscent of this brand of colonial management of "trouble."

Using violence against unarmed students dangerously jeopardized the post-colonial state's legitimacy. Throughout the 1960s, student politics remained isolated from society. Students rarely received support outside of campuses. As one former student from the 1960s remembers it, "every time Lovanium students denounced the regime through demonstrations, the public understood it as a manifestation of youth's unbridled unruliness. People did not dare mixing with protesters … ; on the contrary, they would run away in their houses, yelling: '*Ba Etudiants ba bandi lisusu mobulu na bango*' [Students are starting to make trouble again]."[8] Regardless of their lack of success in attracting a following among Kinshasa's non-educated urban masses—a failure that was repeated on 4 June 1969—students were not legitimate targets of state violence in the public's mind. Students were seen as children in need of protection, as well as the emerging social fraction through which the promises of "development" would be accomplished. Ordinary Congolese interpreted the 1969 massacre—the unrestrained use of violence against a vulnerable part of the national body—as totally illegitimate.[9]

For the students themselves, the event marked a turning point. Pius Ngandu Kashama's autobiographical novel *La mort faite homme* takes place on 4 June 1969, and poetically articulates how the massacre came to define his own student generation.[10] Their dead comrades, deprived of a proper burial, remained haunting presences in the consciousness of the marchers of June. Concurrently, Joseph Mobutu, the Congo's president since 1966, and the man unanimously held as responsible for the massacre, came to embody the figure of death after 1969 in the eyes of many students. Mobutu remained in power for nearly 30 more years after the massacre, and the memories attached to him are very complex.[11] Nevertheless, 4 June 1969 is often remembered as a turning point in the history of his regime.

The antagonism between the state and the students at the end of the 1960s—dramatically manifested in the 1969 killings—remained centered on issues directly related to the organization of the higher education system. In spite of this, the conflict about the future of universities produced effects that were felt outside of campuses. Indeed, in the process, certain forms of political imagination disappeared and were replaced by a new political vocabulary. Lovanium was both the source of student contestation and at the same time provided the regime with a legitimizing rhetoric.

Decolonizing the University

> Beware! International imperialism is making plans for the future.
> Its method: leading insidious surveys on tomorrow's elites. Scrutinize their private lives. Get to know their secret motives. This is
> the case of the current survey led by a German team. … Foreign-

ers are still seeing us as their guinea pigs. They take advantage of our weaknesses and divisions. You are young, refuse to be colonialism's guinea pigs.[12]

Global 1968 offered an interpretive context against which the Kinshasa demonstration was read and understood by the different actors, and many in the Congo had paid a lot of attention to the French case in particular. The influence of Benoît Verhaegen, a Belgian professor of political science and the director of the Institute of Social and Economic Research based at Lovanium (IRES), can be traced even more easily.[13] A self-proclaimed Marxist, Verhaegen offered students an entry to revolutionary ideas that lacked a relay in Kinshasa in the mid 1960s. Even though the Congolese student association officially opted for socialism in the early 1960s and some semi-clandestine Marxist reading groups existed on Congolese campuses,[14] Marxism retained an exotic flavor, especially at the very Catholic Lovanium. Verhaegen certainly played a role in the articulation of the student rhetoric at the University. As one former student remembering Lovanium's intellectual environment in the 1960s told me,

researchers … were ordering books for the library from [the Parisian leftist editor] Maspero, [such as those of Frantz] Fanon. When we were reading these books in 1968, we did not even know that these people were dead. We thought they were still alive. And then, May '68 happened, of course. … All those ideas … and Verhaegen's conferences … and we were receiving a lot of guest speakers on campus. There was a real circulation of ideas that made certain things impossible for us to accept.[15]

Verhaegen strongly opposed Lovanium's alienation from Congolese society. To a great extent, the University, created by Belgian Catholics in the mid 1950s, remained a foreign body in the independent Congo. The great majority of professors were foreigners. Academic life and programs totally mirrored the Belgian system. Academic authorities adopted elitism as their official religion, and a great number of students failed every year.[16]

In 1964, at the occasion of Lovanium's 10th anniversary, Verhaegen gave a talk, during which he attacked the institution and condemned its inability to remake itself in the post-colonial context. This intervention influenced the General Assembly of Students at Lovanium (AGEL) that led an impressive successful strike on the campus a few weeks later. Student leaders were in agreement with the Belgian professor that while the country needed a form of "authoritarian socialism," universities had to be democratized. The strike succeeded in creating awareness and fostering unity across the campus. A great number of students took an oath and swore fidelity to the "revolution" and to the student movement. Nevertheless, the strike ended after one week, when AGEL believed it could obtain satisfaction through negotiations. This strategy ultimately failed, as professors and academic authorities allied to block most of the students' claims.[17]

AGEL's unsatisfied demands reappeared regularly in the following years, and the strike's memory continued to fire student leaders' imagination. This greatly contributed to the antagonistic atmosphere at Lovanium, while more activists on other campuses started to mobilize their peers on a similar basis. In 1967, Lovanium's authorities expelled a few students after yet another strike on the pretext of violent acts committed against security agents. The government ordered the Belgian Monsignor Gillon, Lovanium's rector, to reintegrate the students. He was then forced to resign and Tharcisse Tshibangu, a Congolese, became the new rector. Students interpreted the event as a clear victory in their fight for the University's Africanization.[18]

Others signs let students think that they could find an ally in Mobutu's regime. Mobutu's sudden rediscovery of Lumumba particularly helped galvanize the student left. Mobutu had seized power with the support of Western governments. However, influenced by some former leaders of the Congolese Student Union (UGEC), he progressively oriented his political discourse toward nationalism in 1966–1967. The regime's new rhetoric legitimized protests against the enduring colonial nature of universities.

By 1968, the student movement's political platform more clearly than ever centered on the issue of decolonization. Most students were very familiar with the main issues: *co-gestion, Africanization, démocratizasion,* and *déconcentration.* The movement's main grievances only targeted power structures inside universities. Students were not opposing the state—on the contrary, they tried to mobilize the government as an ally in their attempt to promote a reform of universities.

As polarizing as Patrice Lumumba remained in Congolese society, students held him as a tutelary figure. The tacit alliance between Mobutu's regime and the students was made possible by Lumumba's rehabilitation as national hero. Their quarrel resulted from an incident that also related to Lumumba. On 4 January 1968, the government organized a ceremony to celebrate the memory of the first prime minister and martyr of independence. The government made the serious political mistake of inviting United States Vice President Hubert Humphrey to attend the ceremony. Student activists considered Humphrey's presence as an overt provocation. The anti-imperialist students not only opposed the United States' involvement in Vietnam, but even more so, they could not stand that an American official attended this ceremony while his country was believed to be one of the main organizers of Lumumba's assassination in 1961. UGEC leaders organized a protest on the day of the ceremony to denounce this hypocrisy, and the trust between student organizations and the government disappeared. Between January and March, several leaders were arrested, detained in prison for a short time, and, for some of them, expelled from the university.[19] The crisis ended with the dissolution of UGEC by the government and the forced promotion of JMPR, the youth-branch of the state party, on campuses. This rupture between the student movement and Mobutu was the first step that made June 4th conceivable.

In July 1968, Lovanium's board of directors decided to create a working group in charge of reforming the university's status for good, and putting an end to the continuous tensions on the campus. AGEL and PASCOL (the association of Congolese professors and assistants) refused to integrate the working group unless it received voting rights and included a majority of Congolese participants. The crisis intensified over the fall, and in January 1969, anonymous pamphlets invited students to refuse all dialogue with Lovanium's authorities.

A demonstration was planned for the end of the month, which provoked a reaction from Mobutu. He called a national conference in Goma to discuss the reform of universities. The delegates at the conference, presided over by the minister of education, agreed on "co-responsibility" as the principle that should transform the governance of all institutions of higher education. This did not meet the demands of the most radical student groups—and especially of Lovanium's delegation—but it was at least a first step in the sense of the universities' democratization. However, Lovanium authorities could not accept the principle of voting rights for students in all academic institutions and councils—which was the core of the co-responsibility model. Once the conference was over, they sent a memorandum to the government, making explicit that democratizing universities would ultimately threaten the authority of the government: "The natural form of the nation's organs risks then to be affected by the spirit of this reform, and one should be conscious of this risk."[20] Following the reception of the memorandum, Mobutu dismissed the minister of education and adjourned Goma's decisions. This alienated the students from Kinshasa and pushed them to opt for a direct confrontation with the regime through the organization of a mass demonstration in the city.

Food, Generational Conflicts, and Violence

> Could I imagine, even one moment, being the peacemaker I have always been and the family dad that I am, could I imagine—was I saying—that those I always loved without limits would go so far as, through means unknown to the Congolese people and borrowed from abroad, to force me to announce to the Congolese nation news so sad and so tragic for some households, for some families, and for the whole nation?[21]

Beyond the increasing tensions between Mobutu's government and the student movement, other reasons explain the success of the march of June 1969. Micropolitical stakes also contributed greatly to convince so many students to defy a regime that was not reputed for its tolerance of dissent and opposition. Clearly, many of the students who marched on June 4th cared more about the improvement of their daily life than about the more "ideological slogans" of student groups. Nevertheless, students' displeasure at the amount of state scholarships was highly political. The amount of scholarships in 1969 only represented a fifth of what students received in 1960. And, far from being abstract, slogans such as democratization directly evoked the recent clash with academic authorities over the forced assignation of disciplinary orientation to second-year students.

It was a certain idea of the student and a social status that was defended on June 4th when marchers asked for a re-evaluation of their living conditions. University students were a small elite. Most of them had studied in Catholic institutions, spending many years in boarding schools, separated from their families. Many of Lovanium's students were coming from rural regions—particularly from the Jesuit high schools in Kwilu, Bas-Congo, and Katanga—and once in Kinshasa, they were convinced that all their efforts and sacrifices had paid off and granted them an access to the higher strata of society. Food particularly embodied the work of social differentiation that students expected from their access to higher education. The post-colonial promises of development and of social mobility could be assessed through the quality of food offered on campuses. Complaints about food expressed students' anger at the discrepancy they perceived between their real social status and the hopes they had invested in education. In 1964, the call for the strike issued by AGEL already asked both for a democratization of the University and for better conditions of living, which was expressed through a complaint about food: "We can not accept any longer a diet that is nearly unworthy of dogs"[22] Mundanely, many students at Lovanium rode the university buses for their weekly visits to the *cités*, and used their food tickets —and negotiated their access to University dinners—to seduce the women they were meeting there.

The participation of students in the demonstration of June also happened in a context of particularly tense relations between generations and of generalized indiscipline against authority figures. Yoka Mudaba Lye's fictional narrative on June 4th, about a gravedigger who happens to bury in the mass grave his own son among the other victims of the demonstration, encapsulates one dimension of the generational dynamics at play in the event—and the deceived hopes of social mobility invested in education.[23] Remembering his Catholic education with Belgian missionaries and his access to colonial knowledge in the late 1950s, philosopher V. Y. Mudimbe wrote that he then became his "father's father."[24] In 1969, the generational inversion was pushed even further: in Yoka's story, not only is the son much more educated and politically conscious than his father, but it is up to the father to bury the son.

Memories of the generation that came of age in the 1960s abound with stories in which authority is contested, challenged, and inverted. Anecdotes about conflicts with and rebellions against figures of authority—fathers and uncles, priests, teachers—are often linked to memories of the troubled political context of the Congo in the aftermath of its violent decolonization. Violence remained a prominent dimension of political life during the 1960s. It permeated social relations and figures prominently in stories about generational conflicts.

The student movement throughout the 1960s also used violence to be taken seriously. The threat of violence became a way to assert the students' commitment and force their claims. Already in 1964, AGEL's call for a strike ended with the following capitalized sentences: "TO WAIT ANY LONGER! NO! RESISTANCE AND VIOLENCE! YES."[25] On 21 May 1969, the C.E.K. sent an ultimatum to the government, in which they expressed their "right and duty" to defend their interests "by all means necessary, including revolutionary violence, with the same determination as our comrades from Africa, Latin America, Europe, and Asia."[26] June 4th is remembered as a pacific demonstration—a central point for the accession of the victims of the march to the status of martyrs. Nevertheless, as early as 1971, students reinscribed violence in the narrative of June 4th: "Students were forced to use violence to express their anger. Legitimate anger, anger created by the government. Through its silence in face of students' fair demands, the government invited students to leave their classrooms and to invade the streets."[27]

The student movement's rhetoric of violence ultimately served the narrative of the events of June 4th authored by Mobutu's regime. The official discourse on the demonstration did not deny acts of violence. It worked instead, through a series of moves, to displace the responsibility of violence from the center of power (Mobutu, the government, the army, "real" Congolese) to its outside (the students, the "politicians', "fake" Congolese and "fake" students, communists, foreigners. The regime denounced an anti-Congolese coalition, composed of student leaders, politicians, and malevolent foreigners, and cemented through the circulation of money. Students were accused of "mimicking the Parisian month of May" and of being manipulated by foreign Maoist militants. On 7 June, when Congolese students at the University of Brussels decided to bring a letter protesting the recent killing to the Congolese ambassador and were received by embassy employees armed with metal rods, it was foreigners, once again—"mostly students from Northern Africa, Latin America, and Europe"—who were accused of having caused the trouble.[28]

From the Campus to the Military Camp: Destroying the University

> The African University must understand that what is true in Europe or America may not be so in Africa and that it bears great responsibilities towards the Nation which did so much for its sake. So, while the student from the old World exhausts himself

in paralysing contest without causing much harm, the African student is faced after finishing his studies by the grave tasks of reconstruction and development, and any tiny loss of the little we have acquired can cause regression in the way towards progress.[29]

Our education system must aim at modeling an authentically Congolese youth, that think as Congolese, reason as Congolese, act as Congolese and see the future as Congolese. ... We are now starting back from scratch, because we intend to dispose of disciplined youth and not any more of profaners and uncivil students. Thanks to the army, to the medical inspection we have done, we can see that our youth in Lovanium was rotten, not only morally but also physically.[30]

Mobutu needed to remake June 4th into an insurrectionary and foreign movement in order to restore the legitimacy of his regime. Likewise, by capturing the generational dimension of the movement and replacing himself as the nation's father, Mobutu rewrote, appropriated, and inverted the students' political rhetoric.[31] Two years after June 4th, the regime indeed totally transformed the national higher education system and offered a pyrrhic victory to the student movement.

The dead students' symbolic capital allowed clandestine activists at Lovanium to maintain strong feelings against the regime on the campus after June 4th.[32] Students continued to fuel Mobutu's anger. In 1970, at the occasion of the presidential elections, the only ballots against Mobutu's candidacy in Kinshasa were cast at precincts around the University. More crucially, in May 1971, pamphlets and inscriptions on the University's buildings insulted Mobutu's recently defunct mother, publicly calling her a "whore" who did not deserve the national burial she had just received while the bodies of their comrades had never been given a proper sepulture. So, when a commemoration of the killing was planned on 4 June 1971 at Lovanium, the tension between students and the regime was at its highest. After a mass and the spontaneous building of a memorial to the dead students, the army invaded the campus and arrested the Belgian priest who had led the celebration. A group of students took Lovanium's rector hostage for a few hours, asking for the release of the priest. The army intervened again. Mobutu decided to close the university, and to draft all the 3000 students from Lovanium into the army. Most students were allowed to return to school after a few months of military service, even if they still had to wear their uniform and participate in military exercises. Fifteen student activists were condemned to life-long sentences in prison.

The higher education system was totally transformed. A national university was created, incorporating Lovanium and Kisangani, the two private universities, as well as Lubumbashi, previously the only public institution. The creation of this new entity, Université Nationale du Zaire (UNAZA), entailed many changes for academics, administrative employees, and students. Departments and faculties were spread and redistributed throughout the country: pedagogy and psychology in Kisangani; humanities and social sciences in Lubumbashi; medicine, engineering, sciences, and law in Kinshasa. Material, moral, and political conditions of university life were strongly affected.

By 1971, Mobutu had fully adopted the student movement's vocabulary and appropriated the themes of nationalism, Africanization, and decolonization. When he claimed that military service would reform syphilis-ridden students, he did not diverge from the accusation published by the radical student activists against the moral corruption of prostitution, dime novels, and pornographic movies that they saw plaguing their peers.[33] When he reformed the universities, he seemed to apply the slogans that students proclaimed on June 4th before the army started to open fire against them. Mobutu's tour de force consisted of neutralizing most of the political vocabulary that the student movement had used against him.

Mobutu's nationalization and reform in several ways brought concrete answers to claims long defended by student activists. To some observers, the reform constituted a decisive step in decolonizing and democratizing universities. Nevertheless, the democratization supposedly brought by the reform (i.e., democratization as massification) was irreconcilable with the democratization asked for by the student movement (democratization as *co-gestion*). For a French anthropologist who praised the reform, universities had to be authentically Congolese, which meant breaking their isolation from society. The particular status of students—their privileged access to state resources—therefore appeared as a legacy of colonialism. In this sense, the post-1971 decline of students' living standards and, more generally, the deterioration of the material conditions of teaching was not only inevitable, but welcomed: "In a poor country, there is in nothing shameful for the university to be poor. On the contrary, it must be poor, and it is an act of realism to maintain it in a state of poverty."[34]

The 1971 reform marked a real turmoil for universities. It was a violent disruption of the institutions' daily lives. It displaced entire departments, libraries, and laboratories from one part of the country to the other. It politicized campuses and bracketed academic freedom. It undermined the student movement for years. More students were accepted every year, while less money was spent in education. The reform provoked a physical and intellectual decay in universities that has put their survival into question many times and to this day.

By an ironical twist, Mobutu nearly came to apply the program defined by a radical advocate of the student movement in 1971, for whom Congolese universities and the research conducted inside them did not "serve the knowledge of real persons, real things, or real needs, but it serves the abstract speculation that create a useful smoking screen for imperialism." The remedy was therefore radical and resembled the slogans uttered against bourgeois universities by many other students around the globe: "The University should be neither reformed, neither rethought, nor adapted. The university should simply be destroyed."[35]

Notes

This chapter is based on research led in the Congo and Belgium and made possible by financial support from the Center for African and African American Studies and the International Institute at the University of Michigan. Nancy Hunt and Mblala Nkanga offered decisive advice at the different stages of the research. I am indebted to the former student activists who have shared their stories of 4 June 1969 with me since 2007, especially: A. Yoka Mudiba Lye, J.-B. Sondji, C. Kabuya Lumuna, M. Kayemba, F. Kandolo, V. Milimgo, T. K. Yogolelo, M. Nkiko, G. Muteba, K. Mudjila-Mpiku, P. Malangu Mposhi, G. Kalaba, S. Kivilu, J. Kitemoko, P. Ngandu, J. J. Mukendi, D. Nkanza, Dr. Kalamba, M. M. Mwifi, N. Obotela, and B. Tshungu.

1. Raymond Williams, *Keywords: A Vocabulary of Culture and Society* (New York: Oxford University Press, 1976), 278.
2. On the symbolic capital of dead bodies in a different geographical context, see Katherine Verdery, *The Political Lives of Dead Bodies: Reburial and Postsocialist Change* (New York: Columbia University Press, 2000).
3. On events as unfinished business and stories in need of completion, see Veena Das, *Life and Words: Violence and the Descent in the Ordinary* (Berkeley: University of California, 2007).
4. Interview with J.-B. Sondji, Kinshasa, 7 October 2007.
5. For a published autobiographical narrative mentioning the events in the city center, see D. Gabembo Fumu wa Utadi, "De Lovanium à l'Université de Kinshasa," in I. Ndaywel è Nziem (ed.), *L'Université dans le devenir de l'Afrique* (Paris, 2007), 67–76; in the same volume, see also Nyando ya Rubango, "De Lovanium à la Kasapa via caserne: Mémoire d'un pèlerin métis," 97–124).
6. On the mid-1960s rebellions in the Congo, see C. Coquery Vidrovitch, A. Forest, and H. Weiss (eds.), *Rebellions-Révolutions au Zaïre, 1963–1965* (Paris, 1987).
7. See M. Klein, "Congo (K) Simmers," in *Africa Report* Vol. 15, No. 1 (1970): 10–12.
8. Ngub'Usim M. N., "L'élite meneur d'hommes et agent de transformation en R.D.C.," in S. Kivilu (ed.), *Elites et démocratie en République Démocratique du Congo* (Kinshasa, 2000), 23.
9. On the relationship between the students and the masses in Kinshasa, and more generally on the class dimension of the student movement, see J. Vansina, "Mwasi's Trials," in *Daedalus* Vol. 111, No. 2 (1982): 49–70.
10. P. Ngandu Nkashama, *La Mort Faite Homme* (Paris, 1986), 256.
11. Quite ironically, Mobutu's death body—buried in Morocco—has also become an haunting presence in today's Congo; see Bob White, "The Political Undead: Is it Possible to Mourn for Mobutu's Zaire?" *African Studies Review* Vol. 48, No. 2 (2005): 65–86.
12. Anonymous pamphlet reproduced in P. V. Dias et al. (eds.), *Les étudiants universitaires congolais: Une enquête sur leurs attitudes socio-politiques* (Fryeburg, 1971), 19–20.
13. See notably J. Vansina, *Living with Africa* (Madison, 1995), 162.

14. See V. Y. Mudimbe, *Le corps glorieux des mots et des êtres: Esquisse d'un jardin à la bénédictine* (Paris, 1994), p.89ff.
15. Interview with M. Kayamba, Lubumbashi, 1 October 2007.
16. See B. Verhaegen, *L'enseignement universitaire au Zaïre: De Lovanium à l'Unaza* (Paris, 1978).
17. See A.R. Ilunga Kabongo, "Crise à Lovanium », in *Etudes Congolais* 6, n.4 (1964) : 9.
18. See L. Gillon, *Servir en actes et en vérité* (Brussels, 1988), 218.
19. Tnsivuadi Katamba Kamalondo wa Kalombo, *La participation des étudiants zaïrois à la politique, mémoire présenté en vue de l'obtention du grade de licencié en sciences politiques et administratives* (Lumumbashi, 1974), 24–25.
20. Cited in Bernadette Lacroix, *Pouvoirs et structures de l'université Lovanium* (Brussels, 1972).
21. Mobutu's radio allocution on 4 June 1969, reproduced in "Le President, l'universite et les paras," *Zaire, L'Hebdomadaire de l'Afrique Centrale* N.o 46 (June 1969): 12.
22. H. Makanda, "Pourquoi cette grève du 9 mars 1964?" *Etudes Congolaises* Vol. 6, No. 3 (1964): 104.
23. Yoka Lye Mudaba, *Le Fossoyeur, et sept autres nouvelles primées dans le cadre du Concours radiophonique de la Meilleure Nouvelle de Langue Française* (Paris, 1986).
24. Mudimbe (1974), 28.
25. See Makanda (1964), 105.
26. Lacroix (1972), 77.
27. *Le Furet, Journal des Cancres au Maquis,* 4 June 1971, 4.
28. *Unité: Kinshasa, 4 juin 69: lettre d'un témoin* (Leuven, 1969), 23.
29. "Message from H.E. The president of the Democratic Republic of the Congo, Read by H.E.M. Cardoso, Minister of National Education," in *Report of the Second General Conference of the Association of African Universities held at Lovanium University—Kinshasa: Kinshasa: 19th–21st November 1969* (Khartoum, 1970), 26.
30. Mobutu's interview, reproduced in *Le Soir,* 11 June 1971, 3.
31. On the political significance of family metaphors under Mobutu's regime, see Michael Schatzberg, *Political Legitimacy in Middle Africa: Father, Family, Food* (Bloomington: Indiana University Press, 2001).
32. For a chronology of the deterioration of the relations between the student movement and the regime, and the progressive radicalization of the student demands, see P. Demunter, "Les relations entre le mouvement étudiant et le régime politique congolais: le colloque de Goma," *Etudes Africaines du CRISP* No. 126; and P. Demunter, "Analyse de la contestation estudiantine au Congo-Kinshasa—juin 1969—et ses séquelles," *Etudes Africaines du CRISP* No. 132.
33. *Le Furet,* 4 June 1971, 9.
34. P. Erny, *Sur les Sentiers de l'université: autobiographies d'étudiants zaïrois* (Paris, 1977), 104.
35. E. W. Lamy [J.-C. Willame], "Mort de Lovanium," *Les Temps Modernes* Vols. 301–302 (1971): 374.

Chapter 10

Revolution on the National Stage
Mexico, the PRI, and the Student Movement in 1968

Julia Sloan

Scholars of the 1960s generally view 1968 as the culmination of the global revolution that was that decade. In 1968 the dynamics of the post–World War II era, the realities of the Cold War, and the exigencies of governance and citizenship in a period of globalization coalesced into a groundswell of popular, oftentimes youthful protest in dozens of countries around the world. The target of these protests generally was authority, most commonly governmental, but also sometimes racial, gendered, and socioeconomic. The impact of these protests was felt socially, politically, culturally, and even diplomatically as countries from the developed to developing worlds weathered the unrest and navigated a new post-1968 normalcy.

The character of the 1968 revolts, however, was reflective of changes occurring globally since 1945. Populations and economies boomed. Popular access to education expanded. Bipolarity altered national, regional, and global politics and the nuclear arms race raised the stakes on each. Media, communications, and transportation eased and quickened the movement of people, products, ideas, and information from country to country. Corporate capitalism created global consumers of everything from soft drinks to music. Thus, the protestor in the streets in 1968 was typically a relatively affluent, educated (or in the process of being educated) young person who consumed the same news, entertainment, and commodities as his or her counterparts abroad. The result was a global ideology of protest.[1]

The manifestations of this ideology of protest in Mexico, however, were almost wholly national. The student movement that emerged in Mexico in 1968 reflected all of the global influences mentioned above, but had a profoundly homegrown character as well. As educated, middle-class nationalists who read Herbert Marcuse, cheered Che Guevara, and wore blue jeans and mini-skirts, the Mexican student protestors were products of post–World War II globalization.[2] Their most forceful and ultimately effective attacks on the legitimacy of the Mexican state, however, came not from foreign ideology, but rather from a critique of the core tenets of the dominant Mexican political narrative of revolutionary nationalism.

In the midst of and unquestionably influenced by the global tumult of the 1960s, the student movement and the government of President Gustavo Díaz Ordaz engaged in a battle for control of the contemporary meaning and future of the Mexican Revolution. The protesting students and the ruling Partido Revolucionario Institucional (PRI) had conflicting visions of what that future should be, but drew on the same history of revolutionary nationalism to justify their positions. They waged their battle in the public spaces, the parks, the plazas, and the streets of Mexico City as well as in the hearts and minds of its residents.

An Institutionalized Revolution

It might sound strange to say that in their struggle the students and the government of President Díaz Ordaz were fighting over the future of the Mexican Revolution since the Mexican Revolution lasted officially from 1910 to 1917 and had, thus, been over for five decades. However, the Mexican Revolution was very much alive and part of the political life of 1960s Mexico because of a concept called the institutionalized revolution. The issues that had motivated the fighting in 1910—effective suffrage, land redistribution, workers rights, and economic nationalism—were more than seven years of fighting could resolve. At the end of that fighting and with a new constitution granting important concessions to the major stakeholders, the Mexican Revolution ended and the country started down the path toward institutionalized revolution.

The institutionalized revolution is a political ideology rooted in the idea that Mexico can complete the unachieved goals of the Revolution through politics and government action rather than through violence. The redistribution of land to the peasant revolutionaries, for example, was a massive undertaking that, once agreed to politically, required significant government bureaucracy to accomplish. Similarly, the task of hiring and training the army of teachers needed to make good on the 1917 constitutional pledge of universal education took a generation to come to fruition. Similarly, Mexico waited until 1938 to assert its economic nationalism and expropriate its vast oil reserves from the foreign companies that had been exploiting them for decades. Thus, the institutionalized revolution was a process fueled by a commitment to revolutionary ideals and tempered by the realities of size, scope, and resources.

The institutionalized revolution, however, also became a political ideology in and of itself. The Revolution ushered in a new political elite whose power rested on its ongoing commitment to revolutionary ideals. This elite deeply embedded the institutionalized revolution into the nation's political discourses and culture. Meanwhile *"La Revolución"* itself was becoming a mythic part of the nation's political life. Undertaken by *voceros de la revolución,* or "insurgent literati," *La Revolución* represented an effort in the 1920s and 1930s to create a revolution with a capital *R* and involved the writing of official histories, the use of popular culture, and the manipulation of public space. It meant focusing public attention on a shared past and a collective or official memory that celebrated Mexico's cultural heritage and national achievements while deflecting attention away from the problems still apparent in Mexican society. The words of President Plutarco Elias Calles in 1934 in his Proclamation of Guadalajara perhaps sum up this effort best. Calles said: "We have to enter a new phase, one that I would call the period of psychological revolution: we must enter and conquer the minds of the children, the minds of the young, because they do and they must belong to *La Revolución*."[3] The youth of 1968 were among those whose minds had been "enter[ed] and conquer[ed] under the auspices of President Calles's "psychological revolution."

The symbols of the Revolution, as promulgated by the government, created a "set of social and moral values and a normative 'world view' of social life that had widespread acceptance throughout Mexican society and has served to legitimate the actions of the state." The belief that Mexico did indeed have an ongoing social revolution was the most important national myth.[4] The events of 1968 laid bare that myth and the sizeable distance between it and Mexican reality.

From Schoolyard Brawl to Social Protest Movement

The causes and trajectory of the Mexican student movement of 1968 lie in one basic circumstance, the absence of true and meaningful democracy in Mexico. Mexico under PRI leadership was a bureaucratic-authoritarian regime in which the party was critical to the maintenance of hegemony. The student movement began as a result of an act of police aggression and escalated in response to mounting governmental repression throughout the summer and fall of 1968. On 22 July, when riot police—the *granaderos*—entered a Mexico City campus to break up a fight between youths from rival schools, the events that would culminate in Mexico's most serious social protest movement in decades and most egregious act of state-sponsored violence in a generation were set in motion. The *granaderos'* presence on the campus was a violation of university autonomy, a closely held protection akin to academic freedom but extending to the physical space of the campus as well as the intellectual activities taking place therein. In addition to the violation, the *granaderos'* typically aggressive deportment during the altercation raised claims of police brutality. This seemingly inconsequential event marked the beginning of the movement that would take a still undetermined number of lives, shake the nation's political establishment to its core, and haunt a generation for decades.[5]

Protests over the *granaderos'* violation fell on deaf governmental ears and tensions escalated. The security forces' actions prompted a student demonstration in response to protest the brutality. The demonstration elicited a police presence and once again their efforts to control the scene proved heavy handed. Once again, the youth protested and once again the *granaderos* showed up. The students and the riot police became locked in a cycle where violence begot protest begot violence begot protest and so on.

This student agitation became an organized movement in the wake of a July 26th confrontation with police. Two separate student marches, both with official authorization, converged and turned rowdy in downtown Mexico City. The students broke windows, overturned cars, and clashed with the riot police called in to quell the unrest. Injuries and arrests resulted and eight people were left dead. The day's events served to intensify the scale, scope, and public attention paid to the youthful dissidence. Once again protests met with no governmental concessions or admissions of wrongdoing. After July 26th, the students organized themselves into a National Strike Council (CNH) and their agenda coalesced around the issue of police repression.[6]

The CNH developed a list of demands called the *pliego petitorio*. Their demands were: repeal of the Law of Social Dissolution, removal of Generals Cueto and Mendiolea from their positions as leaders of the *granaderos,* disbanding of the corps of *granaderos,* financial compensation for the victims of police violence and for the families of those killed by the police, governmental admission of guilt, and release of all political prisoners. These six demands remained the centerpiece of the student agenda for the remainder of their movement. While each of these six points related directly to the repression the youth had been suffering at the hands of government forces, each point individually and taken together amounted to a critique of the political status quo in Mexico.[7] The *pliego petitorio* was, in effect, a commentary on the absence of democracy in Mexico and the authoritarian nature of the Díaz Ordaz Administration. As such, it opened the door to a far more sweeping indictment of the president and the PRI, an indictment in keeping with much of the rhetoric of the 1960s circulating elsewhere in the world, but also with Mexico's own revolutionary nationalism.

Global Strategies, Local Resonance

While the youthful participants in the Mexican student movement protested against their government, they also contextualized the global unrest of 1968 according to Mexican political narratives. For example, signs and banners at student rallies often carried slogans in support of Ho Chi Minh and against what the Mexican youth characterized as United States' imperial aggression in Southeast Asia. Many Mexicans felt their own country had too been victimized by the United States and thus felt an affinity for the plight of the people of Vietnam. While the rank and file members of the student movement integrated such international issues into their demonstrations and rhetoric, they never made them their focus.[8]

The focus remained on the failings of the Mexican government. While the government attempted to delegitimize the student cause by alleging its association with foreign entities and its vulnerability to outside agitators, the students focused on Mexican issues and situated their movement and its demands within the narrative of revolutionary nationalism. If the students hoped to have any role in reforming their political system, however, they could not do it alone. Thus, the students took their message to the people, made their demands public, and pressured the government for dialogue by occupying several of the most literally and symbolically significant sites in Mexico City.[9]

No site was more significant that the Zocalo. In the heart of the Centro Historico in downtown Mexico City, the Zocalo is perhaps the site with the strongest literal and symbolic importance in the governance of the nation.[10] The students first occupied the Zocalo in July and occupied it several more times during August and September.

The Zocalo or "*gran tortilla*" as it is also known, has served, since the colonial period, as the locus of some of Mexico's most significant events. As poet Alfonso Chase wrote: "plazas are the palaces of the people." Further, Setha Low argues that the "plaza also provides a physical, social, and metaphorical space for public debate about governance, cultural identity and citizenship." The hotels, cafes, and high-end retail stores that front the Zocalo cater to an affluent, oftentimes foreign clientele and, as such, further reinforce the hierarchical structure of Mexican society spatially displayed on the plaza. Framed on two sides by the National Palace and the Cathedral, the Zocalo also houses the physical manifestations of governmental and ecclesiastical authority in Mexico. As such, the Zocalo has long been a place where those seeking to combat that authority have gathered. This central plaza has also, however, been a place where those seeking to reinforce their authority have come.[11] For example, every year during the Independence Day celebrations, the president performs the *Grito de Dolores* from a balcony overlooking the plaza and the tens of thousands of revelers gathered there.[12] In addition to this traditional event, in 1968 the Zocalo also played host to the opening of the Olympic Games. Thus, the Zocalo occupies a prominent place not just in Mexico's history, but also in its ongoing political discourse.

On certain occasions, however, the students purposely stayed out of the Zocalo. The most notable example was on Independence Day in 1968. As mentioned above, the president gave the *Grito de Dolores* from the Zocalo to symbolize Mexico's continued adherence to and celebration of the ideals of the Liberator, Padre Miguel Hidalgo. By staying out of the Zocalo that night, the students were implicitly rejecting the authority of President Díaz Ordaz. The CNH instead held its own festivities at the University City replete with the *grito* and attended by thousands of people.[13] Thus, the student movement in 1968 was not rejecting the message, just the messenger.

Díaz Ordaz however refused to respond to the nation's youth with anything other than repression. Their repeated requests and outright demands for a public dialogue with the president went unanswered. Díaz Ordaz was a conservative, paternalistic politician who believed the people should look up to him, respect him, and trust him. In his view, the students' repeated criticisms and insults signaled not only disrespect and disloyalty to him, but to Mexico as well. The president and his advisors dismissed the idea of a public dialogue with the students as ridiculous.[14] The students, however, believed it to be in keeping with the highest ideals of the institutionalized revolution.

Meanwhile, the student movement became more organized and more sophisticated in its manipulation of public space and its own public image. No student spectacle reflects this maturation of the movement more clearly than the Silent March. Held on 13 September, this demonstration included some 200,000 students and was, save the sound of thousands of pairs of marching feet, completely quiet. This impressive display of solidarity, discipline, and restraint marked the high point of the student movement.[15] Nonetheless, the prospect of thousands of youth pouring into the Zocalo alarmed those living and working in the Centro Historico. As a result, cafes emptied, stores closed, hotels locked their doors, and the crowds in the streets thinned in advance of the student marchers and the ubiquitous busloads of *granaderos* that were sure to follow. Thus, by virtue of their sheer numbers, the students controlled the public space and influenced the political discourse the moment they assembled en masse. The positive, virtually shocked media coverage of the Silent March signaled a shift in public perceptions of the student movement. The restraint of the individuals and the control of the leadership to successfully conduct such an event brought newfound respect to the student cause.[16]

While clearly of central importance, the Silent March was but one of many student demonstrations and the Zocalo was but one of several sites the students utilized in their assault on the Diaz Ordaz government. Chapultepec Park and the Museo de Antropologia y Historia were also favorite staging grounds for student marches. Oftentimes these marches proceeded down the Paseo de la Reforma, one of Mexico City's central thoroughfares and a key north-south artery. Thus, student marches along the Paseo created severe traffic congestion in the downtown area. Equally if not more troubling for the government than the traffic, however, were the buildings the students passed as they marched. Reforma was home to foreign-owned commercial outlets, banks, hotels, and the United States and Soviet embassies. Several other embassies were located in the immediate vicinity and Mexico City's central tourist area, the Zona Rosa adjoined the far side of the boulevard. Thus, student protests down this bustling street brought the government much unwanted attention and laid bare Mexico's political turmoil for international visitors and the nation's commercial and financial elite. As these marches proceeded onward, they typically moved in the direction of the Alameda Park. Moving through this congested section of the city also guaranteed the students an audience, but in this case, one predominantly Mexican and less affluent. The Alameda, for example, filled up in the afternoon with middle- and working-class Mexicans socializing and enjoying the respite from urban life that the park could provide.[17] These landmarks were historically and culturally relevant points of reference on the Mexico City landscape. The Museum, for example was a crowning achievement in the celebration of "native" Mexico in the post-revolutionary period and artistic chronicler of the institutionalized revolution, Diego Rivera immortalized the Alameda in his work. These locations, however, also were of contemporary importance due to their popularity with residents and the resultant levels of pedestrian and vehicular traffic. Thus, by occupying these areas, the students guaranteed themselves not only a sizeable impact, but also a symbolically significant one as well.

The most infamous of the sites student leaders frequently chose for *manifestaciones,* the Plaza de las Tres Culturas, sat adjacent to a sprawling middle-class housing complex known as Tlatelolco, three miles north of downtown Mexico City. The plaza took its name from Mexico's past and functioned as a tangible reminder of the nation's *mestizo* nature and heritage. The buildings surrounding the 100-square-yard plaza; high-rise apartments, government offices, a school, a church built during the colonial period, and Aztec ruins signified the nation's indigenous, Spanish, and Mexican cultures. The housing complex retained the zone's pre-conquest name. This large plaza, which colonial Spanish chroniclers had said dwarfed the plaza at Salamanca, had been the site of Hernan Cortes's final victory over the Aztec Empire. Despite the area's auspicious place in national history however, for modern Mexicans the name Tlatelolco is synonymous with tragedy.[18]

The roots of that tragedy lie in the confrontation between the students and the government over who would legitimately lay claim to the discourse of revolutionary nationalism and who would exert greater influence on its future course. While the student movement was actively engaged in critiquing Mexico's authoritarian governmental structure and thus implicitly trying to reform it, President Díaz Ordaz was not simply trying to maintain the status quo or prevent the reversal of President Calles's psychological revolution. Rather, the Díaz Ordaz Administration was itself aggressively manipulating revolutionary nationalism as well. Díaz Ordaz's concern, however, was less a domestic audience than an international one. Díaz Ordaz and the PRI over which he presided sought to move Mexico increasingly toward corporate capitalism as practiced in the first world. The PRI, since the 1940s had been increasingly repositioning itself to measure the ongoing success of its institutionalized revolution, not in higher pay for workers or land for peasants, but in infrastructure development, international trade, and technical innovation. The skyscraper—not the *ejido* was—became the new symbol of revolutionary nationalism.[19]

Most visibly in 1968, the Díaz Ordaz Administration was engaging in this effort through hosting the Olympic Games. Díaz Ordaz initially opposed Mexico's bid to host the Games, but upon being elected president became a principal architect of the Mexican Olympic agenda. The centerpiece of that agenda was to improve Mexico's international image by presenting a modern, progressive, stable nation to the world, a nation that was the product of the Revolution and institutionalized revolution.[20]

As such, Díaz Ordaz and Mexican Olympic organizers used symbolic spaces, images, and rhetoric in much the same way the students did. Obviously, the student movement and resultant police repression called the desired image of a modern, progressive, stable Mexico into question. Thus, in the days and weeks prior to the massacre at Tlatelolco, the Olympics and the student movement collided literally and figuratively in the public spaces of Mexico City and the minds of student leaders, government officials, and would-be Olympic visitors. The students declared publicly and repeatedly "we want a revolution, not Olympic Games!" Less enthusiastically, but also publicly, however, the student leadership pledged to do nothing to disrupt the games once they began.[21] Nonetheless, the Mexican government, the International Olympic Committee, and foreign countries sending athletes and spectators to Mexico expressed increasing concern throughout the fall of 1968 over the security of the games. Some such concerns were no doubt earnest given the proximity of Olympic venues to campuses, most prominently the location of the Olympic Stadium adjacent to the campus of the National Autonomous University of Mexico.[22]

The Olympic preparations exacerbated the already hostile relationship between the youth and their government because the games were emblematic of the grievances the students had with the ruling party. The athletes in the Olympic Village enjoyed a standard of living, at government expense, for the brief period of the games that was far better than millions of Mexicans would know in a lifetime. The PRI, not the people, would reap any potential benefits. Similarly, the Mexican Olympic Committee's efforts to portray Mexico as a progressive, modern nation were in sharp contrast to the Díaz Ordaz Administration's response to the youth protests. "Todo es posible en la paz," the Olympic slogan, seemed more than a bit disingenuous coming from a government that was shooting students in the streets of the capital city and holding hundreds of political prisoners in its jails.[23]

The student movement represented a public relations and security liability that threatened Mexico's significant political and economic investment in the games. Whether as a result of that liability or not, the student movement ended suddenly and tragically just 10 days before the start of the Olympic Games on 2 October at Tlatelolco when the government ordered the slaying of the people gathered there. The horror of this event forced student leaders not dead or jailed into exile and signaled the beginning of the end of the movement.[24] It forced the student activists out of the public spaces and the dialogue they had attempted to start with the government out of the national discourse. Meanwhile, the Olympics opened with fanfare, celebrations, the release of doves, and hearty congratulations to Mexico on a job well done. The Olympics, it seemed, signaled Mexico's arrival on the world stage and the success of the games became an enduring source of pride for the nation.

The massacre, however, signaled the end of the president's legitimacy and that of his party and his political style. The student movement, though brutally defeated, in fact, because of that brutal defeat, succeeded in ushering in an era of gradual political reform and democratic opening. It changed the way Mexicans thought about their government and in so doing changed the government itself. Gustavo Díaz Ordaz's successor, Luis Echeverría, moved back toward the PRI's populist roots and future presidents actively sought to incorporate intellectuals and members of the generation of 1968 into the state bureaucracy.[25] The collective popular voice raised in 1968, and temporarily silenced at Tlatelolco, returned stronger and louder to help set the course for the nation's future.

Though chronologically separated by just 10 days, the gulf between the Tlatelolco Massacre and the Olympic Games spanned a great distance. That distance was the difference between the promise and the reality of the Mexican Revolution institutionalized as it was in 1968. The use of revolutionary rhetoric, ideology, and symbolism by both the students and the government reflects the broad-based acceptance of revolutionary nationalism. Consensus as to what revolutionary nationalism should look like in 1968, however, was harder to come by. What *was* clear in 1968 is that while domestic politics were inexorably linked to international circumstances, ideologies, and agendas, the power of Mexican revolutionary nationalism was undeniable. The fight for control of the institutionalized revolution in 1968 was made more intense by the international climate, but was a product of uniquely Mexican realities.

Notes

1. See Paul Berman, *A Tale of Two Utopias: The Political Journey of the Generation of 1968* (New York: W.W. Norton & Company, 1996); David Caute, *The Year of the Barricades: A Journey Through 1968* (New York: Harper & Row Publishers, 1988); Dominick Cavallo, *A Fiction of the Past: The Sixties in American History* (New York: St. Martin's Press, 1999); Robert V. Daniels, *Year of the Heroic Guerrilla: World Revolution and Counterrevolution in 1968* (Cambridge, MA: Harvard University Press, 1989); Karen Dubinsky, et al. (eds.), *New World Coming: The Sixties and the Shaping of Global Consciousness* (Toronto: Between the Lines, 2009); Carol Fink, Phillip Gassert, and Detlef Junker, *1968 The World Transformed* (Washington, DC, and Cambridge: The German Historical Institute and Cambridge University Press, 1998); Greg Grandin, *The Last Colonial Massacre: Latin America in the Cold War* (Chicago: University of Chicago Press, 2004); Gilbert Joseph and Daniela Spenser (eds.), *In From the Cold: Latin America's New Encounters with the Cold War* (Durham: Duke University Press, 2008); George Katsiaficas, *The Imagination of the New Left: A Global Analysis of 1968* (Boston: South End Press, 1987); Martin Klimke and Joachim Scharloth (eds.), *1968 in Europe: A History of Protest and Activism,*

1956–1977 (New York: Palgrave Macmillan, 2008); Arthur Marwick, *The Sixties: Cultural Revolution in Britain, France, Italy, and the United States, c. 1958–1974* (Oxford: Oxford University Press, 1998); Eric Zolov, *Refried Elvis: The Rise of the Mexican Counterculture* (Berkeley: University of California Press, 1999).

2. Herbert Marcuse, *One-Dimensional Man: Studies in the Ideology of Advanced Industrial Society* (Boston: Beacon Press, 1964).

3. Thomas Benjamin, *La Revolución: Mexico's Great Revolution As Memory, Myth, and History* (Austin: University of Texas Press, 2000), 13–14, 20, 32, 37, 95–96, 99, 110, 148.

4. Ruth Berins Collier, "Popular Sector Incorporation and Political Supremacy: Regime Evolution in Brazil and Mexico," in Sylvia Ann Hewlett and Richard S. Weinert (eds.), *Brazil and Mexico: Patterns in Late Development* (Philadelphia: Institute for the Study of Human Issues, 1982), 58, 76.

5. The 22 July altercation is generally regarded as the start of the movement because a direct line of action can be drawn from it to the rapid and steady intensification of the crisis. It is worth noting however, that 22 July was not the first confrontation between students and the *granaderos* and that police on student violence had occurred at least as early as 6 July. For a chronological summary of the movement and its antecedent events, see Gilberto Guevara Niebla, *La democracia en la calle: Cronica del movimiento estudiantil mexicano* (Mexico City: Siglo XXI, 1988).

6. Ibid.

7. Elaine Carey, *Plaza of Sacrifices: Gender, Power, and Terror in 1968 Mexico* (Albuquerque: University of New Mexico Press, 2005), 54.

8. Virtually any source that depicts the student marches reveals this Mexican contextualization of international events. For example, see Elena Poniatowska, *Massacre in Mexico* (Columbia: University of Missouri, 1992).

9. Jonathan Kandell, "Mexico's Megalopolis," in Gilbert Joseph and Mark Szuchman (eds.), *I Saw a City Invincible: Urban Portraits of Latin America* (Wilmington: Scholarly Resources, 1995): 183–187.

10. Setha M. Low, *On the Plaza: The Politics of Public Space and Culture* (Austin: University of Texas Press, 2000), 113–114.

11. Ibid., xxi, 31–33, 119–120, 200.

12. For a discussion of the Independence Day celebrations, see William H. Beezley and David E. Lorey (eds.), *Viva Mexico! Viva La Independencia! Celebrations of September 16* (Wilmington, DE: Scholarly Resources, Inc., 2001).

13. Ibid.; Low (2000), 31–33, 113–120; Poniatowska (1992), 331.

14. On Diaz Ordaz, see Herbert Braun, "Protests of Engagement: Dignity, False Love, and Self-Love in Mexico during 1968," *Comparative Study of Society and History* (July 1997 v. 19 #1): 511–549; Enrique Krauze, *Mexico Biography of Power: A History of Modern Mexico, 1810–1996* (New York: Harper Collins Publishers, 1997): 678–737; Salvador Novo, *La Vida en Mexico en el Periodo Presidencial de Gustavo Diaz Ordaz*, 2 Vols. (Mexico City: Conaculta, 1998).

15. Ricardo Garibay, "El Movimiento Estudiantil: Crisis de Participacion," *Hoy* No. 1479 (28 September 1968): 13, 63.

16. Ibid.

17. "El Problema Agoniza," *Hoy* No. 1477 (14 September 1968): 51–54; Donald C. Hodges, *Mexican Anarchism After the Revolution* (Austin: University of Texas Press,

111–146); Ricardo Garibay, "El Movimiento Estudiantil: Crisis De Participacion," *Hoy* No. 1479 (28 September 1968): 13, 63.

18. Low (2000), 113–114; Mexico 68, Tlatelolco October 2, caja 3, exp. 6, 15, p 1–10, Ludlow, AGN.

19. See Jonathan Schlefer, *Palace Politics: How the Ruling Party Brought Crisis to Mexico* (Austin: University of Texas Press, 2008).

20. For Mexico's Olympic ambitions and accomplishments, see the Avery Brundage Collection. Published sources that provide analysis of Mexico's Olympic agenda and details about the games themselves include: Kevin B. Witherspoon, *Before the Eyes of the World: Mexico and the 1968 Olympic Games* (DeKalb: Northern Illinois University Press, 2008); Joseph L. Arbena, "Hosting the Summer Olympic Games: Mexico City, 1968," in Joseph L. Arbena and David G. LaFrance (eds.), *Sport in Latin America and the Caribbean* (Wilmington, DE: Scholarly Resources, Inc., 2002), 133–143.

21. "Upsurge and Massacre in Mexico, 1968. Part 1: The Youth Revolt," *Revolutionary Worker* No. 975 (27 September 1998): 1–6.

22. Brundage Collection, RS 26/20/37.

23. See Ibid. and Witherspoon (2008); Arbena (2002).

24. For information on the Tlatelolco Massacre, see Sergio Aguayo Quezada, *1968: Los Archivos De La Violencia* (Mexico City: Editorial Grijalbo, 1998); Raul Alvarez Garin, *La Estela De Tlatelolco: Una Reconstruccion Historica del Movimiento Estudiantil de 68* (Mexico City: Editorial Grijalbo, 1998); Rene Aviles Fabila, *El Gran Solitario De Palacio* (Mexico City: Distribuciones Fontamara, S.A., 1998); Julio Scherer Garcia and Carlos Monsivais, *Parte de Guerra Tlatelolco 1968: Documentos del general Marcelino Garcia Barragan. Los hechos y la historia* (Mexico City: Nuevo Siglo, Aguilar, 1999); "Upsurge and Massacre in Mexico, 1968: Part 1: The Youth Revolt," *RevolutionaryWorker* No. 975 (27 September 1998), Mexico Connect, http://www.mexconnect.com/mex_history/tlatelolco/tlatelolco1e.html; "Upsurge and Massacre in Mexico 1968: Part 2: Blood at Tlatelolco," *Revolutionary Worker* No 976 (4 October 1998), Mexico Connect, http://www.mexconnect.com/mex_/history/tlatelolco/tlatelolco2e.html.

25. Schlefler (2008); Jorge G. Castaneda, *Perpetuating Power: How Mexican Presidents Were Chosen* (New York: New Press, 2001).

Chapter 11

Student Activism and Strategic Identity

The Anti-Communist Student Action Front (KAMI) in West Java, Indonesia, 1965–1966

Stephanie Sapiie

This chapter examines the collective identity processes of the Anti-Communist Student Action Front (KAMI) formed in the aftermath of the 1 October 1965 coup in Jakarta. After a discussion of events just prior to and following the coup, I describe and analyze the collective identity processes at work in the formation of this organization. I regard collective identity as a movement's conceptualization of self, or its self-definition as a movement, which is in turn particularly dependent on cognitive frameworks of action, or action-frames utilized by movement participants.[1] A movement's self-definition also includes assumptions about boundaries delineated between allies of the movement and its adversaries.

KAMI protests relied on repertoires that replicated themes in nationalist history, particularly a narrative of young patriotism from the Indonesian revolution in 1945. KAMI activities and marches were deliberately nationalistic and emphasized students' patriotism and identity as opponents of political corruption and tyranny. This would not seem particularly remarkable except for the immense bloodshed and violence that formed the backdrop to KAMI actions. It is estimated that approximately 500,000 Indonesians lost their lives in the killings that took place throughout Central and East Java and Bali in violence carried out by vigilantes and the Army's Special Forces from November 1965 to June 1966. As the countryside ran awash in bodies that clogged rivers and rice-paddies, the urban streets of Jakarta were the scenes of student demonstrations orchestrated by army generals to provide legitimacy for a ruthless seizure of power.

KAMI's emergence was supported by the Indonesian armed forces (ABRI) who had recruited among Catholic and Muslim students at the prominent University of Indonesia amongst students opposed to Sukarno's initiatives in the Guided-Democracy period (1959–1963). KAMI helped accomplish ABRI's objectives of wrestling power from Sukarno during a period when Sukarno had dominated national politics through his own action fronts and his well-known ability to move an audience through speech and rhetoric. KAMI activities, marches, and demonstrations helped establish new symbols designed to supplant the period of Guided Democracy. Student protests relied on symbolic campaigns to demonstrate the ineptitude of Sukarno and his cabinet. Student protests pointedly cast blame at the presumptive culpability of the Indonesian Communist Party (PKI) in the alleged assassination of nine army generals and accused the PKI of sabotage and treachery.

KAMI's development as an action-front demonstrated how its identity shifted from networks of oppositional speech to actual organizations capable of public actions, symbolic protests and recruiting and socializing new members. KAMI's collective identity consisted of particular narratives and repertoires that emphasized student's duty and patriotic spirit. At times, actions resonated with themes from nationalist history, such as the duplication of the 1927 Oath of Youth that KAMI students used as a template to declare their intent to protect the country from the PKI. Other actions were designed to demonstrate a unified presence of youth in the streets. During an era when students routinely served as an audience for Sukarno's addresses, marches and public demonstrations around the capital city, KAMI rallies demonstrated a counter-narrative to Sukarno's power. The spectacle of military-directed student opposition followed years of army mistrust in civilian leaders. Student graffiti against "stupid [government] ministers" were not just immature slogans: they reflected the sentiment shared by both students and the army's young anti-communist officer-corps in civilian leaders' incompetence.

Analysis of KAMI demonstrations shows the symbiotic role between KAMI and ABRI. Students marched on the streets in brigade-style formation. Their marches often followed routes past the private homes of various ministers in Sukarno's cabinet en route to symbolic demonstrations at gas stations and the oil ministry, where students could protest rising gas prices. Student graffiti scrawled public insults against parliamentary ministers closely linked with Sukarno's policies of importing rice. KAMI's identity, however, was one that was not entirely under the army's control. It was also rooted in close identification with academics, many of whom were similarly opposed to Sukarno and his cabinet's economic and cultural policies.

The KAMI-sponsored seminar on the economy at the University of Indonesia ("The Leader, the Man and the Gun,") was a forum which served to legitimize the new regime as well as to signal a shift in political opportunities for formerly dissident economists exiled in the Guided Democracy period. Despite early support for the New Order, academic support for the New Order was short-lived, especially as the regime postponed long-awaited elections and electoral reforms.

The Coup

The events of 1 October 1965 marked the end of a year of rising tensions on college campuses throughout West Java. Politicized under Sukarno's Guided Democracy program, university students were opposed to the curriculum changes and indoctrination implied by new requirements imposed in 1963 under new directives known as the Political Manifesto, or MANIPOL USDEK. The growing number of student groups active with the PKI known as Communist Concentrations or (CGMI) on campus alarmed both traditionally Muslim and Christian students who clashed openly on campus with leftist students over screenings of foreign movies and imported science and economic textbooks. In the post-coup period, the army's role was further institutionalized in universities where the army had formed cooperative bodies with students, ostensibly to train them through marching-drills for military campaigns in West Irian and Malaysia.

The September 30 coup itself was triggered by the discovery of the bodies of six dead generals were discovered in a dry well at the Halim Air Force Base outside of Jakarta. A group of "left wing generals who called themselves the "Revolutionary Council"—all of whom were identified as top-ranking generals who led "luxurious lives," contrary to the national ideology—claimed responsibility for the coup, which was designed at eliminating counter-revolutionary elements in the armed forces. The ABRI's response to the coup was initiated by Suharto, who was one of two senior commanders still alive and who commanded the Army's Strategic Reserve (KOSTRAD) units who would assume the task of establishing control over Jakarta under martial law.[2]

Classes were disrupted in Jakarta by martial law. At ITB students continued to go to campus but stopped attending classes.[3] During this time, university student leaders met informally in private homes and in various organizational headquarters.[4] Mobilization of students in these early days came from those groups that had grievances during the pre-coup period. Confrontations between the Leftist Student Communist Concentrations (CGMI) and the Muslim Student Association (HMI) had become worse. In 1964, HMI had been deposed from the Presidium of the Indonesian Student Federation (PPMI), by CGMI (whose membership had grown in the 1963–1964 period to upward of 32,000,[5] and whose growth had come at the "expense" of HMI).

Among their immediate actions following the coup, the army attempted to mobilize anti-communist youth into an organized federation. This effort depended on demobilizing PKI groups, particularly its leaders and literary (LEKRA) and women's groups (GERMANI). KAMI's ability to act was a function of its collective identity developed under close army supervision. KAMI was closely allied to the army officers, who became the dominant forces in Indonesian politics over the next decade, including Suharto, who was heralded as bringing order to Jakarta in the wake of the coup; the former army chief of staff, General Nasution and Sarwo Edhie, paratrooper commander and an active KAMI promoter. KOSTRAD Commanders Idris and Sarwho as well as Intel members Ali Moertopo and Yoga Sugama acted as intermediaries with student groups at the University of Indonesia. ABRI also provided students with protection and supplies.[6] KAMI was central to the army's efforts to promote a "student opposition" to the

Indonesian Communist Party and against Sukarno. Contact between students at the University of Indonesia, such as with Soe hok-Gie and KODAM Colonel Witono, established the army's preference for what Gie recognized as students' "disciplined nature."

Reacting to the Coup: Youth Mobilization against PKI and PKI-Youth

Collective identity in the immediate post-coup period was constructed around a narrative of an anti-PKI sentiment and revenge seeking in the days immediately after 1 October.[7] Student groups reportedly

> used this as an opportunity not only to suppress leftist Communist opponents more effectively but also as a chance to recast the overlapping structures of the student/youth world in forms more suited to their minority interests. Success, of course, depended upon the coincidence of their limited objective with those of major national forces such as the Suharto group and other sympathetic elements.[8]

Vigilante acts were openly encouraged and students played prominent roles in the efforts to destroy the private home of PKI Chairman D.N. Aidit and ransack the PKI-youth headquarters.[9] In the days that followed the army sanctioned purges of communist-youth groups, closing their organizations on campus and rounding up members of the PKI's women's group (GERWANI) and members of its literary organizations, LEKRA.

Anti-PKI youth groups were mobilized outside Jakarta in the provincial capital of Central Java, Yogyakarta.[10] Anti-PKI youth also congregated "in groups on street corners" outside PKI headquarters in Solo.[11] In Yogya, brawls between PKI-youth and NU-sponsored youth groups took place, while in Bandung students held rallies at CGMI's headquarters the day after the big HMI rallies in Jakarta.[12] The rector of ITB reportedly issued orders forbidding students affiliated with any of the leftist organizations—CGMI, the PKI-youth group Pemuda Rakyat, and communist groups such as Lekra and Gerwani—from attending classes, seminars, borrowing books, or being physically present on campus.[13] At the Institute of Technology in Bandung, students formed night-watch contingents on campus to enforce these orders, and a battalion of students was ordered to assemble. Campus communication was interrupted by the closing down of the student radio station and the daily newspaper, *ITB News*.[14]

Initial opposition in Jakarta came from HMI and PMKRI, the Christian student organization.[15] HMI "urged its members to 'work closely to crush Gestapu ... and the September 30 movement organizationally, all communists and anyone however faintly sympathetic to either to its roots."[16] The PMKRI's parent party also had significant grievances with the Guided Democracy system (the Indonesian Christian party, PARKINDO, had been banned by General Nasution for not conforming to "retooling" of the political party system in 1960).[17] PMKRI, like HMI, had also been presidium members with significant grievances against CGMI. Compared to HMI it was much smaller, with a membership estimated at "several thousand" compared to HMI's nearly 100,000 members.[18]

Abdul Gaffur was a medical student and HMI member in 1965. He recalled HMI's grievances had begun "as early as July 5, 1960 … when the rector of University of Jember Prof. Utrech declared HMI was forbidden to meet. Only at state universities after 1960 was HMI active. HMI was up against other student groups like CGMI, GMNI and Germindo. Utrech's commands to destroy HMI lit the spark."[19]

After the coup, HMI was the most vocal advocate for a quick response.[20] A media frenzy accompanied the desire to purge and HMI members recalled "Pictures of the mutilated bodies of the slain generals were disseminated through newspapers and televisions accompanied by anti-communist propaganda from the army. For the first time in years open criticism of the PKI was legitimized, and … HMI was one of the first groups to exploit this opportunity."[21] Leaders of HMI and the Catholic student group (PMKRI) called for a united student front against these actions.[22] A number of other student groups joined in these events. Students recalled that HMI was the first to act. It was, as Roger Paget (1970) argues, best to act:

> HMI's … advantage in the fall of 1965 was clear innocence of any September 30 movement involvement … [and] freedom from political party strings. … This freedom which had served the group well in the aftermath of PRRI/Permesta … once again proved to be a special advantage in the post–October 1 period. HMI was not a federation or a front and therefore had no incriminating friends. It had great prominence nationally both as the enemy of PKI and a strong, relatively independent minded organization in its own right."[23]

Others soon followed HMI. The Muslim party, Nahdlatul Ulama, and its student youth groups issued a joint statement condemning the "coup" and the 30 September movement.[24]

In the first days after the coup, protests against the PKI were allowed, as were students' actions directed at ransacking and burning down the PKI Party's offices in Jakarta, PKI Chairman D.N. Aidit's house, the headquarters of the PKI-sponsored women's group Gerwani,[25] and SOBSI, the Federation of Labor.[26] HMI organized the first public protest on 5 October, demanding that the PKI be banned.[27] By the end of the first week of October, "HMI and other students demolished the headquarters of the PKI and the home of its first secretary, D.N. Aidit, while armed detachments of the Indonesian army looked on."[28] Paget's descriptions of this period suggest certain actions ("tracking down Communist leaders, sacking their houses, attacking the headquarters of various leftist organizations, including the PPMI building in Jakarta") were carried out by "masses of youth" in "partially spontaneous outbursts."[29]

Paget (1970) described these events as evidence of intensifying "contacts and a mutually beneficial relationship developing between "certain military leaders" and "young people."[30] The military did not immediately restrict all youth groups because, as Vince Boudreau (2005) argued, the army required local youth groups to help their efforts to "organize social support against President Sukarno. ABRI agents worked closely with students and rural Islamic institutions to build anti-communist groups."[31]

Youth, in particular, were described as useful to the military because they could take part in actions that would not identify perpetrators with ABRI agents. Youth

> "Provided a corps of vigilantes for the performance of some tasks such as nighttime interrogations and seizures of property, deemed by officers to be inappropriate activities for their own troops. The army, in part, gave the students much needed protection. ... This political symbiosis came to be called the "partnership"; it was at the core of the movement which crushed the PKI and eventually displaced Sukarno and his guided democracy system."

Counter-mobilization, like the kind undertaken by pro-Sukarno group GMNI, were heavily symbolic, stressing their group's patriotism and calls for "civic clean-up campaigns, national and regional conferences and mass-initiations."[32] To emphasize their patriotism, the youth group affiliated with Sukarno's party, the PNI, pledged their loyalty and allegiance to the president. The emphasis on GMNI's rallies was likely to demonstrate that Sukarno could also quickly mobilize youth in his support.[33]

KAMI's Collective Identity

KAMI activities and marches were deliberately nationalistic and played on sentiments and actions that were associated with themes from the Indonesian revolution. Its oppositional consciousness, at first explicitly anti-communist, also changed through episodes of contention. KAMI marches and demonstrations helped legitimize the Army's consolidation of power by establishing a narrative that the military was capable of restoring order and economic health. KAMI marches were designed to undermine civilian power in the parliament and to question the legitimacy of Sukarno, who called for "calm" in the days following the coup. KAMI marches, seminars, and demonstrations helped the military demonstrate that it was capable of tackling problems that civilian leaders had long neglected.

While there was an identifiable element of KAMI that was evident through its street marches and protests, KAMI became a movement that demanded more than simply a ban on the PKI. By late January 1966, the organization was committed to the articulation of ideas of sweeping reform, to removing ministers from Sukarno's cabinet, and to stabilizing inflation and reorienting the Indonesian economy toward integration in the global economy.[34]

To coincide with the commemorations of the 29 October "Oath of Youth" day, KAMI was officially founded as a "federation" with "territorial level of command and organization."[35] Students asserted that they were essentially committed to "stronger action" against the PKI and its mass organizations, "newspapers," and ideology.[36] They also stated that they were "completely and unreservedly behind H.B. the President/Supreme Commander of the Armed Forces/Great Leader of the Revolution Bung Karno," who was still president, although in name only.

These actions provide important clues to how KAMI would act. First, they stood behind all ABRI objectives. Second, KAMI did not outwardly articulate any of the grievances against Sukarno until late January 1966. This reflected the fact that Sukarno was nominally in charge during this period. However, it also demonstrated that KAMI was controlled by the army. The particular way that KAMI framed its actions, as pledges or pleas to the army to carry out their demands while stating their sincerity, demonstrated the subordination of KAMI to the army's directives.

By January 1966, KAMI's street protests and demonstrations were evidence of an expansion of themes to KAMI's earlier "anti-PKI" identity to include concern for economic matters[37] as well as criticism of Sukarno.[38] Student marches were composed almost entirely of students and professors, with protests targeted at a variety of strategic sites: the homes of government ministers in the elite neighborhoods of Jakarta like Menteng, or at government ministries. When students did assemble outside the private homes of cabinet ministers, they were greeted without hostility.[39]

Student marches began at the University of Indonesia with students and faculty "leaving the university" in the morning[40] in long columns or "lines … emulating military discipline" often in "silence." While professors and students marched together,[41] students deferred to their professors, who led the way.[42] Students shouted slogans, such as "DESTROY THE PKI, HANG INDECISIVE MINISTERS, BRING DOWN THE PRICE OF GAS!"[43] The KAMI marches were regimented walks through Jakarta streets to specific locations.[44] ABRI soldiers helped stop traffic when it was necessary and who provided students with water, snacks, and trips back to campus when people became too tired.[45]

Occasionally, students blocked traffic by sitting down and singing songs or chanting slogans. One such chant went as follows:

Who has never been on a bus?

Who wants to raise the price of gas?

Who likes making empty promises?

Who thinks everyone should eat only corn?

Who are the ones who like to throw money around?

Who saves our national wealth in overseas accounts?

MINISTERS

Do you want to be ruled by people like this?[46]

From 10 to 15 January, students marched daily from the campus in central Jakarta to various locations, including parliament (13 January 1966), the Hotel Indonesia (12 January 1966), the old Jakarta neighborhood of Kota near the docks (14 January 1966), the Presidential Palace (10 January 1966), and the Oil Ministry Pertamina (11 January 1966). According to one account, "students marched down Jakarta's main thoroughfares to outside the presidential palace; we sat down on the ground facing the [Cakrabirawa Regiment guarding the palace] and shouted 'ABRI Live!'"[47]

One of the first street protests KAMI sponsored took place on 10 January 1966 following the increase in gas fares from 4 to 250Rp per liter.[48] The demonstration took two days to coordinate and began at the University of Indonesia's medical school at the campus located in the Salemba area of Jakarta. The march started early with students congregating by eight o'clock in the morning.[49] One observer estimated that more than 200 students took part in these marches.[50]

Participating in the KAMI marches heightened students' awareness of their own unique identity as both provocateurs and moral opponents to a regime entrenched in corruption and scandal.[51] Students wanted to be seen by the people[52]: "The people will see and they will know that students don't just live in an ivory tower. I was the architect of this 'Long March,' although in fact I didn't do that much. I wanted students to come and join us, to boycott class and forget about their lectures for a day. ... It's important to show the people that the university is patriotic."[53]

With the exception of protests outside the Presidential Palace, the Oil Ministry, and the Ministry of Foreign Affairs, students' actions were largely against the main ministers within Sukarno's administration: Chaerul Saleh, the coordinating minister for economic affairs, and Subandrio, the minister of foreign affairs.

During these protests, students chanted,

Near or far, two hundred [referring to the new bus fares]

Lower the price of gas

DPR banci (Parliament is powerless)

[Government] Ministers are stupid

Chaerul is a stupid minister[54]

The KAMI repertoire often involved the written word either through chants like the one above or expressed through "hit-and-run" tactics such as graffiti written in ink or with colored felt-tip pens.[55] As an indication of the lawlessness of the early days of KAMI protests in January 1966, the walls of government buildings, the parliament, and fence posts along the gates outside parliament were filled with angry scribbles. "We put up our posters, wildly yelling in the streets 'STOP IMPORTING WIVES; ONE MINISTER, ONE WIFE, CHAERUL SALEH IS STUPID,' all of this before 10:00 clock."[56]

Chaerul Saleh was coordinating minister for the economy and his decision to raise bus fares was one that particularly angered students. As Harsjah Bachtiar noted,

> the relationship between the students and the central government was aggravated by [Saleh's actions], who attempted to bring some order to the wide discrepancy between official and black-market prices by increasing the price of gasoline from 4 to 250 Rp a liter. ... Most of the students, who were already fighting a frantic struggle against the high cost of living in the urban centers, suffered severely from the increase in the price of gasoline.[57]

Anger over gas prices was no doubt behind the sequence of protests in which students seized gas stations in the old Jakarta neighborhood of Kota.[58]

This event, unlike the KAMI marches and graffiti, did not spread throughout the city, suggesting, "it was an isolated incident rather than the development of a new form of protest."[59] Its meaning was to protest the Coordinating Minister for Economic Affairs Chaerul Saleh's "clumsy" decision to increase fares from 4Rp to 250 Rp.[60] "There, students [began] to block the entrances to the gas stations. I started to think that students could be perceived negatively by the public. The army could also come down on us if we blocked the gas stations. It was a moot point it turned out, the plan to block the gas stations didn't happen that day."[61]

The blocking of gas stations was not repeated; whether this was because students were ordered not to repeat this action is unclear. Student marches did not return, at any rate, to the Kota neighborhood of Jakarta. Instead, the following day student marches were directed toward the Bank of Indonesia where "students were on top of cars and borrowed bikes to form barricades. They were told not to; eventually the army threw tear gas, apologizing first to the students ... from the looks of it, the military supports the students."[62] The protests remained good-humored throughout: "We continued along, blocking traffic when we could. One car was refusing to stop, there was almost an accident. The driver of the car, an important person, got out and started to yell, 'let us pass.' There was no commando in sight, just about 15 students. We let him through."[63]

Despite student protests against "stupid ministers," there was not much animosity between students and ministers. From Gie's journal we know that students were often greeted warmly "with smiles" or "waves" from ministers or were offered rides by them[64]:

> In front of Ruslan Abdulgani's house we yelled "long live Mr. Ruslan!!"—he had a good name among students … he had once joined Sjahrir in the PSI, but then joined the PNI. … Outside the buildings of Parliament, we sat down on its steps in our dirty clothes … students started scribbling on the walls "Ministers Throw Money Around," "Destroy the PKI," "Ministers, don't only find out the hard way." … Indeed a lot of slogans were dirty, but this was the voice of the people. This is what people saw all the time: opportunistic politicians and empty slogans.[65]

Recruitment to KAMI

By the end of January the student movement had expanded beyond its initial organization and participants. Not only had students developed a series of repertoires that became affiliated with the KAMI identity, these were also used by new groups eager to exploit or continue KAMI's popularity. Even groups opposed to KAMI utilized the public poster campaigns and graffiti that KAMI first utilized.

KAMI's activities and reputation created new incentives for new members who were eager to join the action-front in January 1966. As pro-Sukarno youth converged on Jakarta's streets in late January, KAMI began to expand beyond its original size and composition of college students. By the end of January 1966 it changed from a protest movement involving only college students to one increasingly joined by high school–age youths. The entry into activism by a much larger and less disciplined contingent of youth shows the scripted nature of the first protests organized by KAMI.

At the end of January 1966, KAMI protests were attended by more than simply KAMI-organized groups; about 3000 high school students formed new action fronts such as KAPPI (Kesatuan Aksi Pemuda Pelajar Indonesia). 79 instructors from universities in Bandung[66] formed the action front KASI (Kesatuan Aksi Sarjana Indonesia).[67] KASI soon expanded beyond its Bandung contingent to include KASI groups at universities across Jakarta including of about 100 University of Indonesia instructors and their graduates.[68]

From the end of January through March 1966, a period when KAMI was in fact banned and classes resumed, new battle lines were drawn between groups who had begun with the first organized actions of KAMI protests in January and those who became involved as the movement developed in late January. These groups included KAPPI and KASI. When KAMI students returned to classes for a week in February, KAPPI students "staged an impressive demonstration in support [of KAMI] at the University of Indonesia."[69]

While initial protests in January 1966 had focused on early demands of KAMI called the "TRITURA" or "Three Peoples' Demands,"[70] KAMI actions after February focused more specifically on Sukarno and his cabinet ministers. Student groups began to also fight each other and battle the palace guards.[71] KAMI students increasingly sought to defend their movement in the context of actions that had occurred in the past: the counter-revolutionary actions of the coup leaders and the PKI that were supposedly benefiting from the unrest.[72]

By March 1966, KAMI had helped create and legitimize a new role for the student movement. KAMI-affiliated newspapers, journals, art exhibitions, and student-initiated radio stations also created a new sense of energy on campus that appealed to a wide range of students eager to be part of the new movement. In this way, KAMI generated a new interest in the student activism that appealed to students' personal identities and creative inclinations.[73] Thus, while students' antagonism to Communist Concentration CGMI had created in the pre-coup period an initial interest in joining KAMI, many students remained involved in the KAMI "movement" long after KAMI had ceased to function for its participatory culture and student-driven activities, newspapers and journals.

Having been a member of KAMI was also to acquire, for a short while, a new sense of status that conferred upon students in the "New Order" positions of some political prominence. Therefore, KAMI created both a series of short-term opportunities to act—initially based on its anti-communist credentials—as well as longer-term commitments among activists who took part in KAMI marches and meetings. While initially KAMI was formed to demand a ban on the PKI, in the long-term, KAMI mobilization created new opportunities for the student movement as a whole and led to the creation of a student movement that attached prestige and status to membership and participation in student demonstrations and mobilization.

Notes

1. I understand social movements as built out of shared social solidarities, strategies and grievances. My conceptualization of social movements is shaped by Bert Klandermans (1992): For collective action to be accomplished "a group must first define itself as a group, and its members must develop shared views of the social environment, shared goals and shared opinions about the possibilities and limits of collective action." See Bert Klandermans, "The Social Construction of Protest and Multi organizational Fields," in Aldon D. Morris and Carol McClurg, *Frontiers of Social Movement Theory* (New Haven: Yale University Press, 1992), 77–103 and Verta

Taylor and Nella Van Dyke, "'Get Up, Stand Up': Tactical Repertoires of Social Movements," *Blackwell Companion to Social Movements.* Eds. David A. Snow, Sarah A. Soule and Hanspeter Kriesi. (Oxford, UK: Wiley-Blackwell, 2004), 262–293. Understanding social movements as narratives is part of my conceptualization and I draw on the insights of Francesca Polletta's *It was Like a Fever: Story Telling, Protest and Politics* (Chicago: University of Chicago Press, 2006).

2. The coup has been the subject of much academic analysis. Among the first to present analysis of the events were two American academics, Benedict Anderson and Ruth McVey, *A Preliminary Analysis of the October 1, 1965 Coup in Indonesia,* Modern Indonesia Project (Ithaca, NY: Cornell University Press, 1971), in a view which would become known as the "Cornell Thesis." Anderson and McVey's 1971 study was a frank assessment of the data available in the days and months immediately following the coup and their analysis includes, radio transmissions, interviews with key actors, and summaries of newspaper articles around the event. Analysis of ABRI's role in the counter-coup that followed the September 30 killings is discussed in ample detail in Harold Crouch's 1978 classic *The Army and Politics in Indonesia* (Jakarta: Equinox Publishing 2007).

3. Noted Abu Rizal Bakrie, "After the 30th of September we stopped coming to classes; we went only for attendance and then left. Our parents were a little concerned, when would we have time for classes if we were always demonstrating?" See Hasyrul Moechtar, *Mereka Dari Bandung: Pergerakan Mahasiswa Bandung, 1960–1967* (London: Alumni, 1998), 484.

4. Roger Paget, "Youth and the Wane of Sukarno's Government," PhD dissertation, Cornell University, 1970, 219.

5. Harja W. Bachtiar, "1967: Indonesian Students and their Political Activities," paper presented at the Conference on "Students and Politics" sponsored by the Center for International Affairs, Harvard University and the University of Puerto Rico, Condado Beach Hotel, San Juan Puerto Rico, 27–31 March 1967, 33.

6. Bachtiar (1967).

7. This fit with the general "design of the Army" response: to suppress reporting of army and aircraft units' involvement in the coup and to place all blame on the PKI. Anderson and McVey note that this position "had the full support of the major religious political parties," and by implication, their youth groups. Anderson and McVey (1971), 56.

8. Paget (1970), 222.

9. Aidit had been picked up in the early morning hours of the coup, along with Sukarno and Airforce Colonel Omar Dhani, to establish, in varying ways, the culpability of the PKI in the killings of the generals. In the hours after Suharto declared a counter-coup, Aidit and Dhani traveled by plane to Central Java and they were executed in November.

10. Anderson and McVey (1971), 57.

11. Anderson and McVey (1971), 57.

12. Moechtar (1998), 82.

13. Fred Hehuwat interviewed in ibid., 409

14. Moechtar (1998), 83.

15. The early student reaction to the crisis evolved from the first anti-PKI incidents, which in themselves merely amounted to an extension of the pre-coup rivalry be-

tween the HMI and the principal communist student organization CGMI; see Stephen A. Douglas, *Political Socialization and Student Activism in Indonesia* (Urbana: University of Illinois Press, 1970), 155.

16. Paget (1970), 204.

17. Under the guidelines of the commission in charge of "retooling" the political parties, four requirements were put into place. These were: (1) an ideological requirement, that all political parties must accept and defend the official state ideology, Pancasila; (2) that parties must have an all-Indonesia character and have no foreign members or foreign chairmen; (3) that parties must have branches in at least six provinces and in every province they must have branches in at least 25 percent of regencies; and (4) that every party must have a total of 150,000 card-carrying members, while every branch must have at least 50 members sanctioned by the police. See Ruslan Abdulgani, *Nationalism, Revolution and Guided Democracy in Indonesia: Four Lectures* (Clayton, Victoria: Center of Southeast Asian Studies, Monash University, 1973), 49. Christian parties in Indonesia had neither the strength nor numbers to meet these requirements, despite the fact that there had been both many Catholic parties and protestant parties since the 1945 period. These parties would merge as PARKINDO in 1945. Noted Webb (1978), "Forming a political party was hard work. Protestants did not have the numbers ... nor enough people of ability to sit in cabinets. Other parties had already cadres of their own." See Rev. Father R.A.F Paul Webb, *Indonesian Christians and the Political Parties,* South East Asian Monograph Series, No. 2(North Queensland, Townsville: James Cook University, 1978), 48.

18. Bachtiar (1967) and Paget (1970).

19. *HMI: 50 Years Serving the Republic* (1997): 62.

20. "The first spark of explosion occurred on October 5, 1965 when the Islamic Student's Association (HMI) organized and successfully staged a fairly sizeable student rally at which President Sukarno was urged to ban the PKI"; see Douglas (1970), 154.

21. Douglas (1970), 155.

22. Subchan Z.E., vice chairman of the NU, and Harry Tjan, secretary of the Catholic Party.

23. Paget (1970), 203.

24. Paget (1970), 197.

25. Gerwani and the PKI-youth regiment Pemuda Rakyat were responsible for (or at least held responsible for) the killings at Halim Air Force Base. Anderson and McVey report that their participation was predicated on orders from Army officials who told the youth (some as young as thirteen and fifteen) that the arrests were of enemies of the president. The youth were not told the identity of those they killed. See Anderson and McVey (1971), 21–22, where they write "it is evident that these youths and girls were brought in the act entirely without their previous knowledge of what was [to follow] ... the motive for drawing in the Gerwani and the Pemuda Rakyat was to incriminate and compromise the PKI."

26. See Bachtiar (1967), 191.

27. Douglas (1970), 154.

28. Ibid., 155.

29. Paget (1970), 180.

30. Douglas (1970), 161.

31. Vincent Boudreau, *Resisting Dictatorship: Repression and Protest in Southeast Asia* (New York: Cambridge University Press, 2005), 104.

32. Paget (1970), 197.

33. Ibid., 197–198.

34. In October, KAMI gave no indication that it supported economic reforms, only that it supported "aggressive action" against the PKI and "counter-revolutionary" elements. And yet, writes Paget, there were clues that suggested an emerging partnership: "Students also gave important recognition to the army leaders and 'a commitment to work with them—not only in the task of crushing the September 30 Movement but in other spheres as well"; see Paget (1970), 52.

35. "In each branch formation the power structure more or less duplicated the national level"; see Paget (1970), 242. As Paget acknowledges, "neither the cohesiveness nor the territorial levels ever really materialized, and KAMI nationally remained loosely federative."

36. Paget (1970), 44; KAMI called to "ban and dissolve all political parties and massorganizations that were in any way affiliated with the PKI or the Left … the permanent cessation of all implicated newspapers and magazines, such as *Harian Rakyat, Warta Bakhti, Bintang Timure, Kebudajan Baru, Ekonomi Nasional, Gelora Indonesia,* etc., and confiscation by the state of all the possessions of these organizations and elements, to purge counterrevolutionary types from all of the top governmental institutions of the state and from the student/youth federations: Front Pemuda, PPMI and MMI."

37. Noted Gie in his diary, "[Col. Witono's] told he thinks that the opponents of the PKI should stick to identifying with economic issues. If people get involved in a prolonged struggle, it will be chaos. 'It is better to have students involved in the protests,' he told me. 'Students are organized and disciplined; we can take instruction. And more to the point, if ABRI sides with suffering people in the street carrying bayonets… [it could get out of control].'" See Gie's diary entry, 7 January 1966, *Catatan Seorang Demonstran* (also quoted in John Maxwell's 2001 biography of Soe Hok-Gie, *Pergulatan Intelektual Muda Melawan Tirani* [*A Biography of a Young Indonesian Intellectual Opposed to Tyranny*], (Jakarta, Indonesia: PT Utama Grafiti, 2001), 124.

38. KAMI's first task was to issue "Three Demands of the Indonesian People," or TRITURA. These demands included: (1) to dissolve the PKI, (2) to replace the existing cabinet, and (3) to lower the price of goods. KAMI also called on students to "boycott classes" and "to protest the higher transportation fares"; Douglas (1970).

39. Gie noted, "We stood outside of [Education Minister] Prijono's house and yelled 'Hang Indecisive Ministers.' He smiled when he saw us and waved his hand." Gie (1983), 136.

40. We know from Gie's writings that marches left between 9:00 and 10:00 in the morning and that they left on time, as Gie arrived late one morning and worried he would not be accommodated (he was).

41. The literature and psychology students marched together; Gie (1983), 136.

42. From ibid. entry for11 January 1966: "On Tuesday, the Long-March on Salemba [Road] began. About fifty people attended. Professor Sutjipto led us. I was about 5 minutes late getting there, but I managed to still be accommodated."

43. Gie (1983), 136.

44. Among locations students marched to were the parliament, the Oil Ministry, Senayan sports stadium, and the private houses of prominent politicians and cabinet ministers; Gie (1983).
45. Ibid.
46. Ibid., entry for 15 January 1966.
47. Ibid. entry for 10 January 1966; see also his version of events in *Notes of a Demonstrator*, 152.
48. *News and Views* No. 80 (30 November 1965).
49. Gie (1983).
50. This figure represented a very small number. The entire population of the University of Indonesia was over 10,000 students.
51. Gie's observations suggest how students who were part of these marches saw themselves. While Gie was aware that he was privileged, he did not see himself as "rich." As Gie noted, "near the Jakarta by-pass I met rich students in cars of their own. They drove by us. I was mad at them. I yelled at them (I must have sounded hysterical)." The marches also, in his opinion, would demonstrate to the Indonesian people students' sincerity and desire to help.
52. This was not a concern articulated by students in the nationalist/republican era (who wanted to lead the people).
53. Gie (1983).
54. Ibid., 131.
55. Hank Johnston, "Talking the Walk: Speech Acts and Resistance in Authoritarian Regimes," *Repression and Mobilization,* Eds. Christian Davenport, Hank Johnston and Carol Mueller. Social Movements, Protest and Contention Series, Vol. 21. (Minneapolis: University of Minnesota Press, 2005): 77–103.
56. Gie (1983), 136–137.
57. Bachtiar (1967), 35.
58. Douglas (1970).
59. Bachtiar (1967), 35.
60. Ibid.
61. Gie (1983), 145–146.
62. Ibid., 132.
63. Ibid., 136.
64. Notes Gie, "From [Bank Indonesia] they went to Harmoni, in fact, some got a ride from a minister's car ... what did the army do? Nothing, it stayed under control"; ibid., 132–133.
65. Ibid., 136.
66. Moechtar (1998), 160.
67. KASI members were instructors from ITB, UNPAD, IKIP (the teachers' training college) and the Catholic University Parahyangan; Ibid., 160.
68. Bachtiar (1967). 50.
69. Ibid., 51, says that this event became known as the "'KAMI-KAPPI' rendezvous."
70. The demands were: (1) banning the PKI, (2) lowering prices, and (3) changing Sukarno's cabinet. See Douglas (1970) and Bachtiar (1967). The inclusion of groups like KASI in late February brought into the KAMI protests an older group of activists who, unlike KAPPI (the high school student contingent of KAMI), preferred a less direct and spontaneous role for action.

71. Thugs and gangsters were used to infiltrate the Sukarno Regiments and they were not interested in peaceful protests Gie (1983), 162.
72. This was a complaint made by both army leaders and Sukarno—both groups who clearly had different interests in the student movement's presence on Jakarta streets.
73. Which Douglas (1970) has argued found little outlet in the pre-1965 campuses, so lacking were they in extra-curricular activities.

Chapter 12

Putting up a United Front
MAN in the Rebellious Sixties

Erwin S. Fernandez

While in Rome, Claro M. Recto, the vanguard of the Filipino nationalist movement, died on 2 October 1960. His untimely passing signaled the end of the
1950s during which he figured prominently for challenging the pro-American-
ism of Presidents Elpidio Quirino and Ramón Magsaysay by advocating an independent foreign policy, a self-reliant economy geared toward industrialization,
and a sovereign nation free from iniquitous provisions of Philippine–US military
bases treaty. Four days after his death, Philippine Ambassador to London León
María Guerrero spoke before the Manila Rotary Club to pay his last respect to
his mentor and friend. In a splendid delivery with his baritone voice, he correctly
pointed out Recto's pivotal role in the development of what seemed to him the
drama called Filipino nationalism. Wanting to anticipate the next act, now that
Recto was dead, he asked: "What turn of the plot is to be expected? What new
protagonist is to appear upon the stage?"[1]

If Recto's death marked the closing of a scene in Philippine nationalism,
it was also the beginning of another by new protagonists claiming to fill the
vacuum and all proclaiming to be heirs to his legacy. The Movement for the Advancement of Nationalism (MAN) arose out of a desire to resurrect Rectonian
nationalism from its momentary slumber and unify all progressive forces in the
Philippines at a time of crisis in the 1960s. Indeed, the 1960s represents a turbulent era when the confluence of various forces of dissent, often with students
leading the way, surfaced worldwide. The era has been characterized often as the
culmination of resistance directed against the conservatism of the preceding decade. Despite the widespread resistance, each society responded uniquely to the
circumstances they found themselves in. To understand the 1960s in the Philippines, it is necessary to look into the internal processes as well as the external
developments that the main actors reacted to against the backdrop of Philippine
society.[2]

This chapter examines the history of the Philippine Left, particularly the
dynamics in the organization and dissolution of MAN from 1966 to 1971. The
first section deals with the factors leading to the organization of MAN. The next

section discusses contending claims about its creation and the basic principles the group professed. After the split in the communist movement, MAN had to contend with two opposing forces each wanting to get the upper hand. The next two sections look at the vicissitudes of MAN amid these confrontations and contradictions, and its failures and successes until its dissolution. The conclusion assesses the significance of MAN in the context of the history of the Philippine Left.

Magsaysay to Marcos: A Nation in Search of an Alternative

The history of post-war Philippines is a history of a nation in search of an alternative to a corrupt and manipulated society.

In the 1950s it was Recto who articulated nationalism as the way out of this neocolonial condition that Magsaysay misunderstood, thus becoming its defender. Carlos P. García, who assumed the presidency after Magsaysay's death and was also elected to the same position, recognized the validity of Recto's ideas. He launched the "Filipino First" policy to promote national industrialization, earning him enemies from local and foreign quarters.[3]

But the CIA-funded election of Diosdado Macapagal reversed the gains of the policy. He lifted exchange controls, ended import controls, and devaluated the Philippine peso. The net effect was immediate and complete: decontrol allowed the free entry of US-made goods, crippling the Philippine manufacturing sector. Unrestricted flow of imports coupled with the remittance of profits siphoned off the foreign exchange reserves, plunging the Philippines into a debt trap.[4]

Closely monitoring the decontrol measures as they aggravated the plight of laborers, local business, and peasants, the Partido Komunista ng Pilipinas (PKP, Communist Party of the Philippines), which had directed the Huk insurgency in Central Luzon, stepped up its mass actions. It initiated the formation of Lapiang Manggagawa (LM, Labor Party) in early 1963, and the Malayang Samahang Magsasaka (MASAKA, Free Union of Peasants) and Kabataang Makabayan (KM, Nationalist Youth) in 1964. These front organizations spearheaded demonstrations in protest of the Laurel-Langley Agreement and the parity awakening the nationalism and anti-Americanism in the country. The criminal jurisdiction issue in the US military bases stimulated the resurgence of anti-American feelings when American soldiers shot to death two Filipinos in two separate incidents at the bases.[5]

Although Macapagal agreed to send an engineering battalion to Vietnam to appease the US, the latter supported Ferdinand E. Marcos who won the election. While in opposition, Marcos was against Philippine participation in the

Vietnam War. Now in power, Marcos endorsed it and got his wish to send a Philippine contingent to Vietnam. Philippine participation in Vietnam added fuel to the strident nationalist, anti-American, and anti-war sentiment of the more militant sectors of the Philippine Left. A huge student rally led by the KM and workers was held in front of the US embassy and at the Manila Hotel where US President Lyndon B. Johnson and other heads of states were billeted for the October 1966 summit meeting. Accused of being communist inspired, the student demonstrators were severely beaten by the police, which led to a congressional investigation. The KM gathered an assembly to condemn police brutality in November, the same month that an idea was conceived to unify all progressive forces in one movement.[6]

Birth of Unity

As to who initiated MAN, there were three claims. The PKP, one source said, "instigated" its creation. Jose Maria Sison claimed that he "initiated" its formation as the chief liaison of mass organizations like the KM and LM. It seems that the two versions could be reconciled since Sison was a member of the PKP's Executive Committee. It becomes problematic when Sison tries to repudiate his PKP connection more in the spirit of revisionism than historical accuracy. Renato Constantino mentioned a small informal group that included himself and Senator Lorenzo Tañada, Recto's vice presidential candidate in the 1957 election and head of the Citizens Party, which discussed the need to revive the nationalist crusade. He was said to have been instrumental in the idea behind MAN, which was to be a united front of all nationalists from the various sectors of Philippine society. MAN, based on three accounts, was not the initiative of one but a meeting of minds of a select group of people, mainly the leading lights of the nationalist movement at that time.[7]

The informal group took more than three months from November 1966 to February 1967 to gather adherents for its cause from the progressive forces not only around Manila but also nationwide. Through invitations, frequent meetings, and discussions, the group was able to enlist the membership of 12 sectoral representatives: business, labor, peasant, youth and students, women, educators, professionals, scientists and technologists, writers and artists, mass media, political leaders, and civic leaders. Thus, at the outset, MAN was able to rise above ethnic, class, or gender differences. An Organizing Committee was tasked with hammering out its program for the upcoming founding congress set on 7–8 February and coming up with MAN's principles and declarations to be released to the public.[8]

At the National Library auditorium, where the Congress was held, *barong*-clad youthful-looking ushers and granny-dressed usherettes attended to the needs of the delegates. Recto was alive in the atmosphere; the second day commemorated the approval of the 1935 Philippine constitution whose convention Recto had presided over. KM delegates, most of whom were youth and students, were there, including MASAKA, whose members came mostly from Central Luzon barrios. One member got everyone's attention when he stood up and insisted on using Tagalog in all speeches and deliberations. Tañada then mesmerized the audience with impeccable Tagalog while others tried hard to speak the language, eliciting some frowns and grins. Ignacio Lacsina led the LM contingent, some in starched white shirts.[9]

The first day was devoted to listening to speeches containing references to current national issues. Teodoro A. Agoncillo, University of the Philippines (UP) professor and chair of the history department, discussed the development of Filipino nationalism, its causes and transformations from the late nineteenth century to the situation in which MAN had emerged by tackling the Retail Trade Nationalization Law. Suspended to take effect by Macapagal, the law was affirmed by a lower court decision on 16 December 1966 and validated the next day by a Supreme Court decision, jolting American businessmen who were opposing the law because it violated parity. Hilarion M. Henares Jr., former chair of the National Economic Council, after clearly pointing out that "economic peonage" was "the Philippine manifest destiny under American design," demolished the myth that foreign capital was needed to jumpstart Philippine industrialization. Alluding to the Philippine Investment Incentives Act being debated in Congress, Henares argued that although foreign vested interests now acknowledged the Philippine need to industrialize, they wanted to control the type of industrialization. As a colonial strategy this meant tying the light industries they invested in as captive markets with their heavy industrial plants abroad. Dr. Horacio Lava, School of Commerce dean of Manuel L. Quezon University, seconded this thesis on his lecture on "the economics of underdevelopment," underscoring that genuine industrialization was the key to national development and that the presence of foreign capital, instead of accelerating development, actually did the reverse. Lacsina talked about the nexus between Filipino nationalism and labor in the struggle for national development. Dr. Sotero H. Laurel, son of the late nationalist Senator Jose P. Laurel and university president of the Lyceum of the Philippines, emphasized the need to infuse nationalism in Philippine education. Taking pot shots at Marcos' Vietnam policy, Congressman Ramon V. Mitra Jr., the last speaker, echoed what had been said before by Recto that Philippine foreign policy should anchor on what could best serve the national interest.[10]

On the second day, after the keynote address by Constantino, who spoke on the type of leadership Filipinos deserve at a time of crisis, Tañada was chosen executive board chairman. Tañada presided over the deliberations, recalling first his participation in the nationalist movement since 1957, reasserting how nationalism was imperative to Philippine survival and finally defining the tasks of MAN, which was to carry out an education campaign. Deliberation on the ratification of the constitution continued past lunch. In the afternoon sessions,

Sison, elected general secretary, rendered a general report on MAN and oversaw the passing of a general declaration describing MAN as "a national crusade" for national liberation and economic emancipation, and four resolutions calling for the abrogation of the military bases treaty and all unequal agreements with the US, nationalist industrialization, the opening of relations with the People's Republic of China, and the Filipinization of education and mass media. At one point in the sessions, some MAN national council members intimated participation in national and local politics, though in a limited scale by fielding candidates in 1969. Getting elected could be facilitated because its constitution recognized municipal chapters as the basic unit followed by district and provincial chapters envisioned to be organized in the whole country within two years before its second national congress.[11]

With more than 300 charter members from 12 sectors of Philippine society scattered throughout the country, MAN's task of undertaking an anti-imperialist parliamentary struggle seemed possible. Yet, internal discord within the PKP dimmed whatever promise MAN may have had before and after the founding congress.

Unity Doomed: Confronting Issues amid Dissensions

The arrest of Jesus Lava, PKP general secretary, in 1964 marked PKP's transition from armed to legal struggle. The creation of mass organizations like the LM, KM, MASAKA, and the Bertrand Russell Peace Foundation (BRPF) founded in 1965 reflected this tactical shift. The KM, instigated by Sison as head of PKP's youth section (although he would deny that it was a party assignment later on) began a nationalist resurgence campaign among students in leading universities in the city that heightened youth militancy all over the country. Under Sison, KM, however, would pose a serious challenge to Lava leadership resulting in factionalism inside MAN and the Filipino Left as a whole.[12]

Recruited in 1962, Sison developed his own faction inside PKP consisting of loyal adherents from the KM at a time when the Sino-Soviet split escalated and deepened the division between pro-Soviet and pro-Chinese parties in the Comintern. Having been to Indonesia on a study grant, Sison associated with the pro-Peking Partai Komunis Indonesia (PKI) three years before the bloody military coup d'etat. Aspiring for greater leadership in the PKP, he tried to project in a number of speeches and articles his commitment to Maoism. The PKP underwent reorganization in 1965 when the ties with the Communist Party of the Soviet Union (CPSU) was reestablished. This made Sison's posturing for Maoism an obvious deviation from the party line.[13]

Taking stock of the situation in which new recruits had arrived on the scene and veteran leaders were released from prison, the PKP leadership decided to hold a plenum to elect a central committee two months after MAN's inaugural convention. The PKP had now known Sison's critical yet valid review of the leadership, which the old guard, the pro-Lava, could not ignore. To them, however, it reeked of revisionism and manifested an attempt to delegitimize their authority. A rectification campaign began, and the party gradually isolated Sison. Knowing that his clique was outnumbered, Sison refused to attend the plenum and began attacking the PKP publicly. Suspended by the PKP, MAN's general secretary was expelled from the party in April 1967, complicating the fragile alignments inside MAN.[14]

The expulsion did not prevent PKP-allied trade unionists from associating with Sison, perhaps either out of sympathy to his ideas or simply ignorance of the decision. On 1 May, the Socialist Party of the Philippines (SPP) was founded, absorbing Lacsina's LM, one of the founding organizations of MAN. Lacsina was elected chairman, while Sison became its first deputy chairman and Atty. Felixberto Olalia Sr., MASAKA's first president, its general secretary. Lacsina and Olalia held national positions in MAN as member-at-large and labor representative of the National Council respectively.[15]

One could imagine the difficulties arising from mutual suspicions between pro-Lava and pro-Sison camps in the annual meeting of the National Council. It would intensify when the PKP removed their people from the KM to form a rival youth organization in November called the Malayang Pagkakaisa ng Kabataang Pilipino (MPKP, Free Union of Filipino Youth). Presumably maneuvered by Francisco Lava Jr., nephew of Jesus Lava, and a member of MAN's national council, MPKP was born at a congress held in Cabiao, Nueva Ecija. Its 600 delegates were led by MAN charter member Ernesto R. Macahiya, the core of which came from the former KM Central Luzon Regional Center.[16]

Unity among youth and students in MAN was placed in jeopardy. The founding of the MPKP was followed by the creation of other youth organizations. The BRPF, Philippine chapter, suffered a temporary split when its chairman, Francisco Nemenzo Jr., a MAN National Council member, had a misunderstanding with Professor Hernando Abaya, a MAN-education sector member, who formed another faction. It was resolved when Nemenzo received recognition from London for his BRPF group. More serious though was another split in the KM in January 1968. Decrying Sison's authoritarian bent, 26 members of KM's national council led by Vivencio Jose, Perfecto Terra Jr., and Ninotchka Rosca, all writers and artists in MAN, left to form the Samahan ng Demokratikong Kabataan (SDK, Union of Democratic Youth).[17]

Under Tañada and with cooperation of conscientious members, MAN continued to confront issues amid the factionalism and sectarian intrigues. The Laurel-Langley agreement, which would end in 1974, was up for revision and a negotiation between the Philippine and American panels took place in November 1967. Atty. Alejandro Lichauco, MAN national council member, alerted Tañada that a draft agreement was reached between the two panels seeking the extension of parity. At the Senate, Tañada sounded the alarm and found paragraph 26 of the Philippine–US joint preparatory committee report as "nothing else but parity" termed as *national treatment*. He hinted at the special privileges to American firms that would continue under the draft agreement. MAN found an ally in the Civil Liberties Union (CLU) when its head, retired Justice Jesus Barrera, raised another serious charge: that the Philippine panel, in extending parity, agreed to take out the "reciprocity" provision and thus give more rights to Americans than Filipinos in a future agreement. Irritated by these insinuations, Marcos brushed off the allegations, squarely issuing a denial that "parity will not be extended beyond 1974."[18]

The rift widened within the Left when a split occurred in the peasant organization, MASAKA, threatening again the unity inside MAN. Sison wielded influence on one group while the much bigger faction was believed to be Lava partisans. Although affiliated organizations like MASAKA had semi-autonomous existences, the split had the potential to seriously impair the coalition since it was one of the founding organizations, and sent one of the largest delegations from the peasant sector.[19]

While having to contend with this internal problem, MAN continued to engage with national issues. One of these was the study made by a committee on the Americanization of the University of the Philippines (UP). Prompted by a desire to know the primary reason behind UP's continuing alienation from Philippine realities, the study cited Americanization, with the steady influx of aid coming from US agencies one of the major factors. It was submitted to the then UP President Carlos P. Romulo who ordered his officials to prepare a reply. As a rejoinder to the Romulo memorandum, the committee again reconvened to substantiate its allegation, which was said to be "a bogey," "a figment of imagination," and a "patent absurdity." It took them four months to finish and soon a new UP president was appointed.[20]

Since July 1968, the national council, composed of several committees, met in preparation for the second national convention. Constantino, chair of the policy and planning committee, coordinated with the various committees including the program committee to come up with a vision consistent with MAN's overall objectives and the Filipino people's true aspirations for a just and better society. Aside from responding to the points raised in the Romulo memorandum, MAN had to deal with the conflicting positions by various sectors of society on issues such as the role of foreign aid and capital, and the two factions in the communist movement trying to outmaneuver each other, not only in the formulation of the program but also in the entire movement. Obviously, the Maoist faction lost its bid for influence. All the preparatory committees were chaired by moderate nationalists and crypto-communists. Sison's role was reduced to contributing to the draft on foreign policy. By late December, Sison completely broke away from the PKP to establish the Communist Party of the Philippines (CPP).[21]

In early 1969, while MAN was in full swing preparing for its second congress, Tañada, Constantino, and Lichauco met Salvador P. Lopez, the new UP president, and handed him MAN's rejoinder in support of its contention on UP's Americanization during Romulo's time. The rejoinder not only zeroed in on UP's Americanization because of uncritical acceptance of American aid through grants and scholarships, but also pointed to the more menacing consequences of using American social science models that were irrelevant to Philippine reality, the harassment toward activist faculty members, and the discrimination against Filipino faculty and students in contrast with favoritism accorded to foreigners. UP's Americanization happened via indirect American control when Filipino administrators become instruments of American educational policies. Having mentioned particular names of faculty and departments like the School of Economics involved in UP's Americanization, it revealed that Americanization not only permeated the university's financial operations but even more so its policies. MAN was concerned with the crucial role UP would play in the nationalist struggle. They believe that UP, as the leading university, "is in a position to influence and shape the minds of young men and women who will later be the articulate spokesmen of their people—or of their enemies." Lopez promised to hold a university-wide discussion on the issue besides suspending contracts with the US-based Asia Foundation.[22]

Co-Optation and Dissolution

Prior to the planning for its second convention, several MAN representatives were invited to Malacañang to hold a dialogue with Marcos. As early as April 1967, Marcos had met several MASAKA members. MAN was reeling from the intrigues sown by the two factions in the party when they agreed to save the movement because of the possibility of a nationalist agenda under Marcos. The PKP's old guard and moderate elements in the movement were still hoping that a change could be effected in the system—a position contrary to the belief of radical elements represented by Sison's KM and Olalia's MASAKA. Marcos had every reason to deal with MAN since the movement was the largest coalition of nationalists and to pitch his nationalist posture in anticipation of the next elections. In addition, MAN did not pose a direct military threat to the regime and its objectives fit well with his nationalism.[23]

From December 1968 to February 1969 MAN exerted efforts to present a 40-page program entitled *MAN's Goal: The Democratic Filipino Society*. A product of many revisions, reflecting the different minds that tried to come up with a consensus, the program again underwent the familiar process of deliberation after a preconvention meeting. At the SSS Social Hall in Quezon City, the two-day gathering on 15–16 March was attended by 800 delegates from all over the country. MAN, Tañada said in his keynote address, had "in its rolls ... the gamut of Philippine society" and within two years "has carried out its mission quite forcefully and not without some success" because "it has helped—if not to swing official opinion fully to nationalist postures—at least to put public officials ... on guard against the cynical betrayals of the past."[24] Outlining the challenges that MAN should take up in the next two years, he mentioned three: the revision of the Laurel-Langley agreement, which he believed should not be extended; economic development through industrialization and the use of Filipino capital instead of relying on foreign capital; and the constitutional convention, proposing that a parliamentary or a semi-parliamentary government should replace the current model.

The rest of the agenda was devoted to the discussion and ratification of the program and the election of a new national council. Starting with a historical setting of Philippine society from pre-Spanish to the American period, the program singled out US "new imperialism" as the culprit of Philippine underdevelopment in science, culture and education, language, and foreign policy since independence in 1946. Revealing that "colonial industrialization" was the new imperialist tactic in the guise of foreign investments, only "nationalist industrialization" coupled with a "genuine agrarian reform" and cultural reorientation would give way to a "new Philippine society" toward a "Democratic Filipino State: a state governed by Filipinos without foreign dictation and control, which belongs to the people." Containing specific recommendations on how to democratize a "semi-feudal," "capitalist" economic system and its attendant sociopolitical structure, it called for among other things the "expropriation of all big landed estates" and their redistribution to their cultivators, and suggested constitutional and legal reforms. It passed the scrutiny of the majority, although the labor, science, and technology students and professionals all engaged in spirited discussions. In the elections, Tañada remained the national chairman along with others like Lichauco, Lacsina, and Dr. Lava as members-at-large. On the other hand, Bartolome Pasion replaced Olalia as peasantry representative and Macahiya took the place of Nilo Tayag of the KM as youth representative. Regional representatives were increased to 12 while the post of the general secretary held previously by Sison was abolished. Abaya who was elected member-at-large reported on the event: "MAN's basic aim is to change Philippine society, not by violent means, but by the politicization of the masses, educating them properly and developing a national language."[25]

If MAN believed that it could contribute toward that end through legal means, the turn of events during and after the national elections proved it to be hopeless. It encouraged participation in the elections not by fielding candidates but by disseminating nationalist ideas and causes with a sanction that it will not be identified with any political party. Since it did not offer any real alternative to the choices in the November elections, MAN, as a Marxist critique of its program put it, "simply yields its right under a nominal democracy to participate in the determination of its fate, surrendering that right to the repressive system."[26] Marcos got reelected by robbing the national treasury and, thus, placing the national economy in shambles.

MAN continued to hope for the success of its strategy while a new alignment was formed among students between the SDK and the KM. Having established the New People's Army (NPA) to pursue an armed struggle, Sison held an ideological hegemony over the youth and students fed up with the system. Radicalized into action in what is now known as the "First Quarter Storm," in January 1970 students demonstrated in front of Congress where Marcos delivered his inaugural address. This sparked a series of protests and rallies that culminated a year later in the "Diliman Commune" when students barricaded UP.[27] The PKP, which had won control over MAN, alienated many among its ranks as it dissuaded its youth and student section from fully participating in the activities in what it believed to be an imperialist plot. MAN, on the other hand, supported its candidates to the Constitutional Convention (Con-Con) getting Lichauco, Enrique Voltaire Garcia II, and Antonio S. Araneta Jr. elected. At the Con-Con, convened in June 1971, Lichauco, who represented the first district of Rizal, presented a resolution advocating the promotion of "real industrialization." MAN knew at the start that it would not succeed and it did not. *Political Review,* a MAN organ released in March, editorialized: "The ridiculousness of a selfishly partisan, foreign oriented and oligarchy-dominated convention drafting a constitution for the people is at once too obvious to engender reasonable expectations of success."[28] The prospect for a change through the Con-Con was very dim. Martial law, which everyone feared, was eventually declared. Under this stifling environment, MAN's objectives did not prosper.

Conclusion

Writing about MAN's failure, Constantino blamed it on the "doctrinaire and sectarian tendencies" among some people on the left who, according to his observation, were predisposed to treat bourgeois groups as inconsequential except to give a semblance of a united front to the movement. But more crucial than this was the power struggle between the two factions—the Lava and Sison cliques—that, in fact, as he himself acknowledged, dissipated the anti-imperialist resistance. No doubt, the split squandered the opportunity to advance into a nationwide mass movement as the creation of provincial chapters was abandoned after the second congress. Unity from its inception was fragile because the seed for disunity grew when personal interest of individuals triumphed over the collective endeavor. It was a fatal consequence of the inability of the traditional left to constructively engage with a new generation of leftist activists branded as Maoist and build a compromise for the sake of the national democratic struggle. On the other hand, the New Left was fueled more by arrogance and opportunism than the exigencies of building alliance.[29]

In the context of Southeast Asia and Asia in general, MAN was not unique among the social movements that responded to the challenges of nation building, decolonization, and neo-colonialism. For instance, in neighboring Malaya, Singapore, and Borneo, there was a resurgence of left-wing organizations in the sixties as shown in their participation in parliamentary elections while in South Korea an upsurge of social movements was evident. MAN was the most ambitious and most organized nationalist movement in the country since the Democratic Alliance in the 1940s and Recto's nationalist crusade in the 1950s. Although weakened by internal feuds, it managed to create a network of like-minded people from various sectors and from different parts of the country. It was able to put pressure on the policy decisions of the Marcos administration in a number of ways. Because of the nationalist resurgence that it personified, Marcos and the Philippine Congress could not ignore its recommendation on the opening of trade relations with any nation including China, and on economic development. The latter was realized when Congress approved Joint Resolution No. 2 or the "Magna Carta of Social Justice and Economic Freedom," signed by Marcos in August 1969. A repudiation of IMF-WB prescriptions, it contained MAN's basic doctrines on the nationalization of the economy through the imposition of import and export controls, restrictions on multinational corporate activities, the end of parity, and non-alignment in foreign policy. It proved to be short lived and illusory. In January 1970 Marcos devaluated the peso, bowing to multilateral lending agencies. MAN also initiated the decolonization of the UP and inspired the indigenization movements in the academe.[30]

Whatever pretensions MAN had of being a progressive organization "wedged between the Left-of-Center and the extreme Left" was quickly shattered by its helplessness to grasp and adapt to stark realities of the times.[31] MAN was contented with its conservatism and accommodation to the status quo, not knowing that as strategies they were in themselves an endorsement of the regime. So as the tide of history ebbed and flowed, MAN remained true to its bourgeois reformist character. Three years after MAN's dissolution the PKP arrived with an agreement with Marcos. Ultimately, MAN suffered from the schism within the PKP making unity impossible. In any case, MAN lost the opportunity in 1968 to solidify its ranks against the common enemy because the bankruptcy of the old failed to take hold of the new situation and also because the young, though able to comprehend the realities of the present, were in a hurry to rush into the future.

Notes

1. Leon Ma. Guerrero, "Recto and Filipino Nationalism," *Manila Times,* 7 October 1960.
2. Eric Hobsbawm, *The Age of Extremes: A History of the World, 1914–1991* (New York: Vintage Books, 1994), 296.
3. Renato Constantino, *The Making of a Filipino: A Story of Colonial Politics* (Quezon City: Malaya Books, 1969), 140–141, 153, 155–156.

4. Alejandro Lichauco, *The Lichauco Paper: Imperialism in the Philippines* (New York: Monthly Review Press, 1973), 35–37; William J. Pomeroy, *The Philippines: Colonialism, Collaboration and Resistance!* (New York: International Publishers, 1992), 224–225, 238.

5. Pomeroy (1992), 284–286; Ray M. Hizon, "The Left in the Sixties," *Graphic*, 25 February 1970, 12. The Laurel-Langley Agreement extended to 20 years the free trade between the Philippines and the US due to expire in 1954. The parity gave equal rights to Americans vis-à-vis Filipinos in exploiting Philippine natural resources.

6. Lewis E. Gleeck Jr., *The Third Philippine Republic 1946–1972* (Quezon City: New Day, 1993), 331–334; Pomeroy (1992), 258–260; Hizon (25 February 1970), 12.

7. Kathleen Weekley, *The Communist Party of the Philippines 1968–1993: A Story of its Theory and Practice* (Quezon City: UP Press, 2001), 30; Jose Ma. Sison with Rainer Werning, *The Philippine Revolution: The Leader's View* (New York and London: Crane Russak, 1989), 32; Rosalinda Pineda-Ofreneo, *Renato Constantino: A Life Revisited* (Quezon City: Foundation for Nationalist Studies, 2001), 170.

8. Jose Ma. Sison, "General Report," in *Movement for the Advancement of Nationalism: Basic Documents and Speeches of the Founding Congress* (Quezon City: MAN, 1967), vii, 1, 6–7.

9. Monina A. Mercado, "Movement for the Advancement of Nationalism," *Graphic*, 22 February 1967, 24.

10. Ibid.; Agoncillo, "The Development of Filipino Nationalism," 98–99; Hilarion M. Henares Jr., "The Philippine Manifest Destiny under American Design," 110–111; Horacio Lava, "The Economics of Underdevelopment," 123, 125; Ignacio Lacsina, "Nationalism and Labor," 132–137; Sotero H. Laurel, "Nationalism in Education," 138–142; Ramon V. Mitra Jr., "Nationalism and Foreign Policy," 143–148; all in *Movement for the Advancement of Nationalism.*

11. Mercado (1967): 24, 26; Sison (1967), 1–9; Renato Constantino, "A Leadership for Filipinos," 43–54; "General Declaration," 20–25; "Constitution," 27, 32–33; "Resolutions," 35–42; all in *Movement for the Advancement of Nationalism.*

12. Alfredo B. Saulo, "A Second Look at Philippine Communism: 1964: A Turning Point?" *Weekly Nation*, 9 August 1971, 16, 28-P, 39.

13. Pomeroy (1992), 287–288. On the Sino-Soviet rift, see Lorenz M. Luthi, *The Sino-Soviet Split: Cold War in the Communist World* (Princeton, NJ: Princeton University Press, 2008), 273–301.

14. Weekley (2001), 24–25; Pomeroy (1992), 289.

15. Saulo, "A Second Look at Philippine Communism: 1967–1968: Years of Hope and Crises," *Weekly Nation*, 23 August 1971, 38–39.

16. Ibid., 39; Weekley (2001), 30–31.

17. Saulo (23 August 1971), 39–40.

18. Gene Marcial, "Disparity on Parity," *Graphic*, 12 June 1968, 30–33; Gleeck Jr. (1993), 351.

19. Saulo (23 August 1971), 39–40.

20. Ninotchka Rosca, "Whatever Happened to the UP Americanization Charge?" *Graphic*, 26 March 1969, 14–15.

21. Ninotchka Rosca, "Making Democracy Meaningful and Palpable," *Graphic*, 7 May 1969, 16, 54; Saulo, "A Second Look at Philippine Communism: Maoist CPP: Power from Gun's Barrel," *Weekly Nation*, 30 August 1971, 12-B.

22. Rosca (7 May 1969), 14–16, 18–19, 60.
23. Pineda-Ofreneo (2001), 172; Gleeck Jr. (1993), 342.
24. Movement for the Advancement of Nationalism, *M.A.N.'s Goal: The Democratic Filipino Society* (Quezon City: Malaya Books, 1969), 41, 44, 46–52; Rosca (7 May 1969), 54, 56.
25. Rosca (7 May 1969), 56; Movement for the Advancement of Nationalism (1969), 1–60; Hernando Abaya, "Change is Coming but Justice Grinds Slow," *Graphic,* 9 April 1969, 14.
26. Movement for the Advancement of Nationalism (1969), 27; Pomeroy (1992), 261; Crisanto Evangelista Jr. [pseud.]. "A Critique of M.A.N.'s Goal Toward a People's Republic," *Solidarity* Vol. 5, No. 8 (1970): 69.
27. Weekley (2001), 32–34.
28. "Editorial: Farce or Fraud," *Political Review* Vol. 1, No. 5 (July 1971): 2; "The Constitutional Convention: Anatomy of Failure" in ibid., 6.
29. Pineda-Ofreneo (2001), 175–176. About the sixties in Asia, please see the special issue of *Inter-Asia Cultural Studies* Vol. 7, No. 4 (December 2006) where articles about social movements in the sixties in the cited countries are found.
30. Pomeroy (1992), 260–261.
31. Amadis Ma. Guerrero, "The Establishment and the Left," *Graphic,* 25 February 1970, 44.

Selected Bibliography

Ali, Tariq and Susan Watkins. *1968: Marching In The Streets*. New York: The Free Press, 1998.

Alves, Maria Helena Moreira. *State and Opposition in Military Brazil*. Austin: University of Texas Press, 1985.

Anderson, Benedict and Ruth T. McVey. "A Preliminary Analysis of the October 1, 1965 Coup in Indonesia." *Modern Indonesia Project*. Ithaca, NY: Cornell University Press, 1971.

Barber, David. *A Hard Rain Fell: SDS and why it Failed*. Jackson, MS: University of Mississippi Press, 2008.

Barnouin, Barbara and Yu Changgen. *Chinese Foreign Policy during the Cultural Revolution*. New York: Kegan Paul International, 1998.

Berger, Mark T. "The End of the 'Third World?'" *Third World Quarterly*. Vol. 15, No. 2 (June, 1994): 257–275.

Berman, Paul. *A Tale of Two Utopias: The Political Journey of the Generation of 1968*. New York: W.W. Norton & Company, 1996.

Braunstein, Peter and Michael William, eds. *Imagine Nation: The American Counterculture in the 1960s and '70s*. New York: Routledge, 2002.

Bonnett, Alastair. *The Idea of the West: Culture, Politics and History*. New York: Palgrave Macmillan, 2004.

Boon-Cheng, Cheah. "The Left-Wing Movement in Malaya, Singapore and Borneo in the 1960s: An Era of Hope or Devil's Decade?" *Inter-Asia Cultural Studies* 7, no. 4 (December 2006): 634–649.

Boudreau, Vincent. *Resisting Dictatorship: Repression and Protest in Southeast Asia*. Cambridge, UK: Cambridge University Press, 2005.

Bresnan, John. *Managing Indonesia*. New York: Columbia University Press, 1993.

Brewster, Keith. *Reflections on Mexico '68*. Malden, MA: Wiley-Blackwell, 2010.

Brown, Timothy S. "'1968' East and West: Divided Germany as a Case Study in Transnational History." *American Historical Review*. Vol. 114, No. 1 (February 2009): 69–96.

Brown, Timothy S. and Lorena Anton, eds. *Between the Avant Garde and the Everyday: Subversive Politics in Europe, 1958-2008*. New York: Berghahn Books, 2011.

Borstelmann, Thomas. *The Cold War and the Color Line*. Cambridge, MA: Harvard University Press, 2003.

Campbell, Horace. *Rasta and Resistance: From Marcus Garvey to Walter Rodney*. New Jersey: Africa World Press, 1987.

Caute, David. *The Year of the Barricades: A Journey Through 1968.* New York: Harper & Row Publishers, 1988.

Cavallo, Dominick. *A Fiction of the Past: The Sixties in American History.* New York: St. Martin's Press, 1999.

Carey, Elaine. *Plaza of Sacrifices: Gender, Power, and Terror in 1968 Mexico.* Albuquerque: University of New Mexico Press, 2005.

Chakrabarti, Sreemati. *China and the Naxalites.* New Delhi: Radiant Books, 1990.

Chatterjee, Partha. "Empire and Nation Revisited: 50 Years After Bandung." *Inter-Asia Cultural Studies* Vol. 6 No. 4 (2005): 477–496.

Cherki, Alice. *Frantz Fanon: A Portrait.* Ithaca, NY: Cornell University Press, 2006.

Cooper, Frederick. *Colonialism in Question: Theory, Knowledge, History.* Berkeley: University of California Press, 2005.

Craig-Harris, Lillian and Robert L. Worden, eds. *China and the Third World: Champion or Challenger.* Dover, MA: Auburn House Publishing Company, 1986.

Dachs, A.J. and W.F. Rea. *The Catholic Church and Zimbabwe.* Gwelo: Mambo Press, 1979.

Daniels, Robert V. *Year of the Heroic Guerrilla: World Revolution and Counterrevolution in 1968.* Cambridge: Harvard University Press, 1989.

Daly, J.A. and A. G. Saville. *The History of Joint Church Aid,* 3 vols. Kopenhagen, 1971.

Das, Veena. *Life and Words: Violence and the Descent in the Ordinary.* Berkeley: University of California Press, 2007.

Digby, Anne and Howard Phillips. *At the Heart of Healing: Groote Schuur Hospital, 1938 to 2008.* Auckland Park: Jacana, 2008.

Dirlik, Arif, Paul Healey, and Nick Knight, eds. *Critical perspectives on Mao Zedong's Thought.* Atlantic Highlands, N.J. : Humanities Press, 1997.

Duara, Prasenjit, ed. *Decolonization: Perspective from Now and Then.* New York: Routledge, 2004.

Dunn, Christopher. *Brutality Garden: Tropicalia and the Emergence of a Brazilian Counterculture.* Chapel Hill, NC: University of North Carolina Press, 2001.

Dussel, Enrique. *Beyond Philosophy: Ethics, History, Marxism and Liberation Philosophy.* Lanham, MD: Rowman & Littlefield Publishers, 2003.

Dubinsky, Karen et al, eds. *New World Coming: The Sixties and the Shaping of Global Consciousness.* Toronto: Between the Lines, 2009.

Ekwe-Ekwe, H. *The Biafra War: Nigeria and the Aftermath.* Lewiston, N.Y.: E. Mellen Press, 1990.

Elbaum, Max. *Revolution in the Air: Sixties Radicals Turn to Lenin, Mao and Che.* New York: Verso, 2002.

Erbmann, Robert. "Conservative Revolutionaries: anti-apartheid activism at the University of Cape Town, 1963-1973." History Honours thesis, Oxford University, 2005.

Erny, Pierre. *Sur les Sentiers de l'université: Autobiographies d'étudiants Zaïrois.* Paris: La Penseie Universelle, 1977.

Erskine, Noel. *From Garvey to Marley: Rastafari Theology.* Gainesville, FL: University Press of Florida, 2005.

Escobar, Arturo. *Encountering Development. The Making and Unmaking of the Third World,* Princeton: Princeton University Press, 1995.

Fink, Carole, Philipp Gassert, and Detlef Junker, eds. *1968: The World Transformed.* Cambridge: Cambridge University Press, 1998.

Feenberg, Andrew and Jim Freedman eds. *When Poetry Ruled the Streets: The French May Events of 1968.* Albany, NY: State University of New York Press, 2001.

Forsyth, Frederick. *The Biafra Story. The Making of an African Legend.* London: Barnsley House, 2001.

Fredrickson, George. *Racism. A Short History.* Princeton: Princeton University Press, 2002.

Gassert, Philipp and Martin Klimke. "1968: Memories and Legacies of a Global Revolt." *Bulletin of the German Historical Institute* No. 6 (2009).

Geertz, Clifford. "What was the Third World Revolution?" *Dissent* Vol. 52, No. 1 (Winter, 2005): 35–45.

Gerhart, Gail. *Black Power in South Africa: The Evolution of an Ideology.* Berkeley: University of California Press, 1978.

Gibbs, David N. *The Political Economy of Third World Intervention: Mines, Money and U.S. Policy in the Congo Crisis.* Chicago: The University of Chicago Press, 1991.

Gitlin, Todd. *The Sixties: Years of Hope, Days of Rage.* New York: Bantam Books, 1993.

Gleeck, Lewis E. Jr. *The Third Philippine Republic 1946-1972.* Quezon City: New Day, 1993.

Grandin, Greg. *The Last Colonial Massacre: Latin America in the Cold War.* Chicago: University of Chicago Press, 2004.

Gray, Obika. *Radicalism and Social Change in Jamaica: 1960–1972.* Knoxville: University of Tennessee Press, 1991.

Gurgel, Antonio de Padua. *A Rebelião dos Estudantes: Brasília, 1968.* Brasília: Editora Revan, 2004.

Hall, Stuart. "The West and the Rest: Discourse and Power." *Formations of Modernity.* ed. Stuart Hall and Bram Gieben. Cambridge: Cambridge University Press, 1992: 118–130.

Harneit-Sievers, J. O. Ahazuem, S. Emezue. *A Social History of the Nigerian Civil War: Perspectives from Below.* Hamburg: Lit, 1997.

Horn, Gerd-Rainer. *The Spirit of '68: Rebellion in Western Europe and North America, 1956–1976.* Oxford: Oxford University Press, 2007.

Horn, Gerd-Rainer and Padraic Kenney, eds. *Transnational moments of change: Europe 1945, 1968, 1989.* Lanham, MD: Rowman & Littlefield, 2004.

Hunt, Lynn and Victoria Bonnell, eds. *Beyond the Cultural Turn: New Directions in the Study of Society and Culture.* Berkeley, CA: University of California Press, 1999.

Hyam, Ronald and Peter Henshaw. *The Lion and the Springbok: Britain and South Africa since the Boer War.* Cambridge: Cambridge University Press, 2003.

Isaacman, A. "Displaced People, Displaced Energy, and Displaced Memories. The Case of Cahora Bassa, 1970–2004." *International Journal of African Historical Studies* 38, no. 2 (2005): 201–238.

Isaacman, A. and C. Sneddon. "Portuguese Colonial Intervention, Regional Conflict and Post-Colonial Amnesia. Cahora Bassa Dam, Mozambique 1965–2002." *Portuguese Studies Review* 11, no. 1 (2003): 207–236.

_____. "Toward a Social and Environmental History of the Building of Cahora Bassa Dam." *Journal of Southern African Studies* 26, No. 4 (2000): 597–632.

Isbister, John. *Promised Not Kept: Poverty and the Betrayal of Third World Development.* Bloomfield, CT: Kumarian Press, 2003.

Isserman, Maurice and Michael Kazin. *America Divided: The Civil War of the 1960s.* Oxford: Oxford University Press, 2000.

Ivaska, Andrew. "Of Students, 'Nizers,' and a Struggle over Youth: Tanzania's 1966 National Service Crisis." *African Today* Vol. 51, No. 3 (Spring 2005): 83–107.

Joseph, Gilbert and Daniela Spenser, eds. *In From the Cold: Latin America's New Encounters with the Cold War.* Durham: Duke University Press, 2008.

Kapoor, Ilan. "Capitalism, Culture, Agency: Dependency versus Postcolonial Theory." *Third World Quarterly* Vol. 23 No. 4 (2000): 647–664.

Katsiaficas, George. *The Imagination of the New Left: A Global Analysis of 1968.* Boston: South End Press, 1987.

Katz, David. *Solid Foundation: An Oral History of Reggae.* Great Britain: Bloomsbury, 2003.

Klimke, Martin. *The Other Alliance: Student Protest in West Germany and the United States in the Global Sixties.* Princeton, NJ: Princeton University Press, 2010.

Klimke, Martin and Joachim Scharloth, eds. *1968 in Europe: A History of Protest and Activism, 1956–1977.* New York: Palgrave Macmillan, 2008.

Kössler, Reinhart and Henning Melber. "The West German solidarity movement with the liberation struggles in Southern Africa. A (self-)critical retrospective," in: *Germany's Africa Policy Revisited. Interests, Images and Incrementalism.* eds. U. Engel and R. Kappel. Munster: Lit, 2002: 103–126.

Kurlansky, Mark. *1968. The Year that Rocked the World.* London: Vintage, 2005.

Lacey, Terry. *Violence and Politics in Jamaica: 1960–1970.* Great Britain. Manchester University Press, 1977.

Lewis, Rupert C. *Walter Rodney's Intellectual and Political Thought.* Detroit: Wayne State University Press, 1998.

Luthi, Lorenz M. *The Sino-Soviet Split: Cold War in the Communist World.* Princeton, NJ: Princeton University Press, 2008.

Ma, Jisen. *The Cultural Revolution in the Foreign Ministry.* Hong Kong: The Chinese University Press, 2004.

Mabry, Donald J. *The Mexican University and the State: Student Conflicts, 1910–1971.* College Station, TX: Texas A&M University Press, 1982.

MacFarquhar, Roderick and Michael Schoenhals. *Mao's Last Revolution.* Cambridge, MA: Harvard University Press, 2006.

Malley, Robert. *The Call from Algeria: Third Worldism, Revolution, and the Turn to Islam.* Berkeley, CA: The University of California Press, 1996.

Manley, Michael. *The Politics of Change: A Jamaican Testament.* Washington D.C.: Howard University Press, 1975.

Marwick, Arthur. *The Sixties: Cultural Revolution in Britain, France, Italy, and the United States, 1958–1974.* Oxford: Oxford University Press, 1998.

Mcdonald, Peter. *The Literature Police: Apartheid Censorship and its Cultural Consequences.* Cape Town: Oxford University Press, 2009.

Movement for the Advancement of Nationalism. *Movement for the Advancement of Nationalism: Basic Documents and Speeches of the Founding Congress.* Quezon City: MAN, 1967.

———. *M.A.N.'s Goal: The Democratic Filipino Society.* Quezon City: Malaya Books, 1969.

Murray, Bruce and Christopher Merrett. *Caught Behind: Race and Politics in Springbok Cricket.* Johannesburg: Wits University Press, 2004.

Nettleford, Rex, ed. *Jamaica in Independence: Essays on the Early Years.* Kingston: Heinemann Caribbean, 1989

Neuhauser, Charles. *Third World Politics: China and the Afro-Asian People's Solidarity Organization, 1957–1967.* Cambridge, MA: Harvard East Asian Monographs, 1968.

O'Malley, Ilene. *The Myth of Revolution: Hero Cults and the Institutionalization of the Mexican State, 1920–1940.* Westport, CT: Greenwood Press, 1986.

Pomeroy, William J. *The Philippines: Colonialism, Collaboration and Resistance!* New York: International Publishers, 1992.

Poniatowska, Elena. *Massacre in Mexico.* Columbia: University of Missouri Press, 1992.

Prashad, Vijay. *The Darker Nations: A People's History of the Third World.* New York: W.W. Norton, 2007.

Ranger, Terrance. *Peasant Consciousness and Guerilla War in Zimbabwe: A Comparative Study.* Berkeley: University of California Press, 1985.

Roberts, Priscilla. *Beyond the Bamboo Curtain: China, Vietnam and the World beyond Asia*. Stanford, CA: Stanford University Press, 2006.

Rodney, Walter. *Groundings With My Brothers*. London: The Bogle-L'Ouverture Publications, 1969.

Ross, Kristin. *May '68 and its Afterlives*. Chicago: Chicago University Press, 2002.

Rossi, Mario. *The Third World. The Unaligned Countries and the World Revolution*. Westport, CT: Greenwood Press, 1963.

Sauvy, Alfred. "Trois Mondes, Une Planete." *L'Observateur* 14 Aug. 1952: 257–275.

Sayres, Sohnya, ed. *The 60s, Without Apology*. Minneapolis: University of Minnesota Press, 1984.

Schildt, Alex and Detlef Siegfried, eds. *Between Marx and Coca-Cola: Youth Cultures in Changing European Societies, 1960–1980*. New York: Berghahn Books, 2005.

Schlefer, Jonathan. *Palace Politics: How the Ruling Party Brought Crisis to Mexico*. Austin: University of Texas Press, 2008.

Segal, Lauren and Paul Holden. *Great Lives. Pivotal Moments*. Auckland Park: Jacana, 2008.

Skidmore, Thomas E. *The Politics of Military Rule in Brazil: 1964–1985*. New York: Oxford University Press, 1988.

South African Democracy Education Trust. *The Road to Democracy in South Africa*. Cape Town: Zebra Press, 2004.

Stephens, Julie. *Anti-Disciplinary Protest: Sixties Radicalism and Post-Modernism*. Cambridge: University of Cambridge Press, 1998.

Suri, Jeremi. "The Rise and Fall of an International Counterculture, 1960–1975," *American Historical Review* Vol. 114, No. 1 (February 2009), 61–68.

———. *Power and Protest: Global Revolution and the Rise of Détente*. Cambridge, MA: Harvard University Press, 2003.

Swan, Quito. *Black Power in Bermuda: The Struggle for Decolonization*. New York: Palgrave Macmillan, 2009.

Thomas, Nick. *Protest Movements in West Germany: A Social History of Dissent and Democracy*. New York: Berghahn, 2003.

Thompson, Joseph. *American Policy and African Famine: The Nigeria-Biafra War 1966–1970*. New York: Greenwood Press, 1990.

Thompson, Lisa and Chris Tapscott, ed. *Citizenship and Social Movements: Perspectives from the Third World*. New York: Palgrave MacMillan, 2010.

Valle, Eduardo. *El año de la Rebelion por la Democracia*. Mexico, D.F: Oceiano, 2008.

Vansina, Jan. *Living with Africa*. Madison, WI: The University of Wisconsin Press, 1995.

Varon, Jeremy. *Bringing the War Home: The Weather Underground, The Red Army Faction, and Revolutionary Violence in the Sixties and Seventies*. Berkeley: University of California Press, 2004.

Verdery, C. *The Political Lives of Dead Bodies: Reburial and Postsocialist Change.* New York: Columbia University Press, 2000.

Vienet, Rene. *Enrages and Situationists in the Occupation Movement in Paris, 1968.* Brooklyn, NY: Automedia, 1992.

Waters, Anika. *Race, Class, and Political Symbols: Rastafari and Reggae in Jamaican Politics.* New Brunswick, NJ: Transaction Press, 1985.

Weekley, Kathleen. *The Communist Party of the Philippines 1968–1993: A Story of its Theory and Practice.* Quezon City: UP Press, 2001.

Westad, Odd Arne. *The Global Cold War: Third World Interventions and the Making of our Times.* Cambridge: Cambridge University Press, 2005.

Wright, Thomas C. *Latin America in the Era of the Cuban Revolution.* New York: Praeger, 1991.

Young, Cynthia A. *Soul Power. Culture, Radicalism and the Making of a U.S. Third World Left.* Durham: University of North Carolina Press, 2006.

Zolov, Eric. *Refried Elvis: The Rise of the Mexican Counterculture.* Berkeley: University of California Press, 1999.

Notes on Contributors

Editors

Samantha Christiansen is an instructor at Northeastern University. Her research interests focus on youth and student mobilizations in South Asia and Europe and international Left politics. Her dissertation (September, 2012) examines the role of student mass mobilizations in East Pakistan (present-day Bangladesh) and the ways in which student identity empowers young people to make claims against the state. It also explores the relationship of place identity and movement culture. She has taught courses in world history, gender, and the history of South Asia at Independent University Bangladesh and Northeastern University.

Zachary Scarlett is a PhD candidate at Northeastern University who specializes in modern Chinese history and the history of radical social movements in the twentieth century. His dissertation examines the ways in which Chinese students imagined and co-opted global narratives during the Cultural Revolution. He has taught courses at Northeastern University in world history, Chinese history, and East Asian history.

Contributors

James Bradford is a PhD candidate and instructor at Northeastern University in Boston, MA. His research interests include the history of informal economies, political dissent, and drugs in world history. His dissertation is entitled "Seeds of Dissent: Opium, Politics, and Development during the Musahiban Dynasty of Afghanistan, 1929–1978."

Nicholas M. Creary received his BA in history and African studies from Georgetown University, his MA in American history from the Catholic University of America, and his PhD in African history from Michigan State University. He has taught at Georgetown University in Washington, DC, and Marquette University in Milwaukee. His first book, *Domesticating a Religious Import: The Jesuits and the Inculturation of the Catholic Church in Zimbabwe, 1879–1980* (New York: Fordham University Press, 2011) focused on the history of religion in Africa and adaptations of Christianity to African cultures.

Arif Dirlik lives in Eugene, Oregon, USA, in semi-retirement. In 2010, he served as the Liang Qichao Memorial Distinguished Visiting Professor at Tsinghua University, Beijing. He most recently held the Rajni Kothari Chair in Democracy at the Centre for the Study of Developing Societies, Delhi. His most recent book-length publication is *Culture and Society in Postrevolutionary China: The Perspective of Global Modernity.*

Erwin S. Fernandez is an independent scholar who has taught at the University of the Philippines. Founding director of the Abung na Panagbasay Pangasinan (House of Pangasinan Studies), he engages in a wide range of research from Philippine diplomatic, military, and literary history to Arab-Israeli conflict, and Pangasinan history. A poet and a short story writer in his native tongue, he advocates for a just and equitable Philippine society that recognizes its multilingual, multicultural, and pluralistic makeup in a polycentric political economy.

Avishek Ganguly was educated in India and the United States. He received his BA from Calcutta University, his MA from Jawaharlal Nehru University, and his PhD from Columbia University. He is currently assistant professor of English at Rhode Island School of Design (RISD). His research and teaching interests are in modern and contemporary drama, post-colonial and anglophone literatures, the cultures of cities, and literary and cultural theory including globalization and translation studies.

Christoph Kalter holds a PhD from the Free University of Berlin and is an assistant professor at the Friedrich-Meinecke-Institut (Department of History) of the Free University of Berlin. He published a revised version of his thesis as "Die Entdeckung der Dritten Welt: Dekolonisierung und neue radikale Linke in Frankreich" [The Discovery of the Third World: Decolonization and the New Radical Left in France] with Campus-Verlag, Frankfurt, Germany (2011).

Konrad J. Kuhn holds an MA in history and popular culture studies from the University of Zurich and received his PhD from the University of Zurich in 2010. He is currently a research fellow at the Research Center for Social and Economic History (FSW) at the University of Zurich. His research focuses on the history of development policies, social and protest movements, and the field of politicized public history. He has published on international solidarity in Switzerland, on Fair-Trade-Campaigns, and on the commemoration of slave trade in Europe.

Pedro Monaville is a PhD candidate in history at the University of Michigan. He is currently working on a history of the student and left activisms in post-colonial Congo. Some of his writings on colonial culture, decolonization, and post-colonial history can be found at http://sitemaker.umich.edu/monaville/home.

Stephanie Sapiie is assistant professor of political science at SUNY Nassau Community College in the History, Political Science, and Geography Department. Her chapter is based on a chapter of her dissertation, "Free Spaces, Identity and Student-Activism: Repression and Student Activism on West-Java, 1920–1979," written at the City University of New York (CUNY) Graduate Center, PhD Program in Political Science, and defended on 14 July 2010.

Chris Saunders is an emeritus professor in the Department of Historical Studies at the University of Cape Town. He has published widely on the history and historiography of southern Africa. He is at present working on a new edition of R. Davenport and C. Saunders, *South Africa A Modern History* (5th ed., 2000).

Julia Sloan earned a PhD in Latin American History from the University of Houston. She joined the faculty at Cazenovia College in 2004 and currently serves as an associate professor of social science and director of the International Studies Program. Her research interests include modern Mexico, the 1960s, and popular culture. Her teaching interests include Mexico, Latin America, world history, comparative social and political institutions, and social theory.

Colin Snider completed his PhD in history at the University of New Mexico in 2011, where he has also spent the last two years as a teaching associate. He has begun revisions to his dissertation for a future book project on middle-class identities and higher education in Brazil, as well as a handful of articles on Brazil's military dictatorship (1964–1985).

Index